ESSENTIAL
—LAW—
FOR CATERERS

2ND EDITION

ROGER PETERS

Hodder & Stoughton

A MEMBER OF THE HODDER HEADLINE GROUP

Cataloguing in Publication Data is available from the British Library

ISBN 0 340 630 787

First published 1992
Second edition 1996
Impression number 10 9 8 7 6 5 4 3 2 1
Year   2000 1999 1998 1997 1996

Typeset by Wearset, Boldon, Tyne and Wear.
Printed in Great Britain for Hodder & Stoughton Educational, a division of Hodder Headline Plc, 338 Euston Road, London NW1 3BH by Redwood Books, Trowbridge, Wilts.

Preface

The law is believed to be correctly stated as at 1 July 1995 although some laws coming into effect after that date have been incorporated, notably the new food hygiene regulations and food temperature controls.

I am very grateful to John Bailey FHCIMA, Senior Lecturer and HCIMA Course Director at Brighton College of Technology for his assistance in trying to make sure this book covers the needs of students on various hotel, catering and hospitality management courses.

Contents

CHAPTER 4   BUSINESS CONTROLS

CHAPTER 5   THE CUSTOMER RELATIONSHIP

CHAPTER 6   CONSUMER PROTECTION

CHAPTER 7   FOOD SAFETY AND HYGIENE

Chapter 1

THE LEGAL SYSTEM

WHAT IS LAW?

At its basic level, law is merely a set of rules to govern the conduct of people in a civilised society. The expression 'law and order' is appropriate because, without laws, a civilised society would degenerate into disorder.

Viewed as a set of rules, the law can be likened to the rules of club or the rules for playing a game. All the club members or all the game players must abide by the same rules. If they do not, the club breaks up or the game cannot be played. The same applies to laws – for a civilised society to exist, everyone must abide by the same rules. The rules may be of different types in different situations, for instance, laws as to which side of the road to drive on and laws prohibiting murder.

Laws must be acceptable to society. In a democracy this is achieved by the government of the people, by the people through their elected government. But from time to time laws are made which are not acceptable to a proportion of the community. There will be objections to that law in some way or another, such as demonstrations, strikes and petitions.

Laws can be said to be the rules of a civilised society which society itself sets, so as to ensure a continuing civilised pattern of life.

The degree of sophistication of laws depends on the sophistication of the society. In earlier times when communities were basically agricultural without a developed transport system, there was no need for sophisticated laws. Today we live in a complex society and laws are more complex.

Essentially, the law is a set of rules that controls relationships within society, but the rules change constantly, so as to reflect the generally accepted standards of society. Certain behaviour which is considered to offend against those standards is made unlawful. Murder has already been mentioned as being outlawed but so are numerous other antisocial actions such as mugging and dropping litter. These laws are for the protection of society as a whole to ensure that any member of society can walk through the streets without fear of being murdered, mugged or having to climb over mountains of litter.

Other laws are concerned with the relationship between individual members of society. Laws of contract are concerned with trade, and laws of property provide a set of rules for property ownership. Other laws govern relationships between neighbours, business partners or husband and wife.

CRIMINAL AND CIVIL LAW

Some antisocial behaviour is regarded as an offence against society as a whole. Because of this, society collectively enforces those laws in order to check or prevent such behaviour. This is called criminal law. Enforcement of criminal law may be by the police who will attempt to discover the identity of the wrongdoer, and society will then prosecute that person for the crime. Other crimes involve other enforcement agencies, such as trading standards officers or factory inspectors, but in all of these cases it will be the community or society as a whole which pays for the detection and prosecution of the offender, and it will be the community which punishes the offender, either by extracting a fine or putting the offender in prison or imposing some other sanction.

Civil laws are the laws which govern relationships between individual members of the community. Examples are the rules of defamation of character, trespass on land, wrongful dismissal of an employee and divorce. These are not matters which will involve the police or any other enforcement agency of the society. Instead, it is for the individuals involved to sort out their differences. But society recognises that those differences are best sorted out in a civilised way rather than by pistols at dawn and, therefore, society provides not only a set of rules, but also courts to apply those rules for the resolution of such differences.

There are many differences between crimes and civil wrongs. The most important is that crimes are punished, but civil wrongs are remedied. Although the punishment must fit the crime, punishment is designed to penalise a wrongdoer and deter others from committing crimes.

Another important distinction between civil and criminal law is that a person can insure against committing a civil wrong, but not against committing a crime. Therefore, if someone carelessly drives his car and knocks down a pedestrian, the insurance company will pay the compensation awarded by the civil courts to the pedestrian for his or her injuries, but the insurance company will not pay the fine the driver has to pay when found guilty of the crime of careless driving.

Because of their different nature and the different consequences, crimes and civil wrongs are dealt with in different courts, and the court structure will be looked at later in this chapter.

State subsidised legal aid is also split along the same lines. If an individual wishes to bring, or to defend, a civil court case, but does not have the means to do so, then they can apply to the Legal Aid Board for financial assistance. The criminal legal aid scheme, however, is administered by the criminal courts.

How laws are made

So having seen what law is and the basic distinction between civil and criminal law, now take a look at how laws are made. To do this it is necessary to consider three types of laws, and this introduces yet a further categorisation of law

- the common law – the law made by judicial decisions
- UK legislation – the law made by, or under the authority of Parliament
- European law – law resulting from our membership of the European Union.

In one sense, it is possible to say that just as our laws have become more complicated with a more complex society, also the methods by which laws are made have become more complex as society has expanded out of the village community into the European context.

Common law (judicial decisions)

The common law first started to develop after the Norman Conquest when a strong central government set up a national courts system. The judges had no central laws to guide them and although it would be an oversimplification to suggest they made their own rules as they went along, it would not be far off the mark. Someone had to do the job and the laws they developed became national as the rules were applied around the country.

The 'common law' (which, unfortunately, is an expression with more than one meaning, but only one needs to be considered in this book) was, therefore, the body of law developed over many years from judicial decisions, and was common throughout the country.

The need for judge-made law has diminished as other methods of lawmaking have become established but it is far from dead and, in some areas of the law – such as the law of negligence – it is still very much alive and kicking.

When the decision in a case is important because it establishes new law, or develops or explains existing law, then it is likely to be reported. This means that the judge's reasons for the decision are printed in one of the many law reports.

There are many types of law reports. The official law reports are published by the Incorporated Council of Law Reporting for England and Wales. There are also many commercial law reports, some of which are general and some deal with particular topics, but all use the names of the contestants in the court case and the year of the case as its title. Criminal cases show the name of the prosecutor, for example, 'R' indicating either the Queen or King.

◆ R v DUDLEY AND STEPHENS **(1884)**

Shipwrecked sailors were prosecuted for murder. The prosecution arose from the fact that, to stay alive while they were shipwrecked, they killed and ate the cabin boy. Had they not done so they would all have been dead before they were rescued. The sailors were convicted of murder and the case established that necessity is not a defence to murder.

Civil cases show the names of the contestants known as the plaintiff and defendant or, in Scotland, the pursuer and defender.

◆ RYLANDS v FLETCHER **(1868)**

The defendant constructed a reservoir on his land but water from the reservoir flooded the nearby coal mine owned by the plaintiff. The plaintiff sued the defendant who had to compensate him. The case established an important principle that if a landowner collects on his land anything not naturally there, he is liable for the consequences of its escape, even if he has not been negligent.

Case names are usually followed by various numbers and letters to indicate where the case report can be found. Those details are not included in the text of this book, but are shown in the case index.

UK legislation

UK legislation is the law made by, or under the authority of, Parliament. Strictly, it is the power of the Queen in Parliament and it takes precedence over the common law, so legislation can – and often does – replace, change or merely codify the common law. There are two types of UK legislation

- Acts of Parliament – also known as statutes
- statutory instruments – also known as delegated legislation

and they become law by different processes.

Parliament is made up of two Houses. The House of Commons is the elected part of Parliament. The House of Lords is made up of various people who are there either by appointment, birthright or position, but it provides an extremely useful balance within Parliament.

Most legislation sees the light of day because the government, which is the majority political party in the House of Commons, wishes to make such new laws as part of government policy. Some new legislation is preceded by discussion within the government, or externally. The government might decide the laws need to be changed, but invite views as to how to proceed, and they will do this by issuing a 'green paper'. In other cases, the government merely announces its intentions. The best known example of this is the budget statement made every year, which then becomes the annual Finance Act. Some legislation may become law at the instigation of an individual Member of Parliament.

An Act of Parliament only becomes an Act once it has been passed by both Houses of Parliament and received the royal assent.

The procedure is that a 'bill' (which is a draft Act of Parliament) is drafted by a parliamentary draughtsman. The bill is then formally introduced into one of the Houses of Parliament, usually the House of Commons. This is when the title is read out but, at that stage, there is no debate on its contents. That is known as the first reading. At a later date, the bill is debated in the House of Commons and voted on, this is known as the second reading. If there is a majority in favour at this stage, then the bill goes to the committee stage where it is scrutinised in detail. Usually, the committee is one of the standing committees of the House of Commons.

The next stage in the bill's progress is the report stage, when the bill is debated again in the House of Commons after having been amended and knocked into shape by the committee, this is referred to as its third reading. A further vote is taken and, if in favour, it is then passed and goes to the House of Lords where it follows a similar procedure.

There are various conventions for dealing with amendments or outright rejection by the Lords, but assuming it passes through the Lords it then receives the royal assent – which is when the bill is signed on behalf of the Queen – and ceases to be a bill and becomes an Act of Parliament.

Some bills start off life in the House of Lords, for instance – the Food Safety Act 1990 was introduced in the House of Lords. If that happens, then the same procedure is followed, except that it completes its passage through the House of Lords first before going to the House of Commons.

Theoretically, the Queen retains a right to refuse to sign an Act of Parliament, but if the bill has passed through all its constitutional stages the royal assent will not be refused. The last time the royal assent was refused was in the eighteenth century.

An Act of Parliament becomes law on the day it receives the royal assent unless the Act specifies a later date, or provides that it only comes into effect on a date or dates to be specified by delegated legislation.

Each Act of Parliament has a name and year, for instance, the Environmental Protection Act 1990. Each Act also has a Chapter number which, in the case of the Environmental Protection Act 1990 is C43 of 1990.

A printed copy of any Act can be bought from Her Majesty's Stationery Office (HMSO) and there are also commercially produced prints of Acts of Parliament, which can be found in most large public libraries. Each Act has numbered paragraphs which are called sections, and often there are also Schedules.

Parliament also delegates the power to make legislation, usually to certain government ministers, and it is quite usual for Parliament to pass an Act of Parliament which delegates the power to make all kinds of detailed legislation.

There is no power for government ministers to make delegated legislation without having been given the power by an Act of Parliament. Delegated legislation is made by statutory instruments which are useful because they enable technical and detailed laws to be made in a much simpler fashion. They can also be changed more easily and, therefore, can be kept up to date.

The procedure for making statutory instruments may involve a consultation period beforehand, but the instrument itself has to be put back to the House of Commons and either specifically approved, or not objected to, within a period before it becomes law.

Statutory instruments are either Orders or Regulations and each has a number after the letters SI. For example, the Environmental Protection Act 1990 (Commencement Number 2) Order 1990 (SI 1990/2243) brought certain parts of the 1990 Act into force on the 13 November 1990.

In this book, the statutory instrument number is not quoted in the text, but is shown in the list of legislation. Regulations made under an Act of Parliament must not be confused with EC regulations, which will be looked at later.

EC law

To understand EC law it is necessary to understand the history of the European Union. In the mid-1950s, the main continental countries of Europe decided to create an economic unity within Europe to try to avoid Europe being torn apart by war again.

These countries were Belgium, France, West Germany, Italy, Luxembourg and the Netherlands. They entered into three treaties, which created 'economic communities', of which the most important was the Treaty of Rome in 1957. That treaty created what was then known as the European Economic Community (EEC). The other two treaties covered coal and steel and atomic energy and are not relevant to the subject of this book. In 1973, the UK joined the European Communities at the same time as Denmark and the Republic of Ireland. Since then, Greece, Spain, Portugal, Austria, Finland, and Sweden have joined, and Germany has become enlarged by the unification of West and East Germany. This makes 15 members in total.

Most law affecting businesses which is of European origin arises from the Treaty of Rome of 1957 and such law is referred to as EC law. The Treaty contains numbered paragraphs called Articles. The scope and aim of the Treaty was amended in 1986 by the Single European Act and in 1993 by the Maastricht Treaty. Both were separate treaties which added to and amended the 1957 Treaty.

When the Treaty of Rome was amended in 1993 by the Maastricht Treaty (officially called the Treaty on European Union) the three original treaties were given a collective name of the European Union (EU) and the Treaty of Rome also became known as the EC Treaty. The term EEC is no longer used.

Treaties are international agreements between countries but they are not law. The agreement reached in a treaty needs to be made law. When the UK joined the EEC in 1973, it did so by the UK Parliament passing the European Communities Act 1972, which made the Treaty of Rome part of the law of the UK. The Single European Act was incorporated into UK law by the European Communities (Amendment) Act 1986 and the Maastricht Treaty by the European Communities (Amendment) Act 1993.

So the slightly confusing situation is reached that the UK is a member of the EU but the main body of law resulting from that membership is known as EC law.

The picture is even more confusing because Norway and Iceland have become associate members of the EU and the area covered by both full and associate membership is known as the European Economic Area (EEA). The benefits of associate membership of those two countries are achieved in the UK by the European Economic Area Act 1993.

In passing the European Communities Act 1972, the UK Parliament gave up its supremacy to make laws in certain matters. EC laws have supremacy over UK laws and, as a consequence, the UK and all member states of the EU have lost their sovereignty in those areas covered by the EC Treaty (as amended). The supremacy of EC laws is demonstrated by the following case.

◆ **FACTORTAME LTD. V SECRETARY OF STATE FOR TRANSPORT (1991)**

The Merchant Shipping Act 1988, a UK Act of Parliament, imposed conditions which had to be met if a fishing vessel was to be registered as British. The conditions included one that it had to be British owned. The applicant company was owned and controlled by Spanish nationals. The company owned and operated fishing vessels which, prior to the 1988 Act, were British registered and so could fish against the British Fishing Quota. The company could not meet the new conditions in the 1988 Act.

The company alleged that the 1988 Act was contrary to EC law and that question was referred to the European Court of Justice for a decision.

The European Court of Justice decided that the UK's 1988 Act was in breach of Article 52 of the EC Treaty and was, therefore, ineffective.

The important point about this case is that Article 52 of the EC Treaty took precedence over a UK Act of Parliament so as to render the latter partly ineffective.

But EC law is not only contained in the EC Treaty (the Treaty of Rome) because the Treaty itself provides for EU institutions to be able to make secondary legislation.

> **EC Treaty Article 189**
>
> *In order to carry out their task, the Council and the Commission shall, in accordance with the provisions of this Treaty, make regulations, issue directives, take decisions, make recommendations or deliver opinions . . .*

The effect of regulations, directives, etc., will be discussed later, but now to look at how the EU makes this secondary legislation.

To do this it is necessary to know something about EU institutions. Apart from the European Court of Justice, there are three principal institutions of the EU.

- The Commission initiates community legislation by bringing forward proposals for legislation and putting the proposals to the Council. It also enforces community law by ensuring that member countries embody those laws into their national laws. The Commission has a number of Commissioners, drawn from all member countries. The UK has two Commissioners. The Commission is organised into different departments known as Directorates General, each responsible for an area of policy.
- The Council consists of one representative at senior government level from each member country. The Council decides on policy because the Council votes on EC legislation, but since the Single European Act a unanimous decision is not required on all matters. The Council is assisted by a

committee of permanent representatives (known as COREPER) consisting of officials of the member states who do much to agree detail and set agendas for Council meetings.

- The European Parliament (originally called the European Assembly) consists of Euro MPs directly elected by the whole electorate of the member countries of the EU every five years. Unlike the UK Parliament, it has no supreme legislative powers, that is, it cannot make any laws itself, but the Council must ask the European Parliament for its opinion before the Council makes any new laws on a subject, and the Maastricht Treaty has given the European Parliament greater powers.

All EC secondary legislation (regulations and directives) has to be seen to develop EC Treaty objectives. There are three different procedures by which EC secondary legislation is made. These procedures are known as the consultation procedure, co-operation procedure and the co-decision procedure.

The final stage in all procedures is the adoption of the legislation by the Council. The Council adopts such legislation either unanimously, or by a qualified majority (each member state has a number of votes). Whether unanimity or only a qualified majority is needed depends on which procedure is used and what route is taken through the procedure. If the Council uses the wrong procedure, the European Court of Justice can declare the relevant legislation to be invalid.

HOW LAWS ARE ENFORCED

The UK has a hierarchy of courts – courts where cases are dealt with first of all (courts of first instance) and appeal courts.

The courts system is divided into two categories – the civil court system and the criminal court system. In the criminal court system, proceedings are usually commenced on behalf of the state, either by the Crown Prosecution Service or some other enforcement agency. In civil cases, one party to a dispute will commence proceedings, in the case of High Court cases, this is done by issuing a writ.

The civil courts

In England and Wales, there are two civil courts of first instance – a county court and the High Court. A county court is for most civil disputes, but for matters where the value of the dispute in money terms is high, then the matter may have to be commenced in the High Court. The High Court has specialised divisions dealing with particular laws, and with judges familiar with those laws.

Appeals from both a county court and the High Court go to the Court of Appeal (Civil Division) and further appeals from there go to the House of Lords.

In addition to the courts system there are various tribunals with limited jurisdiction. These are informal courts and the best known are industrial tribunals. Appeals from industrial tribunals go to the Employment Appeal Tribunal.

The criminal courts

A person accused of a crime will be tried in either a magistrates' court or in the Crown Court according to the seriousness of the alleged crime.

Magistrates' courts often comprise two or more Justices of the Peace (JPs) who are not legally qualified, but they are advised by a legally qualified clerk of the court and they deal with all less serious crimes.

Crown Courts have a legally qualified judge. They deal not only with the more serious crimes, but also with appeals from magistrates' courts. Appeals from Crown Courts go to the Court of Appeal (Criminal Division), and further appeals from there go to the House of Lords.

European courts

Before looking at the European courts, it is important to say that EC law is part of the law of the UK, and is enforced and applied by the UK national courts in exactly the same way as the UK courts deal with national laws.

The European Court of Justice (ECJ) consists of 16 judges, one from each member state and a president of the court. The ECJ is assisted in its duties by a number of Advocates General who assist it by preparing, in advance, detailed opinions on the laws on each case, which they then present to the ECJ with recommendations.

The ECJ has extremely wide terms of reference, which include dealing with actions against member states for failure to implement any EC law (Articles 169 and 170 of the EC Treaty).

The ECJ can assist national courts in dealing with European law. The procedure operates under Article 177 of the EC Treaty. If a national court of a member state is dealing with a dispute in which a question arises under EC law, and the answer to the question is necessary for the court in the member state to come to a decision, then that court can refer the question to the ECJ to give a preliminary ruling.

Decisions of the ECJ are published throughout the European states in the various different languages and, in this way, European law is developed and explained consistently throughout all member states.

There is also a European Court of First Instance which, among other things, has jurisdiction to deal with certain trade competition matters.

The ECJ should not be confused with the European Court of Human Rights which is an entirely separate court formed under a separate treaty, the European Convention on Human Rights.

Lawyers

Each country has its own lawyers. In England and Wales there are two branches of lawyers – barristers and solicitors. Barristers deal with two types of work. First they are specialist advocates, that is, lawyers who appear in all courts to question witnesses and argue the case on behalf of their clients. Secondly, they are available to give opinions on the law on any set of facts but barristers only accept instructions from solicitors and certain other professional categories of people – they do not deal directly with the public.

Solicitors are the lawyers to be found in most towns dealing with a wide variety of legal matters and usually as firms of solicitors. They deal directly with the public and they can appear as advocates in magistrates' courts and county courts. Additionally solicitors with relevant experience can be authorised to be advocates in the High Court.

How laws apply

Judicial precedent

The common law, that is, judge-made law, developed from judges' reasons for decisions in particular cases. A decision in a case sets a precedent which is followed in subsequent cases. This system of judicial precedent requires two basic features

- a hierarchy of courts
- a law reporting system.

The hierarchy of courts is important because the higher up the system the decision is made, the more authority the decision has. Accordingly, decisions in the House of Lords are very important in setting a precedent for future cases, but magistrates' court decisions do not set any precedent for future cases. The need for law reports is so that there is a reliable written record of the reasons for a decision.

By this system of judicial precedent, the law is developed and explained in a structured way so business can be conducted and people go about their ordinary lives relying on that settled structure.

Legislation in force

One of the problems with UK legislation is discovering what legislation is in force. Acts of Parliament come into force when they receive the royal assent, but often the Act itself will provide that it will not come into force until dates to be specified in a commencement order, or even a series of commencement orders for different sections. Also a later Act of Parliament may repeal or amend an earlier one. The same applies to secondary legislation.

The only practical way of discovering which legislation is in force and whether it has been amended is to refer to specialist publications.

Judicial interpretation of legislation

Legislation is a written set of rules decided on by a law-making body which lays down rules to govern a range of situations. It is difficult, if not impossible, for one set of rules to cover every possible situation. To add to the confusion, sometimes legislation may be ambiguous or difficult to understand.

The job of the courts in applying or enforcing legislation is to make decisions as to what it means, and then to apply it to the set of facts in a particular case. This task of deciding what the legislation means is called 'interpreting' the legislation.

To complicate the issue further, there are different rules for interpreting UK legislation and EC legislation (including UK legislation passed to implement EC directives). When the UK Parliament passes laws, the reasons for the laws are not stated, but with EC laws the reasons are given. Also, if UK laws are made to implement EC directives there is always the directive to refer to, to see how far the UK law has been successful.

In the case of EC laws (including UK laws implementing EC directives), the courts look at the reasons for the legislation (and the directive being implemented) to interpret the purpose and the wording of the directive as illustrated by the following case.

◆ LITSTER V FORTH DRY DOCK COMPANY LIMITED (1989)

A ship repairing company became insolvent and a receiver was appointed. The receiver agreed to sell the assets of the insolvent company to another company, but the purchasing company did not want to keep the existing workforce of the insolvent company because it had its own employees who were paid less.

At 3.30pm the receiver dismissed the employees without notice and, an hour later, the transfer to the purchasing company took place.

The Transfer of Undertakings (Protection of Employment) Regulations 1981 provide that, on the transfer of a business, the staff who are employed in that business 'immediately before the transfer' also transfer with the business together with all their existing rights.

The 1981 regulations were made to implement EC directive 77/187, and the purpose of the directive was to provide protection for employees in the event of a change of employer and, in particular, to ensure the safeguard of their rights.

Because the receiver had no money to pay the employees, they claimed unfair dismissal compensation from the purchasing company.

The purchasing company answered the claim by saying that the employees did not transfer to it with the business because they were not employed in the business 'immediately before the transfer' there had been a gap of one hour.

The case went on appeal all the way to the House of Lords where it was decided that it was necessary to interpret the 1981 regulations as applying, not only to employees in the business at the time of its transfer, but also those who would have been employed at that time had they not been dismissed before and because of the transfer. Unless the 1981 regulations were read in that way, then the purpose of the EC directive would not be achieved.

But, for UK laws which are not made to implement an EC directive, the courts work on the basis that the words of the legislation must be given their ordinary meaning, even if that might mean that Parliament's intentions may be thwarted unless the wording is ambiguous. If there is an absurdity (and that does happen) then the courts will interpret the legislation so as to avoid an absurd result.

The strictness of this literal interpretation rule has recently been relaxed by the House of Lords in a decision which has shown a move towards the European approach.

◆ PEPPER (INSPECTOR OF TAXES) v HART (1993)

An independent boys school offered places not taken by fee paying pupils to the sons of teachers and other staff at one-fifth of the normal fees. That reduced level of fees was sufficient to cover the additional cost to the school of educating those boys – that is the extra cost which would have been avoided if the places had been left unfilled.

Nine teachers and the bursar who were having their sons educated at the school under the scheme were assessed liable to tax on the cash equivalent of the benefit. The law which created liability to tax on benefits in kind was ambiguous. The court decided to look at the reports of the parliamentary debates (*Hansard*) at the time the law was being discussed to see if those reports threw any light on what was intended. From the debate it was clear that it was not the intention to tax such benefits where the fees paid covered the additional cost involved. As that was the case here the House of Lords decided that no tax was payable because that was not the purpose of the particular tax law.

Application of EC laws

EC laws are still in their infancy – they have been around for less than 40 years – while English law has developed over at least 900 years. How EC law applies is still being worked out in practice.

As already seen, the primary legislation of the EU is the Treaty of Rome (as amended). Much of the Treaty is only a framework of loose expressions of policy. The Treaty of Rome is part of UK law and, as such, is said to be 'directly applicable'.

There are, however, specific and quite precise areas of the Treaty which create legal rights and obligations capable of being enforced by individuals in their own national courts. Such parts are referred to as having 'direct effect'. One such part is Article 119 of the Treaty.

Article 119 EC Treaty

Each member state shall . . . maintain the application of the principle that men and women shall receive equal pay for equal work.

◆ **DEFRENNE V SABENA (1975)**

Ms Defrenne was an air hostess employed by the Belgian Airline, Sabena. Male air stewards employed by Sabena were paid more than air hostesses despite their jobs being identical.

Ms Defrenne took court action against the airline basing her claim on Article 119 of the EC Treaty. The question which had to be decided was whether the somewhat general statement in Article 119, which appeared to be a duty directed to member states, gave any rights to employees of private employers.

The European Court of Justice decided that Article 119 had direct effect and, therefore, conferred rights enforceable by Ms Defrenne.

EC secondary legislation consists of regulations, directives, decisions, recommendations and opinions. Regulations are of general application and binding in all member states. Once made by the EU institutions, they form part of the law of each member state without the need for any further action. They have immediate 'direct effect'.

Article 189 EC Treaty

. . . a Regulation shall have general application. It shall be binding in its entirety and directly applicable in all member states.

A Directive shall be binding, as to the result to be achieved, upon each member state to which it is addressed but shall leave the national authorities the choice of form and methods.

A decision shall be binding in its entirety upon those to whom it is addressed.

Recommendations and opinions shall have no binding force.

Unlike UK regulations, EC regulations are known by their number and year rather than their title. For example, EC Regulation 1612/68 has as its title 'Regulation Number 1612/68 of the Council of the 15 October 1968 on the Freedom of Movement for Workers within the Community'.

Directives are directions given to member states to make national laws by a certain date to achieve certain results.

As a matter of logic, directives cannot have direct effect, because they do not become law in each state until the national law is made. However, for a number of years, individuals have endeavoured through court cases to take advantage of 'rights' contained in EC directives which have not been incorporated into the national laws. All those attempts failed where the date for implementation of the directive had not expired, but what if the date had expired and the national legislature had not implemented the directive?

◆ MARSHALL V SOUTHAMPTON AND SOUTH WEST HAMPSHIRE AREA HEALTH AUTHORITY (1986)

Miss Marshall was employed by the Area Health Authority. The Authority had a compulsory retirement age equivalent to the state pension age, namely, 65 for men and 60 for women.

Miss Marshall did not want to retire when she reached 60, and the Authority allowed her to stay on, but compulsorily retired her when she was 62. Miss Marshall alleged that this was in breach of EC directive 76/207 which required national laws to be implemented to eliminate sex discrimination at work and establish the principle of equal treatment as regards dismissal and retirement.

She was unable to rely on the Sex Discrimination Act 1975 because that Act permitted different retirement ages. The date for the implementation of EC Directive 76/207 had passed.

The case went to the European Court of Justice where it was decided that

- the directive required the national state to implement laws outlawing different retirement ages
- the date for implementation of the directive had passed
- as the Area Health Authority was essentially a part of the state, the Area Health Authority could not set up as a defence the failure of the state to fulfil its EC obligations
- Miss Marshall could accordingly rely upon the directive.

This means that when directives have passed their 'implement by' date, they can have a direct effect between the defaulting state and an individual. The relevant provisions of the Sex Discrimination Act 1975 were promptly amended by the Sex Discrimination Act 1986, to give effect to the EC Directive 76/207.

Miss Marshall only won her case because she was employed by the state (or an organ of the state). The result would not have been the same had she been employed by a private employer.

This unsatisfactory state of affairs creates a division of the principle of 'direct effect'. Vertical direct effect is rights and obligations enforceable between the state and citizens within the state. On the other hand, horizontal direct effect refers to rights enforceable and obligations between individuals.

So, after Miss Marshall's win, it could be seen that EC directive 76/207 had vertical direct effect, but not horizontal direct effect. The latter was only achieved when the Sex Discrimination Act 1986 was passed.

To use another example, in Ms Defrenne's case (the Belgian air hostess), Article 119 not only had vertical direct effect, but also horizontal direct effect.

But the unsatisfactory state of affairs of unimplemented directives only having vertical direct effect and not horizontal direct effect was to some extent corrected by the following case.

◆ FRANCOVICH V ITALIAN REPUBLIC (1992)

The Italian Government had failed to implement Directive 80/987 to set up a compensation scheme for employees whose employers become insolvent.

Mr Francovich was owed money by his insolvent employers. He sued the Italian Government for the money due to him.

The European Court of Justice decided that if a directive gives rights to individuals and has not been implemented then an individual who suffers loss as a direct result of the failure to implement the directive can sue the government to recover that loss.

  Accordingly despite the fact that the compensation scheme had not been established Mr Francovich was able to get compensation from his government because of their failure to set up that scheme.

EC directives, like EC regulations, have wordy titles. The EC directive in Miss Marshall's case is the 'Council Directive of 9 February 1976 on the Implementation of the Principle of Equal Treatment for Men and Women as regards Access to Employment, Vocational Training and Promotion and Working Conditions'. In practice, EC directives are known by numbers, and sometimes by short titles, for example, the Equal Treatment Directive.

  EC recommendations as indicated in Article 189 have no binding effect, but can be taken into account when the court comes to make some sense of any national legislation passed to give effect to the recommendation.

Some aspects of civil law

There are numerous classifications of civil law, many of which will be met later in this book. In particular, land law is looked at in detail in Chapter 3. But three types of civil law are outlined here before moving on.

Contract

A contract is an agreement which has legal consequences. An agreement to meet for lunch is not a contract. An agreement to buy a business will be a contract.

  Every contract has more than one party – usually two. A contract arises by the acceptance of an offer, where the parties intend that their agreement will create a legally binding relationship.

  An essential ingredient in a binding contract is that there must be what is called 'consideration', that is, what is given in exchange. If a person buys a meal in a restaurant, the restaurateur provides consideration (the meal) and, likewise, the customer (money in payment). If there is no consideration, for example, a promise to provide a customer with a free meal, there is no contract which can be enforced in the courts by the customer. If, however, there was some consideration for the promise, for example, a free meal in return for the customer not suing the restaurateur for having poured gravy all down his suit, then there is consideration because consideration does not have to be financial.

All commerce is based on the enforceability of laws of contract and the courts will either enforce a contract by an order compelling the defaulting party to carry out his or her obligations under the contract, or will make the defaulting party pay the other party sufficient money to compensate him or her for the breach of contract.

Tort

A tort is a civil wrong where one person's conduct causes harm to another – it is based, not on the contractual relationship between the parties, but on a duty owed by each member of society to each other. There are numerous classifications of tort, but those most often met are

- defamation
- trespass
- negligence

The latter (negligence) is the breach of a legal duty of care towards another resulting in damage.

Most tort is either still based on common law or is now to be found in statute law, which codifies the original common law principles.

Breach of statutory duty

Criminal and civil laws are quite distinct. They are administered in separate courts and create quite separate rights and duties.

Merely because someone breaks the criminal law, does not mean that an individual harmed by that breach can sue the person in the civil courts. For example, the Food Safety Act 1990 creates a criminal offence of selling food which fails to comply with the food safety requirements. The guilty person can be punished for that crime but an individual cannot sue in the civil courts basing the claim on that breach of that criminal law. Instead, an individual who wants to sue must find some basis for that claim in civil law.

But there are some situations in which an individual can sue another basing the claim on breach of a criminal duty. This is referred to as the tort of breach of statutory duty.

The general rule is that, where criminal duties are imposed for the protection or benefit of the public generally, then a breach of those duties will not give rise to civil remedies. So in the case of a breach of any of the criminal duties under the Food Safety Act 1990, an individual has no civil remedy merely because of the breach.

If, however, criminal duties are imposed for the benefit or protection of a particular category of individuals, then any of those individuals who are harmed by a breach of those criminal duties can generally sue for the tort of breach of statutory duty, rather than sue for negligence or some other civil remedy.

As will be seen in Chapter 3, the Workplace (Health, Safety and Welfare) Regulations 1992 create criminal offences, but it is one of those situations where a breach of a criminal duty can be relied on to give a civil remedy.

◆ SELF EXAMINATION QUESTIONS ◆

1 The Unfair Contract Terms Directive (Council Directive 93/13/EEC) requires member countries to make laws to comply with the directive no later than 31 December 1994 to be applicable to all contracts made after 31 December 1994. The Unfair Terms in Consumer Contracts Regulations 1994 implement in the UK that directive but only as from 1 July 1995. Explain what is a directive and implementing regulations and also explain what consequences could arise as a result of the six months delay in implementation.

2 Klaus runs a functions catering business. Recently he did the catering at a function but afterwards 12 people became ill from food poisoning. The cause of the poisoning was found to be the cold meat buffet prepared by Klaus. Consider the criminal and civil consequences for Klaus.

See Appendix for suggested answers.

Chapter

THE BUSINESS ENTERPRISE

TYPES OF BUSINESS ORGANISATIONS

SOLE TRADERS

PARTNERSHIPS

COMPANIES

OTHER ORGANISATIONS

FRANCHISES

Types of business organisations

The types of business or commercial organisations in the UK can be divided into four categories

- sole traders
- partnerships
- corporations
- other unincorporated organisations.

Each of these will be looked at in turn, but only a particular type of corporation will be considered – a company which has been incorporated under the companies legislation.

What distinguishes a corporation from any other form of business organisation (in England and Wales) is that it is legally a 'person'. This means that a company can be a party to a contract, can commit a crime, can own land, in fact, can do almost all the things that a natural person can do, except think for itself.

Different types of corporations exist including

- building societies
- local authorities
- corporations formed by Royal Charter or Act of Parliament
- companies formed by registration under the Companies Acts.

It is this latter category of corporations which will be considered in this book because that is the only form of corporate business organisation available to the hotelier and caterer.

Sole traders

The most basic type of business enterprise is the sole trader, that is one person who runs his or her own business with or without the help of employees. Sole traders are a feature of the building and property maintenance industries where self-employed plumbers, electricians etc., run their own businesses, often without business premises. But small catering establishments, especially cafes and take-away food premises, are also run by sole traders. A sole trader is referred to as the 'proprietor' of the business.

The drawback to being a sole trader is the fact that the proprietor must provide all the capital for the business, and takes all the risk. The proprietor has unlimited liability, so that if the business fails, it is not only his or her business assets which can be used to pay creditors, but also personal assets.

If the business becomes insolvent, then the sole trader may have to be declared bankrupt, which is an order of the court under which a trustee is appointed to sell all the trader's assets to pay his or her creditors.

There are advantages of being a sole trader. It is the cheapest method of setting up in business, all the profits of the business belong to the sole trader and the sole trader is his or her own boss.

There are no special laws which apply to sole traders as there are with partnerships and companies.

If the business is successful and expands, there comes a point where the business becomes too large for a sole trader and at that stage the trader may have to convert to one of the other forms of business organisations, for instance, take in a partner so as to become a partnership, or incorporate the business and run it through a company.

PARTNERSHIPS

Nature of partnerships

A partnership is two or more people who work together as joint proprietors of a business to make a profit by their joint efforts.

Partnership Act 1890 Section 1

Partnership is the relation which subsists between persons carrying on a business in common with a view of profit.

No special formalities are needed to create a partnership: whether a partnership exists is a question of law to be decided by the courts. But most partnerships are created by a partnership deed which is essentially the partnership's constitution.

Partnerships are common in the case of professional businesses such as solicitors and accountants. A partnership is collectively known as a 'firm' and usually trades under a business name (see Chapter 4 for details).

The members of a partnership are usually individuals, but there is nothing to prevent a partnership in which the partners are all companies or a mixture of companies and individuals.

Unlike a company, a partnership (firm) is not a separate legal entity (see below for Scotland) and each partner is liable jointly with the other partners for all the debts and other obligations of the firm (section 9 Partnership Act 1890). This is because they are, in essence, a collection of joint proprietors.

Because a firm has no separate existence, it cannot own land, make contracts, sue or be sued in the firm's name, instead these things are done by the partners personally. The latter rule has been eased by court rules to permit a firm to sue and be sued in the firm's name rather than naming all the individual partners.

In Scotland the rules are slightly different because a Scottish firm is a separate legal entity, although the partners still have unlimited liability.

A partnership does not usually become a large organisation and the reason for this is that the number of partners is limited to 20 (section 716 Companies Act 1985) except in certain professional partnerships where there is no limit on the number of partners.

Partnership as a business organisation is suitable for a business where the partners put up the capital and run the business themselves. They take the risks personally of commercial success or failure.

The partnership relationship

The rights and duties as between the partners is controlled by the partnership deed. If there is not a deed or it does not cover the particular matter, then the Partnership Act 1890 provides some rules which apply unless something else is agreed.

In particular, section 24 Partnership Act 1890 sets out some basic rules which apply in the absence of some other agreement, for example all partners share equally in profits but must also contribute equally to make up losses.

No new partner can be introduced without the unanimous consent of the existing partners and no partner can be expelled unless there is a power in the partnership deed to do so.

A partnership can usually be terminated by any of the partners giving notice to the others. Also, the death of a partner will terminate the partnership, but the remaining partners will be able to form a new partnership and carry on the business without a break.

Limited partnerships

A limited partnership is one where at least one partner has unlimited liability for the partnership debts and liabilities, but some, or all, of the others can have limited liability rather like the shareholders in a company. Such partnerships are governed by the Limited Partnerships Act 1907, but are rarely met in practice. They have many of the drawbacks of companies concerning the need for registration but without the advantage of being a separate legal person.

Advantages and disadvantages of partnership

The formation and maintenance of a partnership involves considerably less formality and cost than setting up and maintaining a company, and the regime under the Partnership Act 1890 is far less rigid than for companies under the Companies Acts. For instance, if the partners wish to increase the capital of the partnership by putting in more money, they merely agree to do so. On the other hand, if a company wishes to increase its capital, then it is necessary to comply with the procedures laid down in the Companies Act 1985.

There are taxation differences between companies and partnerships which can influence which type of business organisation is chosen to run the business.

Where a company is of advantage is that it is the appropriate business organisation where the capital is provided by people who do not necessarily wish to run the business.

COMPANIES

The type of companies considered in this book are companies which are incorporated under the Companies Acts and are 'limited by shares' (the expression 'limited by shares' will be explained below).

There are two other types of companies which can be formed under the Companies Acts

- companies limited by guarantee
- unlimited companies.

Of these, the former are usually only non-commercial organisations, and the latter are extremely rare.

A company limited by shares has shareholders who are also referred to as 'members' of the company and who collectively own the company and provide the capital for the business. A shareholder's liability is limited to the amount payable under his or her share or shares. If the shares are fully paid up and the company has to be wound up because it is insolvent, then a shareholder cannot be required to pay any more money, he or she just loses what he or she has put in.

In this way, shareholders in a company enjoy an advantage over other business owners because their liability is limited and they do not place their personal assets at risk by being the owners of a business. It is this limitation of liability which is probably the greatest attraction of a company as a business organisation.

Every company limited by shares has to have a minimum of two shareholders but a private limited company (see below) can have just one shareholder in which case some special rules apply. (Companies (Single Members Private Limited Companies) Regulations 1992).

Ownership of shares in a company is recorded in each company's shares register and usually a certificate, 'a share certificate', is issued to each shareholder, but section 207 Companies Act 1989 envisages shares being issued without a certificate.

Private and public companies

Companies are divided into two further categories – private and public. A private company cannot offer shares to the public and is therefore appropriate for the small or family business or where a partnership is incorporated. Such companies have to have the word 'limited' as the last word of their name although in use the word limited may be abbreviated 'Ltd'.

Public companies have to comply with a whole range of requirements in the Companies Act 1985 including having a minimum capital and the words 'public limited company' must be the last words of its name, which may, in use, be abbreviated to 'plc'.

A private company can re-register as a plc, and vice versa. The advantage of being a public limited company is being able to raise capital by issuing shares to the public for example to enable the business to expand.

Formation of companies

A company is formed by delivering certain documents to the Registrar of Companies and paying a fee. If these are all in order and the name of the company is acceptable, then the Registrar will issue a certificate of incorporation, and the company then comes into existence. The certificate of incorporation will state the date of incorporation, the company name and the company number.

Constitution of companies

The constitution of a company is contained in two documents called the memorandum of association and the articles of association. These documents are prepared before the company is incorporated and are some of the documents to be delivered to the Registrar in order to incorporate the company.

The memorandum of association is a very formal document which specifies (among other things) the name of the company and the purposes of the company (its objects). Traditionally the objects of a company have been set out in length with every conceivable commercial activity so as to give the company scope to do anything. Section 110 Companies Act 1989 now allows a company memorandum to state that the object of the company is to carry on business as a general commercial company, in which case, the company will be able to carry on any trade or business and do anything needed for that purpose, for example borrow money, own land and take on employees.

The articles of association set out the rules for regulation of the company including the rules about general meetings, appointment and powers of directors, accounts and audits etc. There are standard articles of association which may be used or modified as appropriate.

Management of companies

A company must have directors. In the case of a private company, there has to be at least one director, and for public companies the rule is that there must be a minimum of two directors. The articles of association will usually specify a maximum number of directors.

Every company must also have a company secretary. The secretary's tasks are not managerial but administrative. There are numerous legal duties, including keeping the register of shareholders. Usually a director can also be the secretary, but if the company only has one director then someone else has to be the secretary.

There are two categories of directors – executive and non-executive. The former are generally full time. A non-executive director is a person who is appointed for some special quality which is useful to the company but who does not normally work in the company.

Directors meet as the board of directors and make decisions (known as resolutions) at board meetings. The quorum for a board meeting is usually fixed by the articles of association. The job of the board of directors is to manage the business of the company in accordance with the memorandum and articles of association.

Shareholders

The shareholders (members) of the company are collectively the owners of the company and they exercise control over the company through the meetings of the company which they are entitled to attend. Every company must have an Annual General Meeting every year. The business at the Annual General

Meeting will include a report from the directors, consideration of the accounts, the auditors' report, the election of directors and appointment of auditors.

Any meeting for all shareholders other than the Annual General Meeting is known as an Extra-Ordinary General Meeting, at which the business conducted depends on the purpose of the meeting. There may be different classes of shareholders according to the nature of their shares and they may have different voting rights.

Decisions at shareholders' meetings are also called resolutions, and some resolutions may require more than a majority to be passed, for instance, a resolution to wind up the company will generally be an 'extra-ordinary resolution' which requires a majority of three quarters of members who vote on the proposal.

Accounts and annual return

Every company must keep sufficient accounting records of company transactions to show the financial position of the company at any time. Failure to keep these accounts places criminal liability on the company directors.

Every company must have a financial year and at the end of the financial year a balance sheet and a profit and loss account must be prepared. These accounts, which are known as the annual accounts, together with a directors' report containing a fair review of the business over the year must be presented to the Annual General Meeting of the company (sections 226 and 234 Companies Act 1985).

Every company must complete certain forms and send them, with certain information and copies of the annual accounts, to the Registrar of Companies. This is known as 'filing' the annual return. The annual accounts to be filed every year at the Companies Registry (also known as Companies House) must contain all the information and comply with the requirements of Schedule 4 to the Companies Act 1985. However, small companies can take advantage of certain exemptions so that only a summary balance sheet needs to be filed. Medium-sized companies can also supply less information than the full requirements of Schedule 4, but more than a small company. The definitions of a small- and medium-sized company are set out in the Companies Act 1985 and depend on turnover, assets and number of employees.

There are time limits within which companies must file their annual returns at the Companies Registry. Private limited companies must file their annual returns within ten months from the end of their financial year and public limited companies within seven months. Companies who file their returns late are 'fined' late filing penalties which can be heavy.

All companies must have their accounts audited except for small companies unless at least 10 per cent of the shareholders request an audit.

The annual return sent to Companies Registry becomes a public document so that anyone can look at it at the Registry. The information in the annual return gives useful information to all varieties of businesses including credit reference agencies. The requirement to file annual accounts at the Companies Registry and for those accounts to be public is the price to be paid for the benefit of limited liability.

Where a company is part of a group of companies (for example one or more companies substantially owned or controlled by another company) then in addition to individual accounts for each company a set of group accounts must be prepared (section 227 Companies Act 1985). Group accounts comprise a consolidated balance sheet and a consolidated profit and loss account which show the financial state of the business of the whole group as if the individual companies were merely divisions of the one business. Small groups do not need to prepare group accounts.

Disqualification of directors

Under the Company Directors Disqualification Act 1986 a person can be prohibited from acting as a director in any company if a court makes a disqualification order.

There are various grounds under the 1986 Act for making an order but section 6 of the 1986 Act requires a court to make a disqualification order against a person who is a director of a company which has become insolvent, and the conduct is such that he or she is unfit to be involved in the future management of a company. The aim of section 6 is to prevent a person allowing a company to sink into insolvency, abandoning that company, and then starting up again with a new company.

OTHER ORGANISATIONS

There are other types of organisations which may be formed for various purposes, but only two of these have any real relevance to the hotel and catering industry – clubs and joint ventures.

Clubs

There are two sorts of clubs – proprietary clubs and members' clubs. A proprietary club is a business operated by a proprietor (which may be a sole trader, partnership or company) for a profit. An example is a country club run by a company and which people can join as members, usually on an annual basis, by paying a fee and can use the facilities of the club. Such a club is only a club because membership is necessary to use the facilities. In all other respects a proprietary club is no different from any other business. A members' club is entirely different. It is a number of people who associate together for non-commercial reasons often for social or sporting purposes. Such a club is not a partnership because there is no intention to make a profit, but a club can be incorporated (be a company). The club's rules are its constitution. The rules will say what is the club's purpose, who can be members, who runs the club etc. If the club is very large, there may be a management committee.

A members' club has the advantage that instead of obtaining a licence for the sale of alcohol it can become registered under section 40 Licensing Act 1964 which confers certain benefits, principally the permitted drinking hours.

A members' club is not a separate legal entity and cannot, for example, own land. If a club buys a clubhouse, it will be put in the names of trustees on behalf of the members of the club.

Joint ventures

A joint venture is well described by its name; it is where two or more people or companies co-operate for a commercial venture. The venture may be to run a business or achieve a particular objective. The co-operation is similar to a partnership but most joint ventures operate either through a company set up for the purpose or through contractual arrangements between the parties. In the latter case the relationship is usually referred to as a consortium.

Joint ventures may be created because the resources needed are beyond the abilities of the individual members, for example to build a channel tunnel or to operate a credit card company. Other joint ventures are created because the skills of the participants are complementary and necessary for the objectives of the joint venture.

There are no separate laws controlling joint ventures. The venture itself, and the rights and obligations of the participants, are controlled by the legal documents prepared for the operation of the venture. However, competition law has considerable effect on the setting up of joint ventures. Joint venture arrangements invariably include restrictions on the participants of one sort or another, such as not to compete with a joint venture. Such restrictions must be tested for validity by looking at Article 85(1) EC Treaty and the Restrictive Trade Practices Act 1976 (see Chapter 4).

FRANCHISES

Franchises are difficult to define. They are not a type of business organisation, but more a business system which a business organisation permits another to use. The business system will usually be a complete set of rights involving business name and trade mark, business get-up, for example layout, design, decoration of premises, and standard menus, business method and standards for example standard recipes. Franchises are well established in the hotel and catering business, especially in the fast food sector.

A franchise is based on a contractual relationship. The franchisor permits the franchisee to carry on a business under the franchisor's business system, including using the business name belonging to the franchisor. The franchisor will, under the contract, retain certain controls over how the business operates, mainly to ensure that the use of that name is enhanced and not damaged by the franchisee's use of the system. The franchisee may be required to buy supplies from the franchisor for instance, food, menu cards and staff uniforms, and the franchisee will pay a periodic fee to the franchisor for the use of the franchise system. The franchisor will also usually undertake not to grant any other franchise within the area covered by the franchisee, and will often be responsible for certain advertising for the benefit of the franchise system. The franchisor will, generally, undertake to carry out training for the franchisee and franchisee's staff.

The franchisor may endeavour to create a national network of outlets all run by different businesses but using the franchise system, so that all of the businesses are 'clones' despite the fact that they are run by different business organisations. In this way, the individual businesses benefit from the increased awareness created by the national identity of the franchise network.

The attraction of a franchise is that the franchisee benefits from having the business system already set up. If a franchise is operating successfully in one town there is every reason to expect that it can operate successfully in another. A person taking on a franchise which has a successful track record should have a better chance of making a success of the business than starting up without the backing of a franchise.

Franchises and EC competition law

In Chapter 4 the topic of competition law is considered, in particular Article 85 EC Treaty, which prohibits all agreements which could affect trade between member states and which prevent, restrict or distort competition within the European Union.

Franchise agreements contain a whole host of restrictions which can affect trade. For some time it was uncertain how Article 85 EC Treaty related to restrictions in franchise agreements. The matter was brought to a head in the following case.

◆ PRONUPTIA DE PARIS GMBH V SCHILLGALIS (1986)

A franchisor, Pronuptia de Paris, entered into franchise agreements with franchisees for the sale of bridal gowns and wedding attire. Mrs Schillgalis had a franchise agreement with Pronuptia de Paris which gave her the exclusive franchise in Hamburg, Oldenburg and Hanover.

The franchise agreement provided for various matters including for Mrs Schillgalis to pay to Pronuptia franchise fees of 10 per cent of her turnover. She did not pay and she was sued by Pronuptia, in the German courts, for the money.

Mrs Schillgalis countered the claim by saying that she was not liable to pay anything because the franchise agreement was in breach of Article 85 EC Treaty and therefore void. The German court asked the European Court of Justice for a preliminary ruling as to the applicability of Article 85 to the franchise agreement.

The result in the Pronuptia case was interesting. The European Court of Justice decided that some of the provisions of a franchise agreement could breach Article 85, in particular market sharing provisions (that is giving certain territories exclusively to some franchisees) and also practices which control prices.

This decision caused some consternation in EC institutions. Franchises were seen on the one hand as successful means for small businesses to enter a competitive market, while on the other hand, franchises could be viewed as anti-competitive in many respects. It was a question of steering a middle course.

Under Article 85 there is power to grant block exemptions which enable potentially infringing agreements to be exempted. Largely due to the decision in the Pronuptia case, the EC Commission issued a block exemption for franchises and this is to be found in EC Regulation 4087/88.

The terms of the block exemption are detailed, complex and beyond the scope of this book, but the advantage is that if a franchise agreement is drawn up so as to be within the block exemption, then it does not fall foul of Article 85 and is valid.

─────────◆ **SELF EXAMINATION QUESTIONS** ◆─────────

1 Angela is proposing to start up her own function catering business. Explain what two forms her business organisation could take and discuss some of the advantages and disadvantages of each.

2 Angela's friend Beatrice is willing to help Angela by providing some of the capital to start up the business. Beatrice does not want to lend the money to Angela but wants to have a stake in the business because she believes it is likely to be a success. What methods could be used for this purpose?

3 Angela's business becomes highly successful. She wants to use her business formula to expand the business further afield but she appreciates the problems of running the expanded operation herself. Consider the options available.

See Appendix for suggested answers.

───────────────────────◆───────────────────────

Chapter **3**

BUSINESS PREMISES

❖

OWNERSHIP

BUSINESS LEASES

FIRE PRECAUTIONS

COVENANTS AND TIES

OCCUPIERS' RESPONSIBILITIES (CIVIL)

OCCUPIERS' RESPONSIBILITIES (CRIMINAL)

TOWN AND COUNTRY PLANNING

HIGHWAY AMENITIES

CAPITAL ALLOWANCES

BUSINESS RATES

❖

OWNERSHIP

Every country has its own laws of ownership of land. It is a rule of international law that land law is governed by the law of the country where the land is, even if the land is owned by someone who lives in another country.

Scottish and English laws differ, and this is particularly true of land law. There are, however, sufficient similarities to make some general statements. In both countries the theory is that the Crown owns all land, and although in common parlance someone is said to own land, in fact, they own an intangible item which in England is called an 'estate'. This is a legal concept which is useful as it creates a greater degree of flexibility than is possible by attaching ownership directly to the soil, bricks and mortar.

Freehold

By section 1(1) Law of Property Act 1925, there are only two 'estates' in land in England and Wales

- freehold – technically known as 'the fee simple absolute in possession'
- leasehold – technically known as 'a term of years absolute'.

A freehold estate is for an unlimited period of time, but a leasehold estate is limited in time. Leasehold can either be for a fixed period, for instance, a lease of 99 years which comes to an end when the lease term expires, or it can be a periodic tenancy, such as a weekly or monthly tenancy, which is a leasehold which continues until brought to an end usually by a notice.

Both freehold and leasehold estates can, and often are, affected by other 'interests'. The main ones are

- rights of way and other easements
- mortgages
- restrictive covenants.

Leasehold

A leasehold estate for a term of more than three years must be created by a legal document known as a deed, and is generally known as a lease. A leasehold estate for three years or less may be created informally.

A headlease is a lease created by a freeholder. An underlease is a lease which is created out of a lease, and must be shorter in time than the lease out of which it is created. In theory, there is no limit to the number of underleases, sub-underleases, etc, which may be created out of one freehold.

A lease is usually a lengthy document. It is a species of contract. The lease will describe the property in precise terms – this is especially important where what is being leased is only part of a building, for example, a ground floor restaurant in a building. The lease will also contain various covenants by the tenant and some by the landlord. A lease will invariably provide for the landlord to be able to terminate the lease if the rent is not paid on time, or if there is some other breach of the lease. Such a provision is known as a forfeiture clause.

In a lease for a period of more than about five years, there will often be a rent review clause, which provides that the rent for the first few years will be at a stated amount and thereafter will increase to an amount calculated in accordance with a formula. This is designed to ensure that the rent payable under the lease keeps pace with inflation and rents generally. A long-term lease will probably provide for rent reviews about every three years.

Licences

The word 'licence' means permission. A liquor licence permits the licensee to sell alcoholic drinks. A licence of land is a permission given by the owner or occupier of that land to permit someone to use or occupy that land for some purpose.

At first sight, a licence appears to be indistinguishable from a lease, but the main difference is that a lease creates a leasehold estate in land (as already seen), but a licence creates no estate and is generally only a personal permission.

Because of the different legal consequences of a document being a lease or a licence, it is important to distinguish between the two but that is not always easy. The courts are often called on to decide whether the document is a lease or a licence. What the parties call the document is not conclusive. The courts have to consider the substance of the relationship rather than the document's label. The following case was an important House of Lords' decision.

◆ Street v Mountford (1985)

Mrs Mountford signed an agreement which permitted her to occupy two rooms. By the agreement she had to pay a weekly rent and give 14 days' notice to terminate the agreement. The agreement contained the following:

'I understand and accept that a licence in this form does not and is not intended to give me a tenancy protected under the Rent Acts.'

The agreement gave Mrs Mountford exclusive possession of the rooms. The House of Lords decided that an agreement which gives exclusive possession is a lease and not a licence, unless the arrangement taken as a whole points convincingly the other way. Accordingly, Mrs Mountford had a lease not a licence, despite the declaration in the agreement.

This means that if there is no right to exclusive possession, then only a licence is created and generally the converse will apply, that is, if the agreement gives the occupant exclusive possession, then generally a lease will exist.

When a hotel guest books into an hotel they have only a licence of the hotel room. The hotel proprietor continues to have control of the room, retains a key, cleans and services the room and the hotel manager would restrain improper use of the room. This type of licence is known as a contractual licence, and most people would be able to see the distinction between that and a lease at a glance.

Other cases are less easy to distinguish. The catering concession at a theatre may only create a licence for the caterer to use the kitchen and servery rather than create a lease even though the agreement is for a fixed period, for example, a year.

The distinction between a licence and a lease is important for a number of reasons. For instance, a landlord, when granting a lease, does not give any implied warranty that the premises are fit for use for the purpose for which it is leased, but such a term is implied when a licence is granted. So a person proposing to take a lease of an hotel would be wise to have a survey of the property beforehand, but a guest booking into an hotel does not need to have a surveyor check the room to see if the floor is liable to give way during the night.

Another distinction between leases and licences is that business leases come within the security of tenure provisions of the Landlord and Tenant Act 1954, but licences do not.

BUSINESS LEASES

'Tenure' is a legal expression the history of which dates back to the Norman Conquest. Today, in broad terms, it is an expression to differentiate between freehold and leasehold. If a person runs a hotel or restaurant, then the goodwill of that business tends to be associated with the premises where the business is carried on. If the proprietor owns the freehold of the premises, then he or she is not worried about the right to remain there because a freehold estate is unlimited in time. If, on the other hand, the proprietor only owns a leasehold estate, then the proprietor will be concerned about what happens to the business and its goodwill when the lease period comes to an end.

This is where the security of tenure provisions of Part 2 Landlord and Tenant Act 1954 (as amended by the Law of Property Act 1969) come into play. In outline, the 1954 Act (as amended) gives a tenant of business premises the right to a new lease or compensation at the end of the lease. The Landlord and Tenant Act 1954 (the 1954 Act) does not apply in Scotland, but similar provisions do apply to many business premises.

Leases covered by the Landlord and Tenant Act 1954

The 1954 Act applies if

- the tenant or sub-tenant actually occupies the business premises for the purpose of his or her business
- the lease is for more than six months or is a periodic tenancy but not a licence to occupy, and
- the 1954 Act has not been excluded by a court.

Prior to the Landlord and Tenant (Licensed Premises) Act 1990, leases and tenancies of public houses and certain other licensed premises were excluded from the operation of the 1954 Act, but currently they are included.

It is possible for a landlord and tenant to contract out of the operation of the Landlord and Tenant Act 1954 by agreeing before the lease is granted that the Act will not apply and by making a court application for approval of that agreement. If the court approves the agreement, then the security of tenure provisions of the 1954 Act will not apply (section 38). Otherwise, the Act cannot be excluded.

Operation of Part 2 Landlord and Tenant Act 1954

The scheme of the 1954 Act is simple. Security of tenure is initially established by the simple expedient in section 24 that a business lease does not come to an end unless it is terminated by the procedure set out in the Act. Therefore, even if the lease is for a fixed period, if nothing is done the lease just continues indefinitely.

Although there is a procedure for the tenant to terminate the lease at the end of the lease period (section 27), or to bring the matter to a head by asking for a new lease (section 26), it is usually the landlord who takes some action because otherwise the lease continues at the old rent.

The action to be taken by the landlord is set out in section 25. It involves the service of a notice in a particular form on the tenant to terminate the lease. The notice may be served between six and twelve months before the date on which it is to apply. The date specified in the notice to terminate the lease cannot be earlier than the date on which the lease would end but for the 1954 Act.

So a landlord who serves notice in time, can bring the leasehold to an end on the same date as specified in the lease as the date on which the leasehold expires. The landlord's notice must say whether he/she would object to the granting of a new lease and, if so, on what grounds.

Once the landlord has served notice, the tenant may serve a counter notice saying whether or not he/she is willing to give up possession of the premises on the date specified in the landlord's notice. Assuming the tenant is not willing to give up possession, then there is a procedure to be followed for making an application to the court for a new tenancy.

The court is obliged to grant the tenant a new lease for a period of up to 14 years unless the landlord objects to the grant of a new lease on one of the seven grounds set out in section 30 of the 1954 Act, and is able to establish that objection at court. The seven grounds of objection by a landlord are

- that because of the tenant's failure to comply with repairing obligations he/she ought not to be granted a new lease
- that the tenant has been persistently late in paying the rent
- that because of other breaches of obligations, the tenant ought not to be granted a new lease
- that the landlord has offered the tenant suitable alternative premises
- that the premises are only part of premises owned by the landlord who can raise a substantially higher rent if it is let as a whole rather than in parts
- that the landlord needs possession to demolish or reconstruct the premises
- that the landlord wants to occupy the premises personally either for business purposes, or as a residence.

If the landlord establishes one of these grounds, the court must refuse to grant the tenant a new lease but if the refusal is only because of the last three points, then the tenant is entitled to compensation from the landlord, depending on how long the business has been carried on at those premises. The compensation will be equal to the rateable value of the premises unless the business has been carried on at those premises for at least 14 years in which case the compensation is twice the rateable value (Landlord and Tenant (Appropriate Multiplier) Order 1990).

There is also an option in certain circumstances for compensation to be calculated at a higher multiplier but based on the rateable value prior to April 1990. An agreement in a lease not to claim compensation is only valid in very limited circumstances.

If a new lease is ordered by the court, the contents of the new lease will be as agreed between the landlord and the tenant and, failing agreement, as decided by the court. The court can also fix the amount of rent if not agreed, and will do that on the basis of a formula set out in section 34 of the Landlord and Tenant Act 1954, which ignores any goodwill attached to the premises as a result of the tenant's business having been carried on there. The court can provide for the new lease to contain rent review provisions.

Although many court applications for new leases are commenced, very few applications result in a court hearing because they are resolved without the need for the court to decide.

Provided the tenant continues to occupy the premises for business purposes, he/she retains exactly the same security of tenure at the end of any new lease obtained by the operation of the 1954 Act, so that a tenant may obtain a whole series of renewed leases and, in theory, the business may stay there indefinitely.

FIRE PRECAUTIONS

Hotel fires can have dreadful consequences, especially if they occur at night. But a fire in any premises where people can expect to be found in large numbers can be tragic as has been seen over the years and recently with the Bradford City football ground and the Kings Cross underground station disasters. Fire precautions are therefore the subject of legislation.

The legislation commences at the planning stages for any new building or any extensions to any existing building. The building regulations (in Scotland, building standards) require certain fire preventative measures to be incorporated at the construction stage. This aspect of the subject is, however, beyond the scope of this book.

There is an EC recommendation of 22 December 1986 on fire safety in hotels. The purpose of the recommendation is to set minimum standards of fire safety throughout EC member states but (as will be recalled from Chapter 1) EC recommendations have no legal standing.

The local fire officer will be consulted whenever there is an application for an entertainments licence or a liquor licence and fire requirements may have to be met in order for the licence to be granted.

The main legislation on the subject of fire precautions in existing buildings including newly built buildings is contained in the Fire Precautions Act 1971

(FPA 1971) as amended principally by the Fire Safety and Safety of Places of Sport Act 1987 (FSSPSA 1987).

Fire safety under the FPA 1971 (as amended) is achieved by requiring certain premises to have a fire certificate. It is first necessary to identify those premises.

Premises for which an application has to be made for a fire certificate

Section 1 FPA 1971 (as amended by section 78 Health and Safety at Work etc Act 1974 and section 1 FSSPSA 1987) sets out a list of types of premises which may be designated by statutory instrument as requiring a fire certificate.

Two categories of premises relevant to hoteliers and caterers have been designated as needing a fire certificate.

- Any premises used in the business of a hotelier or boarding house keeper for providing either sleeping accommodation for staff or sleeping, dining or other accommodation for guests but only if at least one of the following conditions apply:

  1 there is sleeping accommodation (whether for staff or guests) for more than six persons, or
  2 there is some sleeping accommodation above first floor level, or
  3 there is some sleeping accommodation below ground floor level
  (Fire Precautions (Hotels and Boarding Houses) Order 1972 and, in Scotland, the Fire Precautions (Hotels and Boarding Houses) (Scotland) Order 1972).

- Any premises used as a factory, office or shop or as railway premises where persons are employed to work (Fire Precautions (Factories, Offices, Shops and Railway Premises) Order 1989).

In the *first* category of premises (hotels and boarding houses) 'guests' means members of the public including travellers and holiday makers for whom sleeping accommodation is provided and does not include the sleeping accommodation used for the proprietor's relatives and friends. In the *second* category (factories, offices and shops etc.) restaurants fall within the definition of shops as do hotel dining rooms open to non-residents, and the hotel reception and office area comes within the definition of offices.

So the position reached so far is that *all* restaurants will need a fire certificate, as will *all* hotels *except* the very smallest, which only have ground and first floor sleeping accommodation.

Premises which are or may be exempted from the need for a fire certificate

There are three provisions which exempt premises, which would otherwise need a fire certificate, from the need for a fire certificate;

- Section 2 FPA 1971 but this now has no relevance to hoteliers and caterers.
- Article 5 Fire Precautions (Factories, Offices, Shops and Railway Premises) Order 1989, which exempts any offices, shops etc., in which no more than 20 people work at any one time and no more than ten work elsewhere than on the ground floor. To see if the maximum has been exceeded it is generally necessary to take the total of all people working in one building so that a ground floor restaurant employing less than 20 people may still need to be covered by a fire certificate if the offices above have more than ten people working there at any one time. Persons working in the premises are not limited to employees, but can include the proprietor, family helping out, trainees etc.
- Section 5A FPA 1971 which was inserted by section 1 FSSPSA 1987.

Section 5A FPA 1971 empowers a fire authority to exempt certain premises from the need for a fire certificate. The premises which may be exempted are any ground floor offices or any offices which are on the ground and first floors only or on the ground floor and basement only or on all three floors (basement, ground and first) provided the basement is separated from the ground floor by a construction which provides resistance to fire for a period of at least 30 minutes. Shop premises may also be exempted but only if they are either limited to the ground floor or if they include a basement, provided the basement is separated by fire resisting construction giving the same 30 minutes protection (Article 6, Fire Precautions (Factories, Office, Shops and Railway Premises) Order 1989). There is *no* power for the fire authority to exempt any hotel or boarding house from the need for a fire certificate.

The fire authority may only exempt premises after inspecting the premises (unless they have been inspected within the last year) and may exempt either on an application for exemption or when an application is made for a fire certificate. The decision whether or not to grant exemption is entirely a matter for the fire authority but the exemption may be given subject to a statement specifying the maximum number of people of any category, for example, customers, who can safely be in the premises at any one time.

An exemption given by a fire authority may be withdrawn by that authority at any time after notice to the occupier of the premises, giving reasons for the withdrawal and providing an opportunity to make comments (section 5B FPA 1971).

If after an exemption has been granted any structural alterations to the premises are to be carried out or if more people than the maximum are to be accommodated then the occupier of the premises must first give notice to the fire authority (section 8A FPA 1971).

It should be emphasised that premises which are exempt from the need for a fire certificate are *not* relieved of all responsibility for fire safety measures and the provisions which apply to exempt premises are considered on page 44.

Fire certificates

A fire certificate is required for premises if designated by either the Fire Precautions (Hotels and Boarding Houses) Order 1972 (or the Scottish equivalent) or the Fire Precautions (Factories, Offices, Shops and Railway Premises) Order 1989 and if not exempted from the requirement for a fire certificate. If premises are used without a fire certificate when one is required then the occupier commits a criminal offence (section 7 FPA 1971).

Application for a fire certificate is made on a prescribed form to the fire authority for the area where the premises are situated. Pending the issue of a fire certificate the occupier must comply with certain basic fire precaution measures in section 5(2A) FPA 1971.

On receipt of an application the fire authority must consider (in the case of premises which qualify for consideration for exemption) whether to grant an exemption from the need for a fire certificate. The premises will be inspected by the fire officer and if the fire authority decides not to exempt the premises and is satisfied as to the adequacy of

- the means of escape and measures for ensuring that escape routes can be safely used in the case of fire
- fire fighting equipment for use in case of fire
- the fire alarms

then a fire certificate has to be issued.

If any such items are not adequate the applicant will be informed what needs to be done and if that is not done within the period specified by the fire authority the application for the fire certificate will be treated as refused. An appeal against refusal of a fire certificate can be made to a magistrates' court.

The fire certificate may well be a bulky document and will specify:

- the use of the premises covered by the certificate
- the means of escape in the case of fire
- the means for ensuring that escape routes can be safely used, for example, emergency lighting
- the type, number and location of fire fighting equipment in the building, for example, extinguishers
- the type, number and location of fire alarms.

The certificate may also specify other matters including ensuring that escape routes are kept unobstructed, the display of exit signs and notices about what to do if a fire occurs, staff training, and limits on the number of persons within premises (section 6 FPA 1971). Much of this may be very detailed. The fire certificate must be kept at the premises.

All of the requirements in the fire certificate must be observed at all times and if any material extension or structural alteration to the premises is proposed the fire authority must be informed.

Fire precautions in exempt premises

Premises which are exempt from the need for a fire certificate, either because of Article 5 Fire Precautions (Factories, Offices, Shops and Railway Premises) Order 1989 or because they have been exempted by the local fire authority, are still covered by certain fire safety measures.

- There is a general duty in section 9A FPA 1971 (inserted by section 5 FSSPSA 1977) for exempt premises to have such means of fire escape and fire fighting as reasonably required. Contravention of this requirement is a criminal offence.
- A code of practice entitled Code of Practice for Fire Precautions in Factories, Offices, Shops and Railway Premises not required to have a Fire Certificate, was issued in March 1989 under section 9B FPA 1971 and although breach of the code is not itself an offence, failure to observe the code may be evidence of a breach of the general duties in section 9A.

The general duty on an occupier of exempt premises to provide fire escape and fire fighting equipment can be enforced by means of an improvement notice (section 7 FSSPSA 1987) which is served by the local fire authority and specifies what measures the fire authority considers are necessary to comply with that duty and a time limit within which to do so. The improvement notice can refer to the Code of Practice (mentioned above) to indicate the necessary remedial steps to be taken. An appeal against an improvement notice can be made to a court but failing that it is an offence not to comply with an improvement notice.

Houses in multiple occupation

A house in multiple occupation (HMO) is defined in the Housing Act 1985 as a house occupied by people who are not one household. This is intended to apply to hostels where people live, rather than hotels and guest houses which provide short-stay accommodation. But the definition is so vague and wide that hotels potentially fall within the definition. Furthermore, some hotels may provide long-stay accommodation in part of their premises or may do so out of season – an example is a seasonal guest house which takes in those receiving housing benefit out of season.

The implications of a hotel or similar establishment being classified as an HMO are that certain standards apply for washing, toilet and cooking facilities but more important is the effect on fire precautions. The legislation on HMOs is enforced by the environmental health department of the local authority and that department can require higher fire precautions standards under the Housing Act 1985 (as amended) than apply either under a fire certificate or to exempt premises. The fire standards for HMOs generally depend on the number of storeys in the building. If a property is classified by the local authority as an HMO but that classification is disputed then the matter can be appealed to a county court.

Prohibition notices

The original section 10 FPA 1971 was completely replaced by a new section 10 by the FSSPSA 1987. The original section 10 empowered the courts, on an application by the fire authority, to make orders prohibiting or restricting the use of premises where a serious fire risk existed. The new section 10 allows the fire authority to serve a prohibition notice in such circumstances with a right of appeal against such a notice to a court. Therefore, application to the court is not now needed for the prohibition to be effective.

If the fire authority considers the risk to people on the premises if a fire occurs to be so serious that the use of those premises should be prohibited or restricted, then the fire authority can serve a prohibition notice on the occupier. The premises may be almost any premises whether or not covered by the requirement for a fire certificate.

A prohibition notice must specify the risk and the prohibition or restriction which applies until that risk has been removed or reduced. Such a notice can take immediate effect where the risk of serious personal injury is imminent, otherwise the prohibition notice takes effect from the date specified, letting the occupier take appropriate remedial steps and have the notice withdrawn before it becomes effective.

COVENANTS AND TIES

There are three categories of covenants which may attach to ownership of land or be binding on the owner or occupier

- covenants which are binding on successive freeholders of the land and are unlimited in time and benefit nearby or adjoining land
- covenants imposed for some limited period, for example, in a lease or mortgage
- planning obligations imposed under section 106 Town and Country Planning Act 1990.

These covenants may have particular effect on those running or wishing to run a hotel and catering business on those premises. The third category, planning obligations, is dealt with later in this Chapter.

Covenants attaching to land

Covenants are contractual promises and are enforceable by and against the parties to the contract. However, some covenants can be enforced against successive owners of the land – this is described by lawyers as the covenant 'running with the land'.

For a covenant to 'run with the land' three conditions must be satisfied, and, simplified, these conditions are that

- the covenant must be negative in nature, that is, not require expenditure of money for its performance
- the person imposing the covenant must have nearby land which will benefit from the covenant, and
- the burden of the covenant must be intended to be binding on successive owners of the burdened land.

If these three conditions are satisfied, then the owner for the time being of the land which has the benefit of the covenant can enforce the covenant against the owner for the time being of the burdened land.

Because the covenants are negative, they are generally referred to as 'restrictive covenants'. Many of these restrictive covenants were imposed before the first legislation on town and country planning and consequently often have a quaint ring about them. One common restrictive covenant met in practice is one which prohibits the sale of intoxicating liquors or the use of land as 'an inn or public house'. Brewers who dispose of licensed premises now can not impose a restrictive covenant preventing the use of the premises as licensed premises (Supply of Beer (Loan Ties, Licensed Premises and Wholesale Prices) Order 1989).

Restrictive covenants do not become extinct by passage of time but remain enforceable for ever and a day. If a restrictive covenant has been breached for many years without being enforced it may become enforceable. Sometimes it is difficult to find out whether a covenant is enforceable or who may be entitled to enforce it, and in those circumstances it may be possible to obtain insurance against the possibility of a court enforcing such a covenant.

Section 84 Law of Property Act 1925 does provide a method to bring a restrictive covenant to an end. The procedure involves an application to the Lands Tribunal to discharge or modify a restrictive covenant on certain grounds, for example, that the covenant is obsolete, or that no one would be prejudiced by its end or modification. Similar provisions concerning the discharge or variation of feuding conditions in Scotland apply under the Conveyancing and Feudal Reform (Scotland) Act 1970.

Brewery ties in leases and mortgages

Leases and mortgages (in Scotland, standard securities) are forms of contracts and both invariably contain covenants. Both leases and mortgages can be lengthy documents setting out covenants in detail. In the case of mortgages, the document is often reduced to a minimum by incorporating printed terms and conditions which are set out in a separate document or, in Scotland, incorporating the standard conditions set in Schedule 3 to the Conveyancing and Feudal Reform (Scotland) Act 1970.

As a matter of practice, lease and mortgage covenants deal with the money side of the transaction (either rent or mortgage payments), the insurance of the property, repairs, use of the property and a whole range of other issues designed to regulate the relationship between the landlord and tenant or the mortgagor and mortgagee.

But one type of covenant which is found in leases and mortgages of premises selling alcoholic drinks is a type of covenant which is known as a 'tie'. This occurs where the landlord or the mortgage lender is a brewery. Such a covenant typically appears in the leases and mortgages of public houses but can be found affecting hotels, wine bars etc. Such covenants are designed to ensure that the tenant or mortgage borrower buys beer and other drinks only from the brewery. Ties can fail to achieve their intended result or be restricted in operation in a number of ways.

The courts, as a matter of policy, will not enforce contracts which are contrary to public policy and agreements in restraint of trade fall within that description. They are void unless reasonable in all circumstances both as between the parties and in the interests of the public.

◆ Esso Petroleum v Harpers Garage (1967)

An agreement was made by the owner of two garages and Esso Petroleum. In the agreement the owner covenanted only to sell motor products supplied by Esso. The covenants were for four years for one garage and twenty-one years for the other. The twenty-one year restriction was in a mortgage. The court considered that the twenty-one year restriction was too long and therefore unreasonable. The four-year restriction was, however, valid taking into account all of the advantages and disadvantages of the agreement.

In Chapter 4, some anti-competitive agreements are considered. The Restrictive Trade Practices Act 1976 does not apply to lease and mortgage covenants but Article 85(1) EC Treaty does need to be considered here in the context of brewery ties. It will be recalled that Article 85(1) prohibits any agreement which could affect trade between member states and which prevents, restricts or distorts competition. Brewery ties can be caught by Article 85(1) because, for example, if a UK brewery ties UK public houses it will be more difficult for a brewery in another member state to sell its beer in the UK.

Article 85(1) can be subject to individual or block exemptions. For brewery ties there is an exemption in EC Regulation 1984/83, Block Exemption for Exclusive Purchasing Agreements. The precise terms of the block exemption depends on whether the brewery provides the premises for the resale of the beer. If the brewery does not provide the premises then the exclusive purchasing agreement (tie) cannot exceed five years if it relates to specified beers and other drinks, or ten years if restricted to specified beers only. If the brewery provides the premises then the tie can effectively be indefinite for beer.

Additionally the European Commission has issued a notice which treats small brewer's ties as exempt from Article 85 as of minor importance if certain criteria are met. If the brewer's total production and market share do not exceed certain limits and if the tie is not for longer than seven and a half years for beer and other drinks or fifteen years for beer only then the tie will not be caught by Article 85.

If a brewery tie falls foul of Article 85(1) of the EC Treaty and is not saved by, for example, satisfying the requirements of the block exemption then a national court has no power to authorise the tie (*Delimitis v Henninger Brau AG 1991*). However, the effect of the nullity of the brewery tie on the rest of the contract is a matter for national courts to decide – does the whole lease fail or can the offending tie be cut out leaving the remaining provisions of the lease valid? (*Inntrepreneuer Estates (GL) Ltd. v Boyes 1993*).

There is also UK legislation which affects the tenants and mortgage borrowers of major UK breweries. The Supply of Beer (Tied Estate) Order 1989 strikes at covenants in leases and mortgages from certain major breweries. Such tenants and mortgage borrowers are no longer restricted by covenants in their leases and mortgages which would prevent them from buying the following from a supplier of their choice

- At least one brand of draught, cask-conditioned beer brewed by a brewer other than the brewer to whom the tenant/borrower is tied
- non-alcoholic and low-alcohol beers
- all other non-beer drinks including soft drinks, ciders, wine and spirits.

Finally, while on the subject of ties, mention should be made of special rules which apply to ties in or associated with mortgages. In the case of mortgages the courts have developed a rule which states that there should be no burden on the right to redeem a mortgage and be able to enjoy the property free from all of the covenants in the mortgage. Typically, this applies to ties of one sort or another. Accordingly, if the owner of a 'free' public house mortgages that public house to a brewery and the mortgage covenants tie the mortgagor to buy only the brewery products then the owner should be rid of that tie when he or she redeems (pays off) the mortgage.

However, if the advantage obtained by the mortgage covenant can be regarded as a separate 'bargain' then the advantage might continue beyond redemption of the mortgage.

◆ KREGLINGER v NEW PATAGONIA MEAT AND COLD STORAGE COMPANY LIMITED (1914)

A meat company borrowed money from a firm of wool brokers by way of a mortgage. In the mortgage was an option for the wool brokers to purchase any sheepskins the meat company had available for sale within five years.

Before the five years were up the meat company repaid the loan and claimed that the option was at an end. The case went to the House of Lords where it was decided that the option was intended to be for five years even if the loan was paid off earlier and therefore the option was still binding on the meat company for the balance of the five years.

However, if a brewery makes a loan or provides other financial assistance in return for a tie, the recipient of the loan or assistance is able to give notice, which the brewery cannot specify to be longer than three months, to repay the loan. When the loan is repaid the tie then ceases (Supply of Beer (Loan Ties, Licensed Premises and Wholesale Prices) Order 1989).

OCCUPIERS' RESPONSIBILITIES (CIVIL)

An occupier of premises has certain responsibilities to people on those premises for their safety. The responsibilities are numerous and in a book of this nature it is only possible to consider the main duties and responsibilities.

Those responsibilities can be conveniently divided into two categories – civil and criminal. In the event of a breach the former involve an action for damages by an injured person and the latter involves prosecution (usually by the local authority). The same set of facts may give rise to both civil and criminal liability. The main civil responsibilities of occupiers are in the Occupiers' Liability Act 1957 (OLA 1957). The subject of safety of hotel guests is looked at in Chapter 5.

The duty of care in the Occupiers' Liability Act 1957

Prior to the Occupiers' Liability Act 1957, an occupier's responsibilities for the safety of people on his or her premises was governed by the common law tort of negligence. Unfortunately, the law evolved somewhat piecemeal so that the standard of care required by an occupier differed according to the reason why people were on the premises.

This was unsatisfactory and so the OLA 1957 abolished the old rules and replaced them with the same standard of care for all persons legally on the premises namely the 'common duty of care'.

Occupiers' Liability Act 1957 section 2(1)

An occupier of premises owes the same duty, the 'common duty of care' to all his visitors, except insofar as he is free to and does extend, restrict, modify or exclude his duty to any visitor or visitors by agreement or otherwise.

But who is an 'occupier' and who is a 'visitor' for the purposes of the OLA 1957?

An 'occupier' is a person who has sufficient control of the premises to be responsible for the safety of persons on those premises. That will usually be the owner or tenant in possession of the premises. There can be more than one 'occupier'.

◆ WHEAT v LACON (D) & CO LTD (1966)

A public house, owned by a brewery, was run by a manager who lived on the first floor above the public house with his wife. With the brewery's consent the manager and his wife took in lodgers using part of the first floor for that purpose. One evening a lodger, who was using one of the two staircases, fell due to the handrail ending before the bottom of the stairs. The stairs were in darkness because the light bulb was missing. The lodger was killed. His wife sued the brewery who denied that they were the occupiers alleging that it was the manager who was responsible. On the facts of the case it was decided that both the manager and the brewery each had sufficient control to be responsible for the safety of visitors and therefore both were occupiers, and both liable for the accident.

Turning now to who is a 'visitor', the OLA 1957 states that the common duty of care is owed to all visitors. This does not just mean guests in an hotel or guest house. It means everyone on the premises other than trespassers – it includes customers, staff, persons delivering goods, the window cleaner and the man or woman who has come to read the meter. Trespassers are not owed the common duty of care in the OLA 1957 but are covered by the Occupiers' Liability Act 1984 (see below).

A person can become a trespasser after having entered premises as a visitor. This happens if his or her permission to be on the premises is limited either in time or in area. So a restaurant diner who hides in the premises intending to steal from the premises after closing time may breach both limitations, both by hiding in a non-public part of the premises, and staying there after the restaurant closes. If he or she then has an accident due to the state of the premises, he or she will not be able to sue the occupier under the OLA 1957.

The court will be reluctant to find that a person has become a trespasser thereby losing his or her rights under the OLA 1957.

◆ STONE V TAFFE (1974)

A committee, of which both the plaintiff and defendant were members, organised a social event in a public house which was owned by a brewery and managed by the defendant Mr Taffe.

The brewery had given explicit instructions to Mr Taffe that no customers or friends should remain on the premises after closing time unless their permission was given. The brewery gave no permission for the social event to go on beyond the normal closing time.

Mr Stone had a fatal accident falling down some narrow, unlit stairs when leaving the function at about 1 o'clock in the morning.

Mr Stone's widow sued both the brewery and Mr Taffe. The brewery alleged that Mr Stone was a trespasser because he was on the premises long after the time set. However as Mr Stone had not been informed of the time limit he was a 'visitor' at the time of his accident.

◆ CAMPBELL V SHELBOURNE HOTEL LTD (1939)

Mr Campbell was a guest at a London hotel. During the night he required the toilet which was along the corridor. The corridor was unlit and he could not find the light switch. He felt along the corridor and found a door which he thought was the toilet but it was in fact the door leading to the basement which was out of bounds to hotel guests. He went through the door and fell down the basement steps. He was not a trespasser because he was making a reasonable search for the toilet and had gone through the basement door in error.

Although the case of *Campbell v Shelbourne Hotel Ltd 1939* predates the OLA 1957, the result would almost certainly be the same now.

The extent of the occupiers' duty of care

The common duty of care is set out in the OLA 1957.

> ### Occupiers' Liability Act 1957 section 2(2)
>
> *The common duty of care is a duty to take such care as in all the circumstances of the case is reasonable to see that the visitor will be reasonably safe in using the premises for the purposes for which he is invited or permitted by the occupier to be there.*

The occupier's responsibility is therefore to take such care as reasonable to see that visitors will be safe in using the premises. That does not mean that if someone has an accident on the premises the occupier is liable for the injuries suffered. In other words, the occupier is not in the position of an insurer who has to pay for any injury however it may be caused.

◆ WOOD V MORELAND & CO (1971)

Mr and Mrs Wood went to a dinner dance at an hotel. It was January and when they left the function to go home at about one o'clock in the morning, they found that the hotel forecourt was covered in frozen snow and hard-packed ice. They had to walk across this to get to a car. While crossing the forecourt Mr Wood slipped and fractured his leg. He sued the hotel proprietors because they had done nothing to clear a safe passage across the forecourt. The claim failed. The hotel was not an insurer of its customers and on the facts it would have been more dangerous to endeavour to clear a path (even if possible) because it would have quickly degenerated into a treacherous slide.

Every case depends on its facts. In *Wood v Moreland & Co*, the injured customer failed in his claim. On similar facts but different circumstances a teacher succeeded in her claim.

◆ MURPHY V BRADFORD METROPOLITAN COUNCIL (1991)

The plaintiff was a teacher at a school. She arrived at the school one morning at about 8.30 a.m. There was snow on the ground and she slipped while on a sloping path in the school grounds which was notoriously dangerous in icy weather. Although the school caretaker had put down some rock salt earlier it had not done the job. Knowing of the dangerous reputation of the path the caretaker should have put grit or cinders down on the path and the failure to do so meant that the council (as occupier of the school) was in breach of its common duty of care to the teacher.

So what sort of things are covered by the common duty of care? First the state of the premises themselves – an unsafe stair handrail, a highly polished floor and a broken stair tread are all matters which could lead to a claim. Failure to take precautionary measures, for example, mopping up water on a marble floor or sticking down a curled up carpet could also lead to claims.

Special categories of visitors

Occupiers' Liability Act 1957 section 2(3)

 (a) *an occupier must be prepared for children to be less careful than adults and*

> (b) *an occupier may expect that a person in the exercise of his calling will appreciate and guard against any special risks ordinarily incident to it so far as the occupier leaves him free to do so.*

So special care is necessary with children, especially in dangerous areas where they may be tempted to play. On the other hand if a builder, window cleaner or electrician is called in to do work then they can be expected to look out for any special risks involved in their job and, to that extent, the occupier has a lesser responsibility. However, that does not mean the occupier can do nothing. It is generally accepted that where a window cleaner has to lean out or sit on a window sill above ground floor level harness anchorage points should be supplied.

Warnings

Occupiers' Liability Act 1957 section 2(4)

Where damage is caused to a visitor by a danger of which he has been warned by the occupier the warning is not to be treated, without more, as absolving the occupier from liability unless in all the circumstances it was enough to enable the visitor to be reasonably safe.

The expression 'without more' roughly translated means 'on that basis alone'. So a warning by the occupier may be sufficient to carry out the duty of care. It will be sufficient if on its own it enables the visitor to be reasonably safe. For example, a notice warning someone to keep to mats placed across a newly polished floor or to use the left banister because the right one is loose may be quite sufficient.

But if the glass in an arcade roof is dangerous and bits are liable to fall out then a warning notice would probably be insufficient and the occupier may also have to hang up some sheeting to avoid falling glass hitting people walking underneath.

Visitors' fault

The common duty of care is to take such care as in all the circumstances is reasonable to ensure that a visitor will be reasonably safe while on the premises. Those circumstances include the conduct of a reasonable person so that an occupier is generally not liable for the failure of a person to use reasonable care to look after their own safety.

Sometimes an accident is caused partly by the occupier's breach of the common duty of care and partly the fault of the person injured. In such circumstances the Law Reform (Contributory Negligence) Act 1945 provides that the claim may still succeed but that any damages awarded to the injured person will be reduced to such an extent as appropriate bearing in mind that person's share of fault.

Faulty work by contractors

If a visitor is injured because of faulty work done by a contractor, for example a visitor is electrocuted because the electrical contractor who wired up a shaving point in a hotel bathroom did so incorrectly, is the occupier responsible under the OLA 1957? The answer, to be found in section 2(4)(b) OLA 1957, is that the occupier is not liable for injury caused to a visitor to his or her premises by the fault of an independent contractor if

- the occupier acted reasonably by entrusting the work to the independent contractor, and
- the occupier took such steps (if any) to check the competence of the contractor and that the work had been done properly.

Accordingly, if an occupier has a need for a specialist – an electrician for rewiring, a gas fitter to service the central heating boiler, a plumber to fit a shower or a maintenance engineer to repair a lift – and is satisfied by the contractor's competence and checks the works afterwards (so far as he or she can), the occupier should not be liable for injury resulting from that work having been carried out incompetently. However, this does not mean that an occupier can escape liability by contracting everything out – it is only if it is reasonable to entrust the work to an independent contractor that the occupier can rely on this provision.

Exclusion of liability

As already mentioned, giving an adequate warning or the employment of competent independent contractors in certain circumstances can mean that the occupier avoids liability. However, both actions (giving adequate warnings and employing specialist competent contractors) should be seen as the occupier taking appropriate steps to comply with responsibilities under the OLA 1957.

To what extent can an occupier exclude liability altogether? Attempts have been made to exclude liability arising to visitors under the OLA 1957 by means of exclusion clauses or disclaimer notices. For example, it was not uncommon at one time to see such notices as 'the proprietor cannot be responsible for any injury caused to persons while on these premises'.

Such attempts are nullified by the Unfair Contracts Terms Act 1977. That Act provides that a person cannot by contract or by notice exclude or restrict liability arising from occupation of premises for business purposes if another person is killed or injured.

Liability to trespassers

The OLA 1957 does not apply to trespassers, instead, the Occupiers' Liability Act 1984 creates a duty by an occupier of a premises to a trespasser to take such care as is reasonable in all circumstances to see that the trespasser does not suffer injury on the premises due to any danger on them if

- the occupier knows (or ought to know) of the danger
- he or she knows (or ought to know) that the trespasser is in the vicinity of the danger or likely to come into contact with it, and
- the risk is one which in all the circumstances should be guarded against.

Liability to trespassers has traditionally arisen where on some premises there is a dangerous attraction for children, for example a building site which presents dangerous opportunities for play and the cases tend to favour child trespassers rather than adult trespassers.

Occupiers' responsibilities (criminal)

There are numerous responsibilities on occupiers of premises which are enforced by criminal sanctions. Some of these such as fire precautions and hygiene of food premises are dealt with elsewhere in this book.

There are two sets of laws to be considered at this point as they impose responsibilities on occupiers of premises and are enforceable by criminal sanctions.

Health and Safety at Work etc. Act 1974

The Health and Safety at Work etc. Act 1974 (H&SWA 1974) is considered in more detail in Chapter 9 because the main function is to protect the health and safety of employees.

However, section 4 H&SWA 1974 imposes a duty on an occupier of business premises to take reasonable measures to ensure, so far as reasonably practicable, that the premises and means of access and exit are safe and without risk to health. The duty is owed to persons (other than employees) who use the premises as a place of work or a place where they may use equipment.

This means that an hotelier owes a duty under section 4 H&SWA 1974 to the self-employed window cleaner or the workmen who come to repair the lift or to decorate the stairway.

Breach of the duty is a criminal offence (section 33 H&SWA 1974) but a breach of this duty cannot be relied on in civil proceedings (section 47 H&SWA 1974).

Workplace (Health, Safety and Welfare) Regulations 1992

The other set of criminal laws is the Workplace (Health, Safety and Welfare) Regulations 1992 ('the Workplace Regulations'). These replace the main parts of the Offices Shops and Railway Premises Act 1963 (OS&RPA) and expand section 4 H&SWA 1974. The regulations apply to almost all workplaces (construction sites, mines and ships being the main exclusions) and so they apply to all catering and hospitality establishments. There are some allowances made for temporary sites such as a beer tent at an agricultural show. Also there are some phasing provisions so that the OS&RPA continues to apply instead of the Workplace Regulations to existing premises (that is premises in use at the end of 1992) until the end of 1995.

The Workplace Regulations are principally safety laws for employees and so the obligations mainly rest on employers in respect of workplaces under their control where employees work. But the obligations are wider and anyone else who, to any extent, controls a place where people work is also responsible under these regulations. So, for example, a hotel proprietor will have a responsibility under the Workplace Regulations for the safety of the hotel premises when being used for delivery of supplies etc.

The Workplace Regulations impose the following obligations.

- The workplace, and its equipment should be maintained in good repair.
- There must be efficient ventilation.
- The temperature should be reasonable and workplace thermometers displayed.
- Lighting (preferably natural) should be sufficient.
- The workplace, furniture and furnishings should be kept clean.

- Rooms should be of sufficient size with enough room for people to get about.
- Work-stations and seating should be suitable both for the work and the worker.
- Floors, passages etc. should be smooth, non-slippery etc.
- Appropriate measures should be taken to avoid anyone falling any distance or anything falling on someone – measures may include securing cellar flaps.
- If appropriate, glass doors etc., should be of safety glass and have a safety sign to show the presence of glass.
- Windows should not open so as to cause any risk (such as risk of anyone falling out) and must be capable of being cleaned safely.
- Traffic routes should be organised to avoid dangers, e.g. to segregate vehicles and pedestrians, escalators should function safely and be equipped with safety devices.
- There should be sufficient toilets and washing facilities and drinking water for people at work.
- People who have to wear special clothing at work should have changing and clothes storage facilities.
- There should be places for rest/meal breaks for example a staff room.

The Workplace Regulations are reinforced by an Approved Code of Practice made by the Health and Safety Commission under the H&SWA 1974. That code of practice gives guidance as to compliance with the Workplace Regulations, for example normal workplace temperatures are given and the minimum numbers of toilets and wash-hand basins are recommended.

Breach of the Workplace Regulations is not only a criminal offence punishable under section 33 H&SWA 1974 but such breach may entitle an injured or ill employee to sue for breach of statutory duty (see Chapter 1 and section 47(2) H&SWA 1974).

Town and country planning

Under the town and country planning legislation, which has been around in substantially its present form since 1947, the state, mainly through local authorities, exercises control over the development and use of land. Prior to the planning legislation landowners were able to build whatever they liked on their land and use the land for any legal purpose. With the social demands of an increasing landowning population that state of affairs could not survive.

The present legislation concerning planning controls is mainly to be found in the Town and Country Planning Act 1990 (T&CPA 1990) as amended by the Planning and Compensation Act 1991.

The control of development

Central to the concept of planning control is the definition of 'development' in section 55(1) T&CPA 1990.

Town and Country Planning Act 1990 section 55(1)

'Development' means the carrying out of building, engineering, mining or other operations in, on and over or under land, or the making of any material change in the use of any buildings or other land.

So 'development' has two sides

- building etc. on land.
- a material change of use of buildings or land.

The rule in section 57 T&CPA 1990 is that planning permission is required for any development. In most cases an application is made to the local authority for planning permission and permission can be granted or refused. If granted it will be granted subject to conditions some of which are obligatory and some are imposed because the local authority considers it appropriate to do so. An appeal can be made against the refusal of planning permission or the imposition of any conditions on a planning permission.

The result is that if someone wishes to build a new hotel or convert a residential house into an hotel then planning permission will be needed and in the latter case even if there is no need to do any work to the building to convert it to an hotel.

Failure to obtain planning permission when it is required can lead to the issue of enforcement action by the local authority which may require the building to be removed or the original use to be restored.

It is only a 'material' change of use that triggers the need for planning permission in the case of change of use of a building or land, so that if a residential house is principally used as a home but one or two rooms are used during the season for bed and breakfast then no planning permission will be required. If the business expands so that the bed and breakfast business becomes the principal use of the building then at that stage planning permission may be necessary.

Similarly it is the primary use of the land and buildings which has to be considered. Therefore if the occupier of a large office building created a staff canteen for the use of office staff, there would be no change of use of the primary use as an office block, and no planning permission would be necessary for the canteen.

The following case illustrates what is 'material'.

◆ EMMA HOTELS LTD V SECRETARY OF STATE FOR THE ENVIRONMENT **(1979)**

An hotel opened its residents' bar for use by non-residents. Even though some 70 to 80 per cent of the customers in the bar were non-residents this did not constitute a material change of use, it was still a hotel and no planning permission was needed to open the bar to non-residents.

Change of use

As seen a material change of use of land or buildings requires planning permission. Section 55(2)(f) T&CPA 1990 provides that in the case of land and buildings which are used for one purpose specified in an order made under the 1990 Act, then the change of use of those land and buildings to another use within the same class specified in that order is not 'development'.

Hence, while a change of use within the same class is outside the need for any planning permission, it will generally be the case that a change from one class to another will require planning permission.

The relevant order is the Town and Country Planning (Use Classes) Order 1987 (generally referred to as the 'Use Classes Order') which lists various uses under various classes. Two classes are relevant.

- Class A3   Use for the sale of food or drink for consumption on the premises or of hot food for consumption off the premises.
- Class C1   Use as a hotel or as a boarding or guest house where, in each case, no significant element of care is provided.

So a change of use from a fish and chip shop (class A3) to a cafe or restaurant, or even a public house (class A3), does not need planning permission. But a change of use from a hairdressers (class A1) to a restaurant requires planning permission. Similarly a change of use from a boarding school or a retirement home (both class C2) to a hotel (class C1) will generally need planning permission.

Having made a change within a class use, it is then possible to change back again because the original use will still be in the same class.

Permitted development

Section 59 Town and Country Planning Act 1990 enables a statutory instrument to be made to grant planning permission for certain specified types of development. This is largely to avoid the planning control system becoming clogged up with applications for permission to carry out development of a fairly minor nature.

Schedule 2 Town and Country Planning General Permitted Development Order 1995 (generally known as the 'General Development Order') grants permission for a whole host of matters for which an application would otherwise have to be made for planning permission. Examples are:

- putting up or altering a boundary fence, wall etc., subject to certain exceptions where the boundary is adjacent to a road
- painting the exterior of a building except for advertisement purposes
- use of land for any purpose not exceeding 28 days in total in any year (e.g. agricultural and trade fairs).

Schedule 2 General Development Order also permits some limited switches between use classes in the Use Classes Order. In particular, premises within class A3 (food and drink) may be changed to either class A1 (shops) or class A2 (financial and professional). The other way around is not authorised. This means that there may be a change of use from a restaurant not only to other premises within its same class, for example a fish and chip shop, public house etc., but also to a variety of uses within Classes A1 and A2 which include building society offices, betting shops, estate agencies, retail shops, post offices, etc.

If there is a change under the General Development Order to a different class use then it is not possible later to change back again.

Outdoor advertisements

The display of outdoor advertisements and signs is governed by the T&CPA 1990 and the Town and Country Planning (Control of Advertisements) Regulations 1992 as amended by the Town and Country Planning (Controls of Advertisements) (Amendment) Regulations 1994. The general rule is in the 1992 regulations.

> **Regulation 5, Town and Country Planning (Control of Advertisements) Regulations 1992**
>
> *No advertisement may be displayed without consent granted by the local planning authority........ ('express consent') or granted by regulation 6 ('deemed consent').*

Regulation 6 of the 1992 regulations permits the display of different classes of advertisements set out in Schedule 3 of those regulations but subject to various conditions. The different classes are detailed but for hotels, catering and other establishments the following are the most important classes.

- Class 2C Non-illuminated signs at an hotel, inn or public house but limited to one sign or, if there is more than one entrance from the road, a sign at each entrance.
- Class 4B Illuminated signs on the business premises (for example shop signs) limited to one on the face of the building and one at right angles to the face of the building such signs showing only the name of the business, its proprietor and the goods, services available. The sign must not flash and only the letters and characters can be illuminated *not* the background.
- Classes 5 and 6 Non-illuminated signs on the business premises or on the forecourt.

There are other classes dealing with such matters as flags and direction signs. Nearly all classes are subject to size restrictions. It is important to appreciate that if an advertisement or sign falls within a relevant class no express permission is needed. If a sign or advertisement is wanted which is outside those classes, for example a larger sign or one which is illuminated but the class only provides for non-illuminated, then such a sign can be displayed if express permission is obtained. However, the Schedule 3 classes can be given a generous interpretation.

◆ **WAVERLEY DISTRICT COUNCIL V VISION POSTERS LTD (1994)**

A poster on the outside wall of a restaurant advertised a particular brand of cigarettes and cigars but with no indication of the fact that the restaurant sold them.

There was no permission for the advertisement and the local authority prosecuted because it considered that in order to take advantage of Schedule 3 to the 1992 regulations any outside advertisement had to relate to the goods and/or services which were the main purpose of the business – in this case cigarettes and cigars – could only be ancillary. The prosecution failed because on a literal reading of the 1992 regulations the advertisement only had to be for goods/services sold on the premises not the principal goods/services of the business.

A local authority may designate an area as an Area of Special Control, the effect of which is that no advertisements can be displayed in that area without express consent except for certain very limited signs (regulation 19 Town and Country Planning (Control of Advertisements) Regulations 1992).

Special and other controls on development or change of use

There are special controls which affect buildings designated as being of special architectural or historic interest (listed buildings) and there are also special controls on areas of special interest or where the character or appearance of the area should be preserved or enhanced – Town and Country Planning (Listed Buildings and Conservation Areas) Act 1990.

It must be said that planning law is complicated in the extreme and the simple rules set out here should only be regarded as a general overview. Sight should not be lost of the fact that whether or not planning permission is required for any alteration to premises or change of use, there may still be a need to obtain consent of or notify other persons beforehand. Examples are

- landlord's consent under the lease covenants
- Building Regulation consent
- approval of liquor licensing justices
- notification to the fire authority under a fire certificate.

Planning obligations

Under section 106 T&CPA 1990 (as substituted by section 12 Planning and Compensation Act 1991) a landowner may enter into a planning obligation which can restrict or regulate the development or use of land either for a fixed period or indefinitely. Also a planning obligation can require land to be used in a particular way. Such an obligation is enforceable against successive owners of the land.

Planning obligations are often used by local planning authorities as supplementary to a planning permission to impose covenants of one sort or another which either might not be suitable to include, or cannot be imposed as conditions, on a planning permission.

HIGHWAY AMENITIES

Pavement cafes and similar business are now a feature of many towns and are on the increase with increasing pedestrianisation of town centre streets. If there is a private forecourt than all well and good but placing tables and chairs on the pavement or in the street is unlawful. A highway is a public right of way whether that right of way is on foot or in a vehicle, putting objects such as tables and chairs on the highway amounts to the criminal offence of obstruction of the highway.

Under section 115E of the Highways Act 1980 (inserted by section 20 Local Government (Miscellaneous Provisions) Act 1982) the local highway authority can give permission to place objects or structures on the highway for facilities for refreshment. The permission can, and usually will, be subject to various conditions in particular to ensure that there is still sufficient room for pedestrians. A payment can be required. Even if permission is obtained, planning permission may also be necessary and if the premises are licensed an amendment may be needed to the liquor licence.

CAPITAL ALLOWANCES

Sole traders and partners in a partnership pay income tax on the profits of their business. Companies pay corporation tax on the profits of their business. The method of calculation of profits is similar in both cases. In particular, in both cases when calculating the profits of the business, no deduction can be made for any capital expenditure (as opposed to revenue expenditure) on capital assets used in the business. For example, although a caterer, in arriving at the taxable profit can deduct the cost of buying the food served to customers, he or she cannot deduct the cost of buying an oven in which to cook the food. The cost of the food is revenue expenditure but the cost of the oven is capital expenditure.

A business would expect to offset the capital cost of an asset used in the business by charging depreciation every year against profits, so as to write off the capital cost against profits over the life of the asset. However, in calculating the taxable profits of a business, no deduction may be made for depreciation.

Instead, tax laws allow certain depreciation of buildings, plant and machinery to be allowed by a system known as capital allowances. The law relating to capital allowances is to be found in the Capital Allowances Act 1990.

Capital spent on building or extending certain qualifying hotels qualifies for capital allowances. The allowances are 4 per cent each year of expenditure or 25 per cent for hotels in Designated Enterprise Zones. To qualify hotels must

- be open a minimum of four months each year in the period April to October inclusive
- have a minimum of ten letting bedrooms excluding staff bedrooms, and
- normally serve breakfast and an evening meal and service the room (bedmaking and cleaning).

Capital expenditure on certain machinery and plant used in a business will also qualify for capital allowances. There is no legal definition of machinery and plant, but one very important distinction for the hotelier or caterer is the distinction between assets used in the business and assets which form part of the premises (or 'setting') in which the business is carried on.

The distinction is important because assets used in the business may qualify for capital allowances but assets forming part of the setting cannot qualify for capital allowances. This rule is softened in practice for the hotel and catering industry because the courts have recognised that the hotel and catering industry is not only selling accommodation and refreshment, but is also creating surroundings which are conducive to the comfort of the customers. In this way, hoteliers and caterers can spend money on the setting and be able to claim capital allowances for it in situations where other traders would have their claims for capital allowances turned down.

◆ INLAND REVENUE COMMISSIONERS V SCOTTISH AND NEWCASTLE BREWERIES LTD (1982)

Scottish and Newcastle Breweries decided to spend money to brighten up its hotels. Their idea was to create a certain character for each hotel. The various premises were treated to aesthetic revamping including various wall decor consisting of murals, wall panels, pictures and decorative items such as bagpipes and axes. In addition, some hotels had sculptures, in particular one representing seagulls in flight at the Atlantic Towers Hotel in Liverpool.

The Inland Revenue considered the items to be part of the 'setting' and therefore not plant and machinery qualifying for capital allowances. The case went to the House of Lords where it was decided that these items were not part of the premises but were items used in creating the correct atmosphere which was part and parcel of the business of hoteliers. The expenditure accordingly qualified for capital allowances.

However, it is still necessary to see whether the various items actually form part of the premises or merely decorate them.

◆ **Wimpy International Ltd v Warland (Inspector of Taxes) (1988)**

Wimpy embarked on a refurbishment programme for its restaurants. It installed new shop windows, suspended ceilings, floor and wall tiles and in some cases, raised floors.

It claimed to be entitled to capital allowances for this expenditure on the basis that the restaurants had quite adequate structure beforehand and the work was all done to make the premises attractive and create the correct atmosphere for the customers.

The court decided that this expenditure was capital expenditure on the premises and did not qualify for capital allowances.

Both of these cases concern refurbishment, but they are just as relevant, if not more so, to setting up a business. The result of the cases is that items which are not part of the structural fabric of the building but which create the correct atmosphere in the premises (and this can include decorative lighting) to attract customers can qualify for capital allowances and hence reduce the tax bill.

Business rates

Non-domestic premises are subject to business rates. This is a property tax payable by the occupier of the business premises. The amount payable is calculated from two elements. First is the rateable value of the property which is generally calculated as equivalent to what rent would be payable by a tenant under a lease where the tenant does repairs and pays insurance and other outgoings. In the case of public houses and licensed premises a different basis of calculation of the rateable value is used.

The second element is the non-domestic rating multiplier which is uniform throughout the country except in the City of London. The business rate payable for a property is therefore the ratable value multiplied by the rating multiplier.

It is only non-domestic property for which business rates are payable. Hotels and guest houses are non-domestic property but the owner's/manager's accommodation in a public house is treated as domestic.

By section 66 of the Local Government Finance Act 1988 (as amended) premises which are used for bed and breakfast but are the proprietor's home and the use for bed and breakfast is subsidiary to use as the proprietor's home are classified as domestic provided no more than six guests can be accommodated at a time. As domestic property council tax will be payable instead of business rates.

A material change in circumstances in non-domestic property, such as an addition to the property, will affect the rateable value of the property and therefore the amount of business rate payable.

◆ SELF EXAMINATION QUESTIONS ◆

1   Edward and Felicity have taken a seven-year lease of a public house from a brewery. The lease includes a clause which requires Edward and Felicity to buy all their beer (as specified in the lease) from the brewery. Edward and Felicity want to be able to offer their customers additionally a beer brewed by a small specialist brewer. Consider their position.
2   The lease encourages Edward and Felicity to expand the trade at the public house. They decide to open up the seven bedrooms to provide bed and breakfast accommodation. If Edward and Felicity do this what are the implications?
3   Edward and Felicity want to advertise the bed and breakfast accommodation on the outside of the public house and also want to put up a sign supplied by the specialist brewer. Consider the consequences of these matters.
4   At the end of the seven years Edward and Felicity want to continue running the public house. Discuss.

See Appendix for suggested answers.

Chapter 4

BUSINESS CONTROLS

BUSINESS NAMES AND REPUTATION

A business name is a name used by a person carrying on a business which name is not his or her own, or, in the case of a company, is not the registered name of the company, or, in the case of a partnership, is not all the names of the partners.

For instance, a company called BNA Ltd, may operate a chain of hotels under the name of Comfort Hotels. BNA Ltd is the company's real name but Comfort Hotels is its business name. A business name is also referred to as a trading name and BNA Ltd can be said to be trading as Comfort Hotels.

There is no requirement to register business names but their use is controlled by the Business Names Act 1985 (BNA 1985). Where an individual, firm or company trades under a business name, then there is a requirement to disclose the true name of the individual, firm or company. This disclosure must be

- by printing the name of the trader on all business letters, invoices, receipts and demands for payment
- by displaying a notice prominently on any business premises stating the name of the business proprietor
- by responding to a request from a customer or other business contact for the name of the proprietor.

Additionally, an address for service of documents must also be stated on all such letters, notices, etc. In this way a person dealing with a business can see with whom he or she is dealing.

It is a criminal offence to fail to display/disclose the true name of the business proprietor as required by the BNA 1985, and if there is a failure to comply with those requirements the business proprietor cannot sue for debts (or enforce any other legal rights) if the debtor (or other party) can show that the failure to disclose the required information has caused some financial loss or as a result has been unable to pursue some remedy.

There are also restrictions on the type of business name which may be used. Certain words or expressions in business names are objectionable and therefore unlawful, because they endeavour to create a false respectability for example by implying some association with a government department or local authority (sections 2 and 3 BNA 1985). Companies cannot be registered with a name which incorporates such objectionable words and expressions (sections 26 and 29 Companies Act 1985).

Passing off

It is a civil wrong (a tort) for a person to conduct business in such a way that customers are deceived into believing that the business is that of another who has an existing goodwill or reputation. It is trading on the goodwill of someone else with the result that there is a risk that the goodwill could be damaged. This civil wrong is known as 'passing off' and arises under common law.

To succeed in a passing-off action, the plaintiff (person suing) must be able to prove that the defendant is conducting business in such a way as to mislead people into believing that it is the plaintiff's business. The plaintiff's business must have some established reputation in the eyes of the public, such as some recognisable appearance to the premises, or a distinctive design, name or logo, or some business prominence which is recognised in some way or the other. That reputation belongs to the plaintiff, who has built up the goodwill and is entitled to protect it.

It is difficult, if not impossible, however, to use a passing-off action to obtain exclusive use to a business name which uses ordinary words.

◆ **PARK COURT HOTEL V TRANS-WORLD HOTELS (1970)**

The owners of the Hotel International at Lancaster Gate in London failed to obtain an injunction to prevent a new hotel being built at the West London Air Terminal being called the 'London International Hotel'. The word 'International' is a commonly used word which can be used to describe a hotel with international guests and although there might be some confusion, that did not mean that there would be any passing off.

However, an invented name is easier to protect. For instance, in the case of *Sheraton Corporation of America v Sheraton Motels Ltd 1964*, a hotel company obtained an injunction to prevent a rival hotel proprietor using its invented name at a hotel intended to open at Prestwick Airport.

Proving a passing-off action is an uphill task, because it is necessary to prove that the plaintiff has an existing business reputation which he/she is entitled to protect and that the defendant's conduct is likely to cause confusion to the plaintiff's prejudice. Some of that task can be avoided by the registration, where possible, of trade marks.

Trade marks

Certain titles, words, designs, labels etc., used in connection with goods or services can distinctively distinguish those goods and services from the goods and services provided by competitors. These are known as trade marks and such marks may be capable of registration under the Trade Marks Act 1994.

Provided the trade mark is capable of being represented graphically and subject to certain exceptions, it can be registered. The advantage of registration under the Trade Marks Act 1994 is that the proprietor of a registered trade mark has exclusive use of that mark for goods or services and can prevent use of the registered trade mark in connection with competing goods or services or any mark which is so similar to the registered mark that it might be mistaken for the registered mark.

Additionally the Trade Marks Act 1994 creates a criminal offence if someone deliberately uses someone else's registered trade mark either for profit or to cause loss to the registered owner of the trade mark. This is particularly important where high-profile brand goods are counterfeited.

The Trade Marks Act 1994 also contains provisions for Community Trade Marks. These allow one registration to be effective throughout the European Economic Area. Registered trade marks can be sold or the owner can permit use by others.

Registration is for ten years but the registration can be renewed for ten years at a time. A trade mark can remain in existence indefinitely, provided it is always renewed.

BUSINESS COMPETITION

EC competition rules

Central to the EC Treaty is the concept of business competition in order to develop the trade in goods and services between member states. The principal provision is as follows.

EC Treaty Article 85

(1) The following shall be prohibited as incompatible with the common market: all agreements between undertakings, decisions by associations of undertakings and concerted practices which may affect trade between Member States and which have as their object or effect the prevention, restriction or distortion of competition within the common market.

The EC Treaty then contains a list of examples of types of agreements covered by Article 85(1) including price fixing and market sharing agreements. It is important to appreciate that European competition rules only apply to agreements and practices which have or are intended to have an effect on trans-European trade.

The prohibited agreements have to be between 'undertakings' (which means any company, trader or other business organisation or entity) but not necessarily in different member states. As has already been seen in Chapters 2 and 3, it is quite possible for an agreement with no connection with a second country to have the potential to fall foul of Article 85(1). So, as seen, brewery tie agreements and franchises which are exclusively limited to one country can still have the effect of distorting trade because such agreements can prevent one party to the agreement purchasing goods from another member state.

If an agreement does breach Article 85, then it is void and the European Commission has power to impose fines for breaches of Article 85 which fines may be up to one million ECU (European Units of Currency) or ten per cent of turnover in the previous year, whichever is greater.

If an agreement could be in breach of Article 85(1), then the parties can apply to the European Commission for 'negative clearance', that is a decision that the agreement does not breach that Article. Application may also be made for an individual exemption under Article 85(3). Block exemptions may also be given in the form of EC Regulations. (See also Chapters 2 and 3, for an outline of two block exemptions, one relating to franchises and the other relating to exclusive purchasing agreements for beer.)

The European Commission has issued a notice as to agreements of minor importance – if turnover and market share do not exceed certain limits the agreements are treated as having negligible impact and not caught by Article 85.

Restrictive trade practices

If an agreement or practice is not caught by Article 85(1) EC Treaty because, for instance, it cannot affect inter-state competition, it may be still be within the Restrictive Trade Practices Act 1976 (RTPA 1976).

The principle behind the RTPA 1976 is simple but the operation of it is complex. The Act is aimed at agreements and arrangements which operate against the public interest. The RTPA 1976 not only makes such agreements and arrangements unenforceable but also prohibits them being put into operation.

What the RTPA 1976 (as amended) does, is to make compulsory the registration of agreements and arrangements between two or more people carrying on business in the UK, which impose certain restrictions on at least two people (including companies). The agreements or arrangements need not be written or legally enforceable, indeed they may be merely understandings, but they must relate to goods or services, or information about goods.

The restrictions must relate to certain matters and these include prices or charges, the terms and conditions of business, the quantity of goods made, or the extent of services supplied, and the persons with whom business is to be done.

By way of example, if the proprietors of hotels in a particular town get together and agree a minimum room price, that is an arrangement or an agreement which is caught by the RTPA 1976. Such agreements are often called cartels.

Details of most restrictive agreements must be registered with the Director General of Fair Trading before the restriction takes effect or within three months after the agreement is made, whichever is earlier. When that happens the Director General must refer the agreement to the Restrictive Practices Court for a decision as to whether the agreement is contrary to public interest.

However, in some situations, the Director General can decide to recommend to the Secretary of State for Trade and Industry that the agreement need not be referred to the Court because the restrictions are not significant enough. Typical of these types of agreements are bulk-buying agreements and codes of practice which impose restrictions, but which are not likely to affect competition, and indeed could be beneficial to the public. For example, if the hoteliers in a town form a hoteliers association and agree a code of conduct which includes beneficial restrictions aimed at the public, the code of conduct should be registered, but will not necessarily have to be referred to the Court.

If the arrangement or agreement is referred to the Restrictive Practices Court then the Court must declare it to be contrary to the public interest unless it can be shown both that the restrictions satisfy one of the eight 'gateways' set out in either section 10 or section 19 RTPA 1976 and that the restrictions are reasonable when balancing the advantages and disadvantages to the public.

The eight 'gateways' are designed to allow restrictions which are required for fair competition or which protect the public.

If the restriction is found by the Restrictive Practices Court to be contrary to public interest, the Court declares the agreement to be void and invariably makes an order prohibiting the parties to the agreement putting it into effect or making another similar agreement. Breach of such an order is a criminal offence.

Some cartels are made and carried out furtively without notifying the Director General of Fair Trading. It is not a criminal offence to fail to register the agreement, but

- if the Director General suspects that there is in operation an unregistered restrictive trade agreement, it can be investigated and an order obtained to prevent it
- anyone affected by such an agreement can sue a party to the agreement for damages.

Monopolies and mergers

The Fair Trading Act 1973 deals with monopolies and mergers. A monopoly is a situation where a company supplies or purchases 25 per cent or more of a particular type of goods or services in the UK or part of the UK. There can also be 'complex monopolies' where different companies, who together have at least 25 per cent of a market, co-operate to affect competition.

A merger happens where two or more companies cease to be distinct. There is no legal obligation to notify an intended merger but many mergers are notified in advance to avoid problems later. Mergers can lead to a monopoly situation.

Neither monopolies nor mergers are necessarily against the public interest but the potential exists for abuse of the power created by a monopoly to the disadvantage of the public. Accordingly the Director General of Fair Trading can decide to refer to the Monopolies and Mergers Commission any monopoly situation or any merger either before it has taken place or up to four months afterwards.

The Monopolies and Mergers Commission will investigate and prepare a report. If the report indicates that the monopoly/merger operates or can be expected to operate against the public interest then government action can be taken to deal with the situation. In such a situation the most common outcome is that the Director General of Fair Trading accepts legally binding undertakings from the company to avoid the adverse effect on the public interest.

Value added tax

Value Added Tax (VAT) is a tax on the sale of goods and services. The tax is administered by HM Customs and Excise.

A taxable person is a person, partnership or company who operates a business selling goods or supplying services and is registered for VAT.

When a taxable person sells goods or supplies services to another taxable person, for example a wholesaler selling to a retailer, the VAT charged by the wholesaler is the wholesaler's 'output tax' and he or she accounts to the Customs and Excise for the tax received from the retailer. The VAT paid by the retailer is 'input tax'. If the retailer then sells those goods at a profit to a customer, he or she will charge VAT on the sale. The retailer will account to the Customs and Excise for the difference between the output tax and input tax. In this way the final non-business customer (the consumer) pays all the VAT but the total tax bill is collected in stages when the value is added at each stage. Table 4.1 will help to explain how the VAT system works. The tax paid to HM Customs and Excise is, in fact, entirely borne by the consumer but funded at each stage by the business community.

TABLE 4.1

Transaction	Price	VAT charged 17.5%	Paid to Customs and Excise
Manufacturer sells to wholesaler	£100	£17.50	£17.50
Wholesaler sells to retailer	£150	£26.25	£8.75
Retailer sells to consumer	£200	£35	£8.75
Total			£35

There are two rates of VAT. The standard rate of VAT is currently 17.5 per cent and the other rate is a zero rate. Additionally, suppliers of goods and services may be exempt.

The principal Act of Parliament is the Value Added Tax Act 1994, but the detailed rules are set out in various statutory instruments (secondary legislation).

A business which has a turnover of taxable (including zero rated) goods and/or services in excess of certain limits (calculated on a quarterly and annual basis) must register for VAT. Below that limit registration is generally voluntary. The limits change, usually annually.

Input/output tax and tax invoices

Input tax is the VAT payable by a business on its purchases and expenses. Output tax is the VAT payable by customers of a business, which business is registered for VAT, on the sales of goods or services to those customers.

The VAT payable is recorded in tax invoices. Whenever a business which is registered for VAT supplies goods or services to another VAT registered business, it must issue a tax invoice containing certain information. The tax invoice must be numbered, and state the name, address and VAT registration number of the person issuing the invoice. The invoice must also give various information including the total VAT payable. If retail sales are made, a tax invoice need only be given if requested, in which case it may be possible to give a less detailed tax invoice which does not show the VAT separately but gives a VAT inclusive price or charge provided that the rate of VAT is stated.

VAT records and accounting

All VAT-registered businesses must keep VAT records and accounts. There is no set way that these must be kept but it must be possible to calculate correctly the amount of input and output tax and for officers from HM Customs and Excise to be able to check those figures. The records and accounts must be kept for six years. All invoices for input tax and copies of all output tax invoices must be retained by the business.

Each business has a tax period which is usually three months, which means that the business must account on a quarterly basis for VAT. Some businesses with a low turnover may account on an annual basis. At the end of each tax period the business must complete and send to HM Customs and Excise, a VAT return for that period.

It is necessary to add up all input tax and the output tax for the period plus certain other adjustments. The output tax is the VAT payable and the input tax, the VAT reclaimable from HM Customs and Excise. If the output tax exceeds the input tax then the difference is payable to HM Customs and Excise. If the input tax exceeds the output tax then the difference can be reclaimed from HM Customs and Excise.

VAT is payable to HM Customs and Excise whether or not the invoice has been paid. If a debt becomes irrecoverable, the VAT can be reclaimed later.

Accommodation

Sleeping accommodation in hotels, guest houses etc. is standard rated. This means that if the business is registered for VAT, then VAT at the standard rate must be charged to the guests staying in an hotel or guest house. The price quoted will invariably be inclusive of VAT. In addition, meals, laundry facilities, telephone calls and other facilities which are provided, are also standard rated.

However, for guests staying longer term the rules change. After the first 28 days, VAT is no longer payable on the accommodation element only of the cost of staying in the hotel or guest house, but VAT must still be charged on the other elements in the charge, for example for meals and other facilities. In any event, at least 20 per cent of the total charge must be allocated to facilities other than the accommodation.

Many hotels, guest houses etc., require a deposit to be paid for advance bookings of accommodation. For VAT purposes these are treated as advance part-payment of the charge for the accommodation. Accordingly, the hotel must treat the deposit as inclusive of VAT at the standard rate as output tax. If the deposit is forfeited because the guest fails to take up the accommodation, the deposit is then treated as compensation for breach of contract and consequently outside the scope of VAT. In those circumstances the VAT already paid on the deposit to HM Customs and Excise can be reclaimed.

But advance deposits should be distinguished from reservation fees. The difference can be seen from the following cases.

◆ **COMMISSIONER OF CUSTOMS AND EXCISE v MOONRAKERS GUEST HOUSE LTD (1992)**

A deposit of 10 per cent was payable at the time of booking. If the booking was cancelled and the room not re-let the deposit was forfeited (that is kept by the guest house). If the guest took up the booking the deposit was part payment of the full price.

◆ **COMMISSIONER OF CUSTOMS AND EXCISE v BASS PLC (1992)**

Hotel rooms were re-let if not taken up by 6pm but if a separate charge was paid at the time of booking the room would be kept for the guest to arrive after that time. The separate charge was not part payment of the full price.

In the first case, a deposit had been paid and in the second, a reservation fee. In both cases VAT is payable at the standard rate in the tax period in which it is received. In the case of a deposit, the VAT may be reclaimed if the customer does not take up the booking but no tax can be reclaimed if despite the reservation fee the customer fails to take up the booking.

Food and drink

Although most food and drink sold in shops is zero rated this does not apply to catering which is standard rated. Accordingly, VAT at the standard rate is charged on

- food and drink consumed on the premises, for example meals in restaurants
- food and drink at functions, for example catering for wedding receptions
- hot take-away food and drink, for example fish and chips, Chinese take-away meals, hot-dogs and cups of tea.

Certain cold food is also standard rated even if it is taken away from the premises for consumption elsewhere. Such cold food includes ice-creams, soft drinks, crisps, alcoholic drinks, chocolate and other confectionery. Apart from these foods any cold food which is to be taken away and eaten elsewhere is zero rated. Service charges are standard rated but any tips freely given are outside the VAT system.

Functions and conferences

If a room is hired with catering such as a wedding reception, then the room hire as well as the catering is standard rated. If a room is hired for a purpose unconnected with catering such as for a conference or seminar then the room hire is generally exempt from VAT (it may be standard rated under the option to tax but that is beyond the scope of this book). If refreshments or meals are supplied to the attendees at the conference or seminar then the refreshments should be charged separately and standard rated.

COMPUTER DATA

The Data Protection Act 1984 (DPA 1984) is all about the protection of individuals and prevention of misuse of personal information held on computers. How it works is to require computer users (known in the DPA 1984 as 'data users') who hold details of living people on their computers, to register under the Act and comply with certain standards of behaviour. These standards of behaviour are embodied in the 'data protection principles'. This is all backed up by rights for individuals to obtain information which is held about them on computers, and have it corrected if it is wrong.

General exemptions

There are various categories of personal data which are outside the scope of the DPA 1984 with the result that keeping such data on computer does not require registration. There are seven categories including

- payroll/pensions etc., for example information kept only for calculating gross and net pay etc.
- accounts of a business including details of creditors and debtors
- club membership records, and
- mailing lists

Personal data used for purposes not covered by the exemptions will mean that the computer user must register with the Data Protection Registrar.

Registration

Failure to register when keeping non-exempt personal data about living people is a criminal offence. Registration is with the Data Protection Registrar who maintains a register containing details, not only of the name and address of the computer user, but also the type of personal information kept, the purpose for which it is kept and to whom the computer user can disclose the information. Registration is usually for three years at a time.

Data protection principles

Central to the operation of the DPA 1984 is the set of standards known as the data protection principles. It is not a criminal offence for a computer user to break these principles which are, in any event, of a very general nature, but the Data Protection Registrar can serve an enforcement notice requiring a computer user to comply with the principles in certain specified ways and failure to comply with that notice is a criminal offence.

There are eight data protection principles.

- To obtain and process information fairly and lawfully.
- To keep the information for particular lawful purposes only.
- To use and disclose the information only in a way compatible with those purposes.
- Not to keep excessive information about individuals.
- The data should be accurate and kept up to date.
- The data should not be kept longer than necessary.
- To provide an individual (on request) with information about the data kept on such a person, and correct it where appropriate.

- To take appropriate security measures against unauthorised access to personal information.

Rights of individuals

Individuals who are the subject of computer data, or who think they may be, have certain rights. The first right is to be told in response to a request whether a particular registered computer user keeps any information about him or her, and if so, what that information is.

If the personal information about an individual held on a computer is inaccurate then the court can order the information to be corrected or erased and a person also has a right to be compensated if they suffer loss or damage as a result of the use of inaccurate computer data.

Disclosure of information

A computer user is entitled to disclose any personal data held on computer to anyone else provided that

- the person to whom the information is disclosed is within the category of persons described in the disclosures section of the computer user's registration entry, or
- the disclosure comes within the categories of permitted disclosures under the Act, for example to the police, or
- the disclosure is with the data subject's consent.

Disclosure of information in breach of these rules is a criminal offence.

INSURANCE

Insurance is a contract under which one party (the insurer) agrees to pay money (or provide some other benefit) to the other party to the contract (the insured) on some future event, which may or may not happen, or might not happen by a certain time. The contract is usually referred to as a policy.

Only persons authorised to carry on insurance business can issue insurance policies. Usually these are insurance companies authorised under the Insurance Companies Act 1982.

Insurable interest

The insured must have an insurable interest in the matter to be insured. So a person who owns a house, or has a mortgage loan secured on a house, can insure that house. A person with no legal or financial interest in the house cannot generally insure it. The reason is that insurance is a contract of indemnity to compensate the insured for the financial or other loss as a result of the occurrence of the event insured against. If a person insures a house in which he or she has no insurable interest it is an unlawful gaming contract.

The type of insurable interest will depend on the type of insurance, so that while a landlord may insure premises used as a restaurant against flood damage if liable to repair the premises, the restaurateur tenant may be able to insure against loss of profits should the restaurant have to close due to flooding.

A seaside hotel may insure against oil pollution on the beach, not because it is liable to clean the beach if there is oil pollution, but because oil pollution may result in a drop of business in the hotel and that possibility gives the hotel proprietor an insurable interest in the beach not being affected by oil pollution.

The insured event

The events insured against will be named in the policy, however, they do not cover events deliberately caused by the insured, so if a person deliberately burns down premises insured, they will be unable to recover under the policy.

Insurance cannot cover criminal liability, so no insurance is possible to insure against fines for a criminal offence, for example for breaches of the Food Safety Act 1990.

The policy

Before a policy of insurance is issued, the insured is under a duty to disclose to the insurer, all facts which might influence the insurer as to whether to insure the risk, and if so, at what premium (price). If a hotel proprietor seeking insurance against damage to the premises fails to reveal to the insurer that the premises are liable to flooding or that tree roots have already caused settlement damage, then the insurer may treat any policy issued as void when that fact is later revealed.

The amount insured under the policy may be limited to an upper limit stated in the policy. In addition, policies often contain an 'excess clause' which requires the insured to be responsible for the first fixed amount of any claim. In this way, the insurer is only responsible for paying under the policy for the excess above that amount. For example, a policy covering loss of money may have an excess of £100 which will prevent minor claims for such things as discrepancies in cash tills.

Another clause commonly found in policies is an under-insurance or 'average clause'. Such a clause provides that if the insured under-insures, for example insures premises for less than their true reinstatement value, then the insured will be treated as his or her own insurer for the proportion under-insured, and if an insured event happens the insurer will only pay for the insurer's proportion of the loss.

The trend with business insurance is for insurers to provide combined policies which provide the insured with a whole range of insurance within one policy. A typical hotel insurance policy will cover accidental damage to the premises and furniture, theft or loss of guests' property, loss resulting from interruption of business, employers' liability, loss, damage or breakdown of computer systems, failure of electricity, gas and other supplies (including loss of frozen foods), loss of liquor licence, legal expenses, and other risks.

OTHER BUSINESS CONTROLS

There are numerous other controls over the way a business is conducted. Many of these controls are mentioned elsewhere, for example, the licensing system for the sale of alcoholic drinks is the subject of Chapter 8.

There are also numerous other controls which are beyond the scope of this book, for example anti-competitive practices under the Competition Act 1980. A number of miscellaneous controls which particularly affect the hotel and catering industry will now be considered.

Late night refreshment houses

A late night refreshment house is a cafe, restaurant, etc., open to serve the public with refreshments at any time between 10pm and 5am the following morning, other than premises licensed to sell alcoholic drinks. The expression therefore covers many fast food restaurants which are open late at night but do not serve alcoholic drinks.

The proprietor of a late night refreshment house needs a licence from the local authority under section 2 Late Night Refreshment Houses Act 1969. Failure to have such a licence when operating a late night refreshment house is a criminal offence. Such a licence is renewable annually on 1 April every year.

If the local authority considers that the premises should be closed by a certain time not earlier than 11pm to avoid disturbance to local residents, then a condition can be imposed on the licence, requiring the premises to close by that time each night.

However, the Late Night Refreshment Houses Act 1969 is not applicable if the premises are within a London Borough which has resolved to apply the London Local Authorities Act 1990 in that borough.

Late night cafes in London

A London Borough Council can pass a resolution to apply in their area the London Local Authorities Act 1990 in place of the Late Night Refreshment Houses Act 1969. The 1990 Act requires cafes which are not licensed to sell alcoholic drinks to be licensed with the local authority if open at any time between 11pm and 5am for public refreshment or between midnight and 5am for the sale of take-away food.

Licenses are for 18 months or shorter periods specified in the licence, but are renewable. Conditions can be attached to licences including the regulating of opening hours to minimise nuisance to residents. The 1990 Act sets out the grounds on which a licence can be refused.

Late night, take-away food shops

The late night opening of take-away food shops can be controlled by an order under section 4 Local Government (Miscellaneous Provisions) Act 1982. A take-away food shop is any shop or other premises where meals or refreshments are supplied to be eaten off the premises other than a late night refreshment house, or premises licensed to sell alcoholic drinks.

If the local authority considers that the late night opening of a take-away food shop should be restricted to avoid unreasonable disturbance to local residents, then it can make an order requiring the named premises to be closed during certain times between midnight and 5am.

Registration of premises

The registration of food premises under the Food Safety Act 1990 is considered in Chapter 7.

Section 49 Offices, Shops and Railway Premises Act 1963 requires an employer who first begins to employ anyone in any office or shop, to serve a notice in a prescribed form on the local authority. This applies to restaurants, wine bars and other premises which fall within the wide definition of offices or shops within the 1963 Act.

There is power in section 17 Development of Tourism Act 1969, for an order to be made requiring all hotels and other establishments which provide sleeping accommodation as a business, to be registered with Tourist Boards. Such an order can provide criminal sanctions for failure to register. No order has been made, and instead, Tourist Boards operate a voluntary classification system for hotels, guest houses etc.

Wet cooling towers and evaporative condensers are components of many air-conditioning systems. Such equipment generally involves the generation of fine water droplets through which air is passed. These are ideal breeding grounds for the bacteria which cause Legionnaire's disease. Because of this the Notification of Cooling Towers and Evaporative Condensers Regulations 1992 require notification to the local authority of all premises containing such equipment.

Baby sitting/listening services and creches

Many hotels, holiday complexes etc., provide baby sitting or listening services or have some organised activities for youngsters. Under section 71 Children Act 1989 a person who provides day care for children under the age of eight on non-domestic premises needs to be registered with the local authority (County Council). A person is not treated as providing day care for children if the total period during which children are looked after does not exceed two hours in any day. Baby listening and baby sitting services are not considered to come within the definition of 'looking after' children and so registration is not considered to be necessary. If, however a creche or entertainment for children under eight years old is organised exceeding two hours then registration is likely. The matter is a question of degree and enquiry may be necessary in the light of the particular facts.

Entertainment licences

If there is public dancing or music, or any similar public entertainment on any premises, then the premises must have an entertainments licence issued by the local authority. The law as to entertainment licences varies slightly between London and the rest of England and Wales. In London, entertainment licences are granted under the London Government Act 1963. Elsewhere the law is set out in section 1 and Schedule 1 Local Government (Miscellaneous Provisions) Act 1982. The main difference is that outside London an entertainment licence is not needed for entertainments in the open air unless the local authority has passed a resolution to bring such entertainments within the need for such a licence.

The need for a licence applies to public music and dancing, including on private premises to which the public is admitted even if there is an admittance charge, but an entertainments licence is not required for a private function such as a private dinner dance.

Entertainment licences need to be renewed annually, although there is power to grant shorter licences or even occasional licences. Licences may be subject to conditions of various sorts and under the Local Government (Miscellaneous Provisions) Act 1982 a local authority can prescribe standard conditions to apply to all entertainment licences granted.

No entertainment licence is required for premises licensed for the sale of alcoholic drinks if the only music or entertainment is by television, radio, recorded sound or music and singing by not more than two musicians or singers (section 182 Licensing Act 1964). But an entertainments licence must be obtained before premises licensed under the Licensing Act 1964 can be granted a Special Hours Certificate.

Music copyright

The copyright in any written music belongs to the composer and/or publisher (Copyright, Designs and Patents Act 1988) except that copyright will expire at a certain date after the death of the composer. Separate copyright exists for the makers of sound recordings.

'Copyright' means a right not to have the music copied, performed in public, broadcast etc., without the consent of the copyright owner. There is no requirement for copyright to be registered because it arises automatically as a result of the original creative work of the composer.

It is the performance in public which generally creates a problem, and public, in this context, means anything outside the normal domestic environment, so it includes not only premises where an entertainments licence is required, but also private members' clubs etc. A performance in this context means either live music, for example by musicians, or recorded music, such as records or tapes.

It would be an impossible task for a hotelier playing piped music in the hotel or a publican with a juke box in the bar, to contact every composer, music publisher and recording company for permission to play such music. The problem is overcome by obtaining licences from the Performing Right Society (representing music composers and music publishers) and Phonographic Performance Limited (representing record companies). These organisations represent almost all copyright owners in respect of most types of music and for a licence fee they permit the use/playing of copyrighted material. The bulk of the fees paid are distributed to the copyright owners as royalties.

Failure to obtain a licence when playing copyrighted music in public could lead to an injunction being obtained by the copyright owners and damages for breach of copyright.

Televisions

Televisions must be licensed under the Wireless Telegraphy Act 1949 as amended. Hotels and other premises where televisions are installed in letting accommodation require a Hotel Comprehensive Licence. Such a licence covers all the televisions installed by the proprietor in the hotel or other establishment, including staff accommodation as well as letting bedrooms. The licence is limited to one site and so does not include a physically separate annex nor does it cover staff (or guests') own televisions. The licence must be renewed every 12 months.

The fee for a Hotel Comprehensive Licence is calculated in multiples of the standard domestic television licence fee. If there are no more than 15 letting rooms (or other units of letting accommodation such as motel chalets) then the fee is the same as the standard domestic licence fee. For up to every five rooms thereafter the fee is increased by the same amount. So the licence fee for a hotel with televisions in 58 bedrooms is 10 times the standard fee (rooms 1–15 = 1 standard fee, rooms 16–55 = 8 standard fees, rooms 56–58 = 1 standard fee).

Gaming

Gaming is the playing of games of chance for winnings and it is controlled by the Gaming Act 1968 (GA 1968). Games of pure skill, for example, chess and darts cannot be gaming even if there is some prize for the winner.

If gaming, other than by gaming machines, is carried on as a commercial enterprise, then the premises have to be licensed or registered under Part 2 GA 1968. However the playing of dominoes, cribbage and certain specially authorised games is permitted on premises licensed for the sale of alcoholic liquor, for example, a public house, without the need for any further permission or licence, but, the drinks licence must be a full on-licence and not a Part 4 licence (section 6 GA 1968).

The general scheme of the GA 1968 is that an applicant for a gaming licence must first obtain a certificate from the Gaming Board. Such a certificate is only issued after the Board has satisfied itself as to the suitability of the applicant for a certificate.

After that, the applicant applies to the local justices for a licence for particular premises. The justices must refuse a gaming licence in certain limited circumstances which are set out in paragraph 22 of Schedule 2 GA 1968, but subject to that, they have a discretion to refuse a licence on any of the grounds in paragraphs 18 to 21 of that Schedule, which includes that there is no demand, or that the premises are unsuitable. Gaming licenses, if granted, are renewable on an annual basis.

Gaming machines are controlled by Part 3 GA 1968 and for most premises a permit is required which is obtainable on application to the local justices. The permit lasts at least three years. The procedure for obtaining a permit for gaming machines is set out in Schedule 9 to the GA 1968.

Waste disposal

The Environmental Protection Act 1990 creates a regime for the lawful disposal of 'controlled waste' which means almost any type of waste to be disposed of even if not hazardous or harmful.

The person who takes away any waste for disposal must be an 'authorised person'. Such authorised persons are local authority waste collectors, registered waste carriers and holders of waste disposal licences. It is a criminal offence to allow someone other than an authorised person to take waste for disposal and so, if that person is not the local authority, it is necessary to check that the person is registered or holds a valid licence.

When waste is taken away, a transfer note must be completed with a description of the waste being handed over. Where one authorised person does regular (for example daily, weekly) collections of the same description of waste (such as waste/surplus food) then an annual transfer note will be sufficient. Copies of transfer notes must be kept by both parties for a minimum of two years.

────────────◆ **SELF EXAMINATION QUESTIONS** ◆────────────

1 Arnold and Bertram are partners in a business, Unwind Caterers. The business operates two hotels, a small chain of restaurants as well as some function catering. The business is registered for VAT. The stationery, invoices and other business documents are due for reprinting. What information should be shown on those documents other than the name Unwind Caterers?
2 The partners have decided to have a logo on the new stationery and business documents and to use the logo on other items such as serviettes so as to create a corporate image. Should Arnold and Bertram register the logo and if so where?
3 One of the hotels run by Unwind Caterers is experiencing a problem with

accommodation bookings which are not taken up. Arnold suggests charging a booking fee of 5 per cent to reserve the room which fee will be deducted from the bill at the end of the stay. What are the VAT implications of this if the suggestion is put into practice?

4 Both hotels have about 30 letting bedrooms each with full facilities including television. In the hotel restaurant/dining rooms (which are licensed to serve alcoholic drinks) recorded background music is played. What licences or permissions do the hotels need in addition to a licence to sell alcoholic drinks?

See Appendix for suggested answers.

Chapter 5

THE CUSTOMER RELATIONSHIP

In this chapter the relationship between the hotelier or caterer and the customer is examined and is almost exclusively concerned with the civil law. Much of the law is also common law (judge-made law) or is derived from such law and so many case decisions will also be met in this chapter.

Chapter 6 looks at the various laws designed to protect the consumer and is largely complementary to this chapter. Those laws affect how hoteliers and caterers conduct their relationships with their customers, but are distinct and almost exclusively statutory. Also, as will be seen in Chapter 6, many of the consumer protection laws create criminal offences.

The relationship between a proprietor of a hotel or catering establishment and the customers is based on contract. A booking of a hotel room or the purchase of a meal in a restaurant creates a legally binding contract. However, before the contract arises there may be some pre-contract discussion or negotiations which lead to the contract being made and it is those precontract matters which are looked at first before considering the contract itself and other matters arising from that contractual relationship.

Misrepresentation

Representations

A misrepresentation is a false statement or representation made by one party to a contract before the contract is made, which representation is intended to induce, and does induce, the other person to enter into the contract. Such a misrepresentation can cause the downfall of the contract or it might entitle the representee (the person to whom the representation is made) to compensation (damages).

A representation is usually an oral or written statement. The statement must usually be of a present or past fact, for example the hotel is 100 metres from the sea. However, the statement could be an opinion or a forecast, especially where the person is qualified to give an expert opinion or forecast.

◆ Esso Petroleum Company Ltd v Mardon (1976)

Esso bought a site on a busy main road which had outline planning permission for a petrol station and it calculated that the petrol station would have an annual throughput of 200,000 gallons as from the third year of opening. When the application for detailed permission was put in, the planning authority required the petrol pumps to be placed at the back of the site and this resulted in access having to be made via a side street, and with lack of visibility from the main road. As a result the petrol station only had an achievable throughput of 70,000 gallons per year.

The petrol station was built, and a prospective tenant, a Mr Mardon, was found. In the negotiations for the tenancy of the petrol station, Mr Mardon was told by Esso that Esso's estimate of throughput was 200,000 gallons per year. Mr Mardon queried this figure, but he was assured the figure was correct and he bowed to the greater knowledge and experience of the Esso 'experts'.

He took the tenancy on a rental based on that throughput. The result was financial disaster. The business failed dramatically and Mr Mardon lost all the money he had put into the business, as well as ending up with many large debts. There was considerable acrimony between Esso and Mr Mardon, who had failed to pay for petrol supplied to him for resale. The dispute ended up in court where the court decided that Mr Mardon had been induced to enter into the tenancy based on the representation made by Esso, who had expertise in the making of sales forecasts for new petrol stations. The forecast was wrong because it had not been revised to take account of the changed circumstances, and so there was a misrepresentation entitling Mr Mardon to a legal remedy.

A representation must be distinguished from mere advertising hype. Expressions such as 'a warm welcome awaits you at . . .' will not generally be regarded by the courts as a representation, and there will not be legal consequences if the welcome is frosty.

Representations can become terms of the contract itself in which case, if the representation is false, the contract will have been breached. If the representation does not become a term of the contract then the law still provides a remedy.

Categories of misrepresentation

A representation becomes a misrepresentation if it is false at the date the contract is made but misrepresentations are divided into three categories dependent on how the falsehood arises

- fraudulent misrepresentations – deliberately false representations or representations made without any belief in their truth
- negligent misrepresentations – untrue representations made honestly but without reasonable grounds for that belief
- innocent misrepresentations – representations which are made honestly and with reasonable grounds for believing that they are true but which turn out to be untrue.

Remedies for misrepresentation

The remedies for misrepresentation differ according to its category.

- Fraudulent misrepresentation – the person induced to enter into the contract may rescind it (treat it as never having been made) or claim damages, or both. Such damages are likely to be heavier than for other categories of misrepresentation.
- Negligent misrepresentation arises under section 2(1) Misrepresentation Act 1967 and the remedies are the same as for fraudulent misrepresentation
- Innocent misrepresentation entitles the representee to rescind the contract, but not to sue for damages, however, in court proceedings concerning an innocent misrepresentation, the court may, in an appropriate case, decide to uphold the contract but award damages instead (section 2(2) misrepresentation Act 1967).

This means that if a hotelier tells an enquirer on the telephone that all rooms have sea views, and the enquirer books a room in reliance on that information, when the guest finds on arrival that the room has not got a sea view, he or she will be entitled to refuse to take the room, and also to damages for the misrepresentation because the hotelier must have been either fraudulent or negligent in making such a statement.

Exclusion of liability for misrepresentation

The contract may try to restrict or exclude the liability of a party for any misrepresentation made by that party. Section 3 Misrepresentation Act 1967 (which was inserted by section 8 Unfair Contract Terms Act 1977) limits the effect of such a provision in the contract.

Section 3 Misrepresentation Act 1967

If a contract contains a term which would exclude or restrict

a) any liability to which a party to a contract may be subject by reason of any misrepresentation made by him before the contract was made; or

b) any remedy available to another party to the contract by reason of such misrepresentation.

that term shall be of no effect except insofar as it satisfies the requirement of reasonableness as stated in section 11(1) Unfair Contract Terms Act 1977; and it is for those claiming that the term satisfies that requirement to show that it does.

Therefore, the exclusion clause must satisfy the reasonableness test, which test is that it was fair and reasonable to include the clause having regard to all the circumstances known or contemplated by the parties when they made the contract. If the exclusion provision fails that test, it will be ineffective.

THE CONTRACT

Formation of the contract

In Chapter 1 it was seen that a contract is a legally binding agreement formed by an offer which is accepted and supported by consideration.

In a contract for the booking of hotel accommodation the contract will be formed by the customer offering to take accommodation and the hotelier confirming the acceptance of the booking. There are many other types of contracts which can be made; bookings for a wedding reception, an outside catering contract or perhaps a short break advertised through the press or by brochures. In each case the contract comes into existence when the 'offer' is accepted.

If a booking is made by post, then the 'offer' will usually be the potential customer writing and asking for accommodation for a certain date, but the contract will be made when the confirmation of the booking is posted back, not when it is received by the potential customer.

Terms of the contract

Where the contract is written, then its terms are usually simple to discover, but if it is oral, it is not always so easy. It is sometimes the case that a contracting party will endeavour to incorporate into the contract some printed standard conditions. The rule is that such conditions must be brought to the attention of the other contracting party, before, or at the time the contract is made, otherwise it will be too late to try and incorporate them later.

◆ OLLEY v MARLBOROUGH COURT LTD **(1949)**

A guest arrived at a private hotel and booked in. She signed the hotel register which contained no notice of any special booking conditions. When the guest went up to the room, she discovered that there was a notice displayed in the hotel bedroom disclaiming liability on the part of the hotel proprietor for articles lost or stolen. Items were stolen from the bedroom. The court decided that the notice was completely ineffective because it was only brought to the attention of the guest after the contract had been made and therefore was not a term of the contract.

The express terms of the contract are those that are agreed between the parties. There are two categories, of contract terms – conditions and warranties. A condition is an essential provision of the contract, the breach of a condition entitles the innocent party both to treat the contract as terminated and to claim damages. A warranty is a less important term of the contract, the breach of which entitles the other party to damages only.

In addition to the agreed terms of the contract, there are circumstances where the law will imply other terms into a contract, even though those terms might not have been discussed or even thought about by the contracting parties. Many of these implied terms are implied by statute law to protect consumers and are considered in Chapter 6, for instance where the Package Travel, Package Holidays and Package Tours Regulations 1992 apply the brochure particulars become implied warranties of the contract.

Other terms may be implied in order to give effect to the unexpressed intentions of the parties, or because the contract would be incomplete without them.

Where a business selling/supplying goods or services enters into a written contract with a consumer (an individual not acting in a business capacity) then under regulation 6 of the Unfair Terms in Consumer Contracts Regulations 1994 the contract must be in plain intelligible language and if there is any doubt about what a contract term means the courts will give that term the meaning most favourable to the consumer.

Exemption clauses

Various attempts have been made over many years by parties to contracts, to exclude or restrict their liability under the contract, for breach of contract, for instance, by providing that a buyer has no remedy for defects in goods or by restricting damages in such cases to a nominal amount. Not unnaturally, both the courts and Parliament have disliked such clauses especially where the other party to the contract is a consumer, that is someone not contracting in a business capacity.

The Unfair Contract Terms Act 1977 (UCTA 1977) nullifies the effect of certain exemption clause and restricts the operation of other clauses. The

UCTA 1977 renders completely ineffective the following exemption clauses.

- An exemption clause which endeavours to exclude or restrict liability for death or personal injury resulting from the breach of any obligation in a contract (express or implied) to take reasonable care or exercise reasonable skill in carrying out the contract (section 2(1) UCTA 1977).
- An exemption clause which, by reference to a so-called 'guarantee', endeavours to exclude or restrict liability for defective products supplied to a private consumer, in breach of a duty of care in the manufacture or distribution of those goods (section 5 UCTA 1977).
- A clause endeavouring to exclude or restrict the liability arising under section 12 Sale of Goods Act 1979 or, liability to a consumer under section 13 to 15, Sale of Goods Act 1979 (section 6 UCTA 1977). The Sale of Goods Act is looked at in Chapter 6.

The UCTA 1977 makes the following exemption clauses ineffective unless, and to the extent that, the clause is fair and reasonable in the circumstances, known to, or contemplated by, the parties when they made their contract.

- An exemption clause which excludes or restricts liability for any loss or damage (other than death or personal injury) arising from any breach of a duty of care in the contract (whether express or implied) (section 2(2) UCTA 1977).
- An exemption clause in a contract which either incorporates standard written terms of business, or which operates against a consumer and which excludes or restricts liability for breach of contract, or failure substantially to perform the contract, or which clause endeavours to allow one party to be entitled to perform its obligations under the contract in a substantially different way from that expected, or even not to carry out his or her contractual obligations at all (section 3 UCTA 1977).
- An indemnity by consumer against any negligence or breach of contract of another (section 4 UCTA 1977).

Similar provisions in sections 15 to 25 UCTA 1977 apply to Scotland. The UCTA 1977 applies equally to displayed disclaimer notices.

In some of the above cases, the UCTA 1977 protects 'consumers' which means people who contract in their private, non-business, capacity, and the other party to the contract makes the contract in the course of his or her business. The following examples will help to make this clear.

- A notice displayed in an hotel foyer which reads 'persons enter and use these premises at their own risk' will be absolutely ineffective (section 2(1) UCTA 1977) but a notice in a guest house which states 'the proprietor accepts no responsibility for loss of or damage to guests' property' might be valid if reasonable (section 2(2) UCTA 1977).

* A mini break booking form for a chain of hotels which states 'the management reserves the right to change the hotel or cancel the break or reduce the period of accommodation' is only valid if reasonable (section 3 UCTA 1977).

If the exemption clause is not struck down by the UCTA 1977, then there are still other hurdles for it to jump before it can be valid. First, the courts will look to make sure it has been validly made a term of the contract (see earlier, *Olley v Marlborough Court Ltd. 1949* page 93). Second, exemption clauses must be worded so that they are unambiguous and cover the matter which arises. If there is any ambiguity about the clause, or doubt whether it covers the loss or damage, or the matter which has arisen, then the benefit of the doubt will be given to the other party, that is against the party whom the clause is trying to protect. Third, an exemption clause may be an unfair term caught and made ineffective by the Unfair Terms in Consumer Contracts Regulations 1994.

Unfair terms

The Unfair Terms in Consumers Contracts Regulations 1994 apply to contracts between a business supplier of goods and/or services and a consumer and implement EC Directive 93/13. To some extent the regulations overlap with the Unfair Contract Terms Act 1977 but there are important distinctions.

* The 1994 regulations only apply to contracts with consumers and only to standard (not individually negotiated) contract terms.
* The 1977 Act only applies to specified clauses while the 1994 regulations affect almost all contract terms.

The 1994 regulations provide that an unfair term is not binding on a consumer but the rest of the contract remains in effect if it can do so without the unfair term. An unfair term is one which

* has not been individually negotiated eg standard printed booking conditions
* does not relate to the main subject matter of the contract
* causes a significant imbalance in the parties' rights and obligations contrary to good faith and to the detriment of the consumer.

Examples of terms which will be regarded as unfair are set out in Schedule 3 to the regulations and include clauses which provide for heavy cancellation charges, allow the business to alter the contract unilaterally without a valid specified reason or allow the business to provide something different than provided for in the contract.

Where a business uses standard contract terms including one or more unfair terms the Director General of Fair Trading can ask for a court injunction to prevent the continued use of such unfair terms or can accept an undertaking from the business not to use those unfair terms in contracts with consumers.

Arbitration clauses

Clauses are sometimes inserted in contracts which provide that disputes or differences will be referred to an arbitrator for a decision instead of the courts. Such clauses are valid and are not treated by the UCTA 1977 as exemption clauses. Arbitration clauses are commonly found in booking forms for package holidays, short breaks etc., and whenever a party might want to try and keep disputes out of the glare of publicity (court cases being held in public, while arbitration is in private).

If, despite a binding arbitration clause, one party issues court proceedings, the other party may apply to the court to stop those proceedings on the basis that the court has no jurisdiction. However, if a contract that has an arbitration clause is made with a consumer, then the Consumer Arbitration Agreements Act 1988 applies. That Act provides that, in most situations, the consumer cannot be compelled to submit a dispute to arbitration if he or she would prefer the matter dealt with by the ordinary courts. The procedure of arbitration is governed by the Arbitration Act 1950, which also deals with the enforcement of arbitration awards.

BREACH OF CONTRACT

If there is a breach of contract, then three questions usually arise. Who can sue? Within what timescale? and what remedies are available?

The person who can sue is usually the innocent party, but there are various rules concerning agency, assignment of contract etc., which are beyond the scope of this book. An important aspect of who can sue is the rule known as 'privity of contract', which will be considered shortly.

If there is a breach of contract, then there is a time limit within which the innocent party must seek a remedy by commencing court proceedings. These time limits are to be found in the Limitation Act 1980 and the general time limit is six years, but in the case of personal injuries and death arising from a breach of contract, the time limit is three years from the later of the date of the breach, or the date the plaintiff acquired certain knowledge as to his or her possible claim.

Generally, the remedies for an innocent party are to treat the contract as terminated (but only in certain situations), seek an order for the other party to perform the contract (specific performance), seek an order to restrain the breach or future breaches of the contract (injunction) and/or obtain compensation (damages).

The question of the amount of damages raises problems in the hotel/catering/leisure industries where the contract may give rise to expectations on one side of an enjoyable experience, for example, a special meal to celebrate an anniversary, a well-earned break or a family holiday. Those expectations may not be realised due to breach of contract, but how far the law can provide compensation for such matters is also considered.

Privity of contract and the block booking

A contract is binding on the parties to it and cannot impose obligations or grant benefits on anyone who is not a party to the contract.

It was the application of this very rule, which in *Donoghue v Stevenson (1932)* meant that the plaintiff had to sue in the tort of negligence rather than for breach of contract.

◆ DONOGHUE V STEVENSON (1932)

A boy and girlfriend went into a cafe. The boy bought the girlfriend a bottle of ginger beer. The girl poured part of the ginger beer into a glass and drank it. She then topped up her glass with the remainder from the bottle, but as she did so, out floated the remains of a decomposed snail. The girl suffered severe shock and became very ill. The girl had no remedy in contract, because she had not bought the drink.

But what if there is a contract which benefits others? Can a breach of contract permit a party to the contract to recover damages for other persons for whom the contract was made?

◆ JACKSON V HORIZON HOLIDAYS LTD (1975)

Mr Jackson booked a holiday through a travel agency for a four week family holiday abroad. He paid £1200 for the holiday which was for himself, his wife and their three children. He required a hotel of the highest standard, and with the adults' bedroom having a communicating door to the childrens' bedroom. The hotel chosen was described as having a swimming pool, mini-golf, excellent restaurant etc. The bedrooms were described as having a private bath, shower and WC.

The holiday was a disaster. There was no proper bath, no swimming pool, and no connecting door. There was mildew and fungus on the childrens' bedroom wall and when the Jacksons complained to the hotel, they were moved after three days into better accommodation, but still very unsatisfactory. The hotel food was distasteful, being cooked in coconut oil.

When Mr Jackson returned home, he sued the travel agency and was awarded damages of £1100, to include compensation for himself and his family. The award of damages for the other members of the family was appealed on the basis that the damages for the distress, discomfort etc., could only be that suffered by Mr Jackson, because he was the only party to the contract, and could not include the distress etc. suffered by Mrs Jackson and the children. The award of damages was confirmed on appeal.

The decision has been criticised in a later case, but in situations where one party generally contracts on behalf of others, such as a family holiday, a school trip with accommodation or a host booking for a party at a restaurant, it is likely that the result in *Jackson v Horizon Holidays Ltd*, will stand the test of time and the damages awarded in future may include damages for the loss suffered by the other persons in the booking.

Damages for disappointment

Normally damages are calculated to compensate for monetary or ascertainable loss, so that in a commercial contract, the innocent party cannot recover damages for distress caused by the breach of contract. But if the contract is for a specific entertainment or enjoyment, the damages awarded may include damages for disappointment.

◆ JARVIS V SWAN TOURS LTD (1972)

Mr Jarvis enjoyed winter holidays. So much so, that he booked well in advance. In 1969, he booked a two week winter holiday in Switzerland with Swan Tours Ltd. The holiday which was described in the brochure as a houseparty holiday, was in an hotel with Alpine bar, English speaking host and set among a wide variety of fine ski runs. Additionally, the facilities were stated to include a welcoming party on arrival, Swiss dinner by candlelight, fondue party, yodeller evening and the services of a representative.

Mr Jarvis was bitterly disappointed by his holiday. The host spoke no English, the second week he was the only person there, which made it a bit difficult to have a party, the ski runs were some considerable distance away, the availability of skis for hire was patchy and even the yodeller evening was a disaster. To make things worse, the bar was in an annexe and open only one evening per week. The holiday was completely ruined. Mr Jarvis sued for damages for the holiday which had cost £63.45 and was awarded £125 damages to include damages for the substantial disappointment.

Other situations readily come to mind where special arrangements are made and booked and where there will be considerable disappointment if the arrangements are broken.

◆ Hotson and Hotson v Payne (trading as Anglia Motel) (1988)

Mr and Mrs Hotson booked the Anglia Motel for their daughter's wedding reception. It was to be an event to remember, with a band, dancing for over 100 guests, sherry reception on arrival and a three-course sit-down meal. Forty-eight hours before the wedding, the motel cancelled the booking. The only alternative venue for the reception which could be obtained at such short notice, was the functions room of a public house. The room was cramped and there was no room for dancing and so the band had to be cancelled and the publican could only put on a cold buffet. The day to remember turned into one to forget. Damages were awarded against the hotel for breach of contract, including not only £265 for the actual loss, such as all the telephone calls to guests and the band's cancellation fee, but £750 for disappointment.

Duties of hoteliers

Certain duties, which are placed on hotel proprietors, apply if the establishment is an hotel as defined as follows.

Section 1 Hotel Proprietors Act 1956

(3) In this Act, the expression 'hotel' means an establishment held out by the proprietor as offering food, drink and, if so required, sleeping accommodation, without special contract, to any traveller presenting himself who appears able and willing to pay a reasonable sum for the services and facilities provided and who is in a fit state to be received.

The definition uses two expressions which need explanation. First, the expression 'without special contract' merely means without previous booking. The expression 'traveller' however, is a little more difficult – it is not, as the name might suggest, someone away from home.

◆ WILLIAMS V LINNITT (1951)

A farmer lived about three miles from Nuneaton and had been one day into Nuneaton. That evening he drove from Nuneaton to the Royal Redgate Inn and on the way he passed his home. He had arranged to meet some friends at the inn for a drink. The case was prior to the Hotel Proprietors Act 1956 but the question arose in a court case brought by the farmer against the proprietor of the inn as to whether the farmer was a 'traveller'. He lived only about a mile from the inn but the court decided that the expression 'traveller' is very wide and means anyone calling at the hotel for accommodation, food or drink, other than the proprietor, his or her family, relatives and personal guests.

The test as to whether an establishment is a 'hotel' depends on whether the establishment satisfies the statutory test in section 1 Hotel Proprietors Act 1956 (HPA 1956). The name of the establishment is not necessarily a guide to whether or not it is a hotel. Neither a private hotel nor a residential hotel (which are distinguished either by the need for prior booking or the unavailability of food and drink for non-residents) are 'hotels' within the HPA 1956 nor is a guest house. On the other hand, a public house which provides bar meals and has a room or two for bed and breakfast will probably qualify as a 'hotel'.

If the establishment is a hotel, then the proprietor has four duties which are all common law duties

- to offer travellers accommodation
- to offer travellers refreshment
- to be responsible for the safety of guests
- to be responsible for loss of, or damage to, travellers' luggage and other goods if they take accommodation at the hotel.

The fourth of these duties is considered on page 103, and the third is considered on page 112.

The first two duties – to offer travellers accommodation and refreshment – are now considered in turn. Both duties create both civil and criminal liability.

Hoteliers' duty to provide accommodation

The obligation is to offer accommodation to travellers at a reasonable price provided the traveller is in a fit state to be received and appears able to pay for the accommodation. There are certain limitations to the duty.

- The traveller must be in a fit state to be received. A hotel proprietor can refuse accommodation to someone, for instance, if they are drunk.
- The traveller must be able to pay for the accommodation and the proprietor is entitled to insist on payment in advance.
- If the hotel is full, that is, all bedrooms taken, the hotel proprietor can turn away the traveller. A stranded motorist is not entitled to demand to sleep in the lounge if all the bedrooms are let.

The duty to provide accommodation is extended to a duty to receive the traveller's luggage and other items. This duty may even extend to the traveller's dog unless the dog is noisy, dangerous or dirty, in which case the dog may be grounds for refusing accommodation for the traveller. There is no obligation to accept luggage or other items alone.

The traveller cannot insist on a particular room even if it is available and a guest who is a nuisance or causes annoyance to other guests may be asked to leave and, if necessary, may be forceably removed.

An offer of accommodation at another of the proprietor's hotels is not sufficient to satisfy the duty if there is accommodation available at the hotel where the traveller wishes to stay.

Hoteliers' duty to provide refreshment

The duty of an hotel proprietor is to supply food and drink by way of reasonable refreshment, at a reasonable price, to any traveller at any time of the day or night. The proprietor may refuse service on reasonable grounds

- if the traveller is drunk or is not suitably dressed or otherwise not in a proper condition to be accepted then those may be reasonable grounds for refusing service
- if the traveller cannot pay then there is no obligation to provide refreshment
- if the hotel proprietor either has no food, or only sufficient for his or her guests and those diners who have booked, then there is no duty on the proprietor to buy in food specially for a traveller.

It is considered to be no justification to refuse service of refreshment if the dining room is full. A meal in the bar or other suitable area should be offered instead.

A person wishing refreshment is not entitled to sit at a particular table or to stay beyond a reasonable time to consume the food and drink.

Enforcement

If a hotel proprietor refuses, without proper justification, to offer a traveller accommodation or reasonable refreshment, then not only may the traveller sue, but also the hotel can be prosecuted.

REGISTRATION OF GUESTS

By the Immigration (Hotel Records) Order 1972, every guest over 16 years of age who takes accommodation at a hotel or other premises where sleeping accommodation is provided in return for payment, must register his or her full name and nationality with the proprietor of the establishment. Each guest must be separately registered even where they are husband and wife.

Where a guest is neither a British nor a Commonwealth citizen, he or she must also supply his or her passport number and place of issue of passport, or details of whatever alternative documents the guest has, which establishes his or her identity and nationality. Such a guest, on or before leaving the establishment, must inform the proprietor of his or her next destination and, if known, the full address where he or she will be staying at that destination.

The proprietor of the establishment is under an obligation to obtain such information and must make a written record of all this information together with the date of arrival of the guest. Those records must be kept for at least 12 months and the information must be available for inspection at any time by the police.

There is no particular form in which the information or record must be kept, except that it must be written. It can be in a book, or separate cards, or however the hotel or guest house wishes to organise its registration records. A print-out of computerised information will be satisfactory.

HOTEL GUESTS' PROPERTY

Conditions for strict liability

The proprietor of a 'hotel' (as defined in section 1 HPA 1956) is strictly liable for loss of, or damage to, a hotel guest's property, and this liability does not depend on the law of bailment (see below). Strict liability is liability which arises without fault or negligence, but is not absolute. Liability arises even if the goods are stolen by a third party or their disappearance or damage is unexplained. There are a number of conditions which have to be satisfied for this strict liability to arise

- the premises must be a 'hotel' within the meaning given to that word by the HPA 1956
- the guest must be a 'traveller' who has taken sleeping accommodation at the hotel
- the loss of, or damage to his or her property must have happened within a certain period
- the property lost or damaged must be of the type to which liability can apply
- the property, at the time of the loss or damage, must be within the 'hospitium' of the hotel.

Before looking at each of these conditions in turn, three other points need to be mentioned. First, the liability attaches to the 'proprietor' of the establishment. This means the person or company which runs the business, *not* the hotel manager nor the person who holds the licence for the sale of alcoholic drinks, (but, of course, the licensee may also be the owner of the business).

The second point to be mentioned is that the liability is strict liability, but that does not mean that the proprietor is liable, in effect, as insurer, because there are defences which may mean the proprietor escapes liability altogether.

Third, the liability is unlimited in amount unless the proprietor restricts the liability by the display of a statutory notice (see below).

Now to look at each of the conditions for liability in turn.

Definition of a 'hotel'

The definition of a 'hotel' is set out in section 1 Hotel Proprietor's Act 1956 and has already been considered as has the definition of a 'traveller'. Basically, the definition is of an establishment, offering food, drink (not necessarily alcoholic) and sleeping accommodation to anyone calling there without the necessity of booking in advance, and who is able to pay for the food, drink or accommodation.

Many establishments which refer to themselves as a hotel are not, in fact, a hotel within the meaning of the HPA 1956, because they do not satisfy the various criteria set out in that Act in one respect or another. For example, many guest houses which refer to themselves as hotels, are not hotels because they do not provide food and drink to people who do not take sleeping accommodation.

Definition of a guest

A traveller becomes a guest when he or she books in to the hotel. In theory, the traveller must be accepted by the proprietor, but in practice this means that they are not refused accommodation. The provision of accommodation to the 'traveller' is the test as to whether a person has become a guest. But the contract for the accommodation may have been booked by a third party, for instance, a tour operator, so for a person to be a guest there is no requirement for the existence of a contractual relationship between the proprietor and the guest.

A person who has become a guest can cease to be one even though remaining in the accommodation because if he or she remains there on a long-term basis, then the guest will cease to be a guest and will instead become a lodger, and the hotel proprietor will then cease to be strictly liable for the loss of, or damage to his or her goods.

Other conditions for strict liability

The guest must have taken sleeping accommodation, so no strict liability attaches to the proprietor of the establishment for the property of a customer who only takes a meal at the hotel or who is at the hotel for a function such as a wedding reception.

The loss of, or damage to a guest's property must occur during the period starting with midnight immediately preceding, and ending with midnight immediately after, the period the person was a guest with accommodation at the hotel.

The hotel proprietor's strict liability does not extend to a vehicle or anything left in it and (shades of a bygone era) any horse or other live animal or its harness or other equipment.

Finally, the goods must have been within the 'hospitium' of the hotel at the time of the loss or damage. The hospitium is the hotel building itself, its grounds and other buildings all used as part of the hotel. So, it will include a swimming pool, car park, gardens etc. It is, however, not necessary for the guest to be within the hospitium of the hotel when the loss or damage occurs.

Defences

If the conditions for strict liability are met, then the hotel proprietor will be liable to compensate the guest for loss of, or damage to the guest's luggage and other property. There are some cases where the hotel proprietor can avoid liability altogether

- if the loss or damage is due to the guest's own negligence, then the hotel proprietor is not liable
- the hotel proprietor is not liable if the guest by his or her actions takes sole responsibility for the goods
- there is no liability on the hotel proprietor for loss or damage caused by enemy action or an Act of God.

The most common of these situations where the proprietor can avoid liability is if the loss or damage is due to the guest's own negligence, but this raises the question as to when a guest is negligent. It is not necessarily negligence not to lock a bedroom door if the hotel is a small country hotel and where people coming into and out of the hotel are all seen by the hotel staff. If the hotel wants the rooms left unlocked so that the rooms may be serviced, then again there can be no negligence on the guest for complying with such a requirement. Similarly, it is not necessarily negligent if the guest does not deposit valuables with the management for safe keeping. The question in each case is whether the guest has exercised reasonable prudence.

◆ Shacklock v Ethorpe Ltd (1939)

A guest at a small country hotel put her jewels in a jewel case which she locked and then put the case in a case with three locks, all of which she locked. She left the case under the luggage stand in her hotel bedroom.

She then went to London for the day but did not lock her bedroom door because it was not the practice of guests to lock doors as the hotel management had no duplicate keys and if the room was locked, the chambermaid could not get in to service the room.

The guest had not been negligent and the guest was entitled to recover for her loss when the jewels were stolen.

◆ Brewster v Drennan (1945)

The guest at a small hotel found that her bedroom had no lock. She mentioned this to the proprietor who assured her that her belongings would be quite safe in her room. While the guest was out, her valuable fur cape was stolen.

The court decided that the guest was not at fault in failing to leave her cape with the proprietor for safe keeping.

Limitation of liability

Section 2 Hotel Proprietors' Act 1956

(3) Where the proprietor of an hotel is liable . . . to make good the loss of or any damage to property brought to the hotel, his liability to any one guest shall not exceed £50 in respect of any one article, or £100 in the aggregate, except where

 (a) the property was stolen, lost or damaged through the default, neglect or wilful act of the proprietor or some servant of his; or

 (b) the property was deposited by or on behalf of the guest expressly for safe custody with the proprietor or some servant of his authorised, or appearing to be authorised, for the purpose, and if so required by the proprietor or the servant, in a container fastened or sealed by the depositor; or

 (c) at a time after the guest had arrived at the hotel, either the property in question was offered for deposit as aforesaid and the proprietor or his servant refused to receive it, or the guest or some other guest acting on his behalf wished so to offer the property in question but, through the default of the proprietor or a servant of his, was unable to do so.

Provided that the proprietor shall not be entitled to the protection of this subsection unless, at the time when the property in question was brought to the hotel, a copy of the notice set out in the Schedule to this Act printed in plain type was conspicuously displayed in a place where it could conveniently be read by his guests at or near the reception office or desk or, where there is no reception office or desk, at or near the main entrance to the hotel.

The notice referred to, in section 2 HPA 1956 is printed in the Schedule to the Act and is shown in figure 5.1

NOTICE

LOSS OF OR DAMAGE TO GUESTS' PROPERTY

Under the Hotel Proprietors' Act, 1956, an hotel proprietor may in certain circumstances be liable to make good any loss of or damage to a guest's property, even though it was not due to any fault of the proprietor or staff of the hotel.

This liability, however –

(a)   extends only to the property of guests who have engaged sleeping accommodation at the hotel;

(b)   is limited to £50 for any one article and a total of £100 in the case of any one guest, except in the case of property which has been deposited, or offered for deposit, for safe custody;

(c)   does not cover motor vehicles or other vehicles of any kind or any property left in them, or horses or live animals.

This notice does not constitute an admission, either that the Act applies to this hotel or that liability thereunder attaches to the proprietor of this hotel in any particular case.

Figure 5.1   A sample copy of a limitation of liability notice

By displaying the notice in the place specified in the Act, the hotel proprietor can limit liability except where the loss or damage was caused by the negligence etc., of the proprietor or the hotel employees or either the guest deposited, or offered to deposit, the property with the hotel proprietor for safe keeping. Failure to display the notice, either at all, or in the proper place, will result in the liability of the hotel proprietor being unlimited.

GUESTS' PROPERTY IN GUEST HOUSES

If the establishment is not a 'hotel' as defined in section 1 HPA 1956, then the proprietor is not strictly liable for a guest's property. Establishments outside the definition in the HPA 1956 will include guest houses, bed and breakfast establishments and private and residential hotels.

Although a proprietor of such an establishment will not be strictly liable, he or she may be liable for the loss of, or damage to a guest's property if the proprietor does not take reasonable care for the safety of the guest's property.

◆ SCARBOROUGH V COSGROVE (1905)

Mr Scarborough and his wife took a room in the defendant's boarding house. They asked for a key to the room as they had some valuables which they wanted to keep safe. That request was refused and a request for a key to the chest of drawers went unanswered. Some jewellery was stolen by another guest. The boarding house keeper was successfully sued for the loss. The court decided that the defendant had failed to take reasonable care for the safety of Mr and Mrs Scarborough's property after having been made aware of the situation.

◆ OLLEY V MARLBOROUGH COURT LTD (1949)

Mrs Olley was a guest at a private hotel. On the day in question she closed the self-locking room of her door. She took the key, which had a disc attached with the room number and put it on the appropriate hook on the keyboard in the reception office and went out of the hotel. When she returned to the hotel, the key was missing. Various valuable items had been stolen from her room by a sneak thief who had come into the hotel, taken the key off the keyboard and helped himself. The proprietor of the private hotel was negligent in not ensuring that a proper watch was kept over the reception office, in particular the keyboard, and as a result, the proprietor was liable for the loss of the guest's property.

If the proprietor of an establishment has been negligent in this fashion, it will then be irrelevant whether the establishment is a hotel within the HPA 1956 or not, because such negligence will mean that if it is a hotel, the proprietor will not be able to rely on the limitation of liability by virtue of the displayed notice, and the result will be the same.

CUSTOMERS' COATS, CLOAKROOMS AND LOST PROPERTY

Hotels often operate cloakrooms for banquets, wedding receptions, conferences and other functions. The waiter in a restaurant may take a diner's coat to put somewhere for safe keeping. A hotel or guest house guest may book out and when the room is later serviced, something may be found left in error in a drawer in the room just vacated. A restaurant diner might hand in a handbag found under the table left by a previous diner. These are some of the many situations where the proprietor of an establishment comes into possession of property and it is necessary to consider these sorts of situations and the liability of the proprietor for the safe keeping of that property.

All of these situations create what is known as a 'bailment'. Bailment is the relationship which arises when one person (the bailee) takes possession (but not ownership) of goods for the owner (the bailor) and is under an obligation to return the goods at some future time. That relationship can happen in a number of ways, for example, a car put into a garage for a service, a video hired or a book borrowed.

Bailment can arise under a contract or outside contract. In very broad terms there are two types of bailment which are known respectively as gratuitous bailment and a bailment for reward. The difference between the two is that the duty of the bailee is slightly different. There must, however, be some assumption by the bailee of responsibility for the safe keeping of the goods.

◆ Ultzen v Nicols (1894)

Mr Ultzen went into a restaurant where the waiter took his coat and hung it on a hook behind Mr Ultzen's seat. When the meal was over, it was discovered that the coat had been stolen. The court decided there was a bailment of the coat by the restaurant and that the restaurant was liable for the failure to take prudent care of the coat.

A gratuitous bailment will arise where there is no payment. Such a bailment creates an obligation on the bailee to take such care of the goods as a reasonably prudent person would take of his or her own goods. If, despite exercising such care, the goods are stolen, lost or damaged, the bailee will not be liable but it is up to the bailee to prove that he or she did take such care and that the loss or damage happened without breach of his or her responsibilities.

A gratuitous bailment will typically arise where a cloakroom is operated without charge or (as in *Ultzen v Nicols*) a restaurant waiter takes a diner's coat. A gratuitous bailee is obliged to hand over the goods to the bailor on request and if this is not done, the bailee can be sued in tort.

If there is a charge for the cloakroom, that is, a fee for leaving coats, bags, umbrellas etc., then the bailment is for reward. Section 13, Supply of Goods and Services Act 1982 obliges the bailee to use reasonable care and skill in looking after the deposited coats etc., and this will generally mean ensuring that the storage place is suitable and security is adequate. This will require a higher degree of vigilance than merely the degree of care that a reasonably prudent person would take of his or her own property.

If there is a loss of, or damage to the deposited goods, the onus is again on the bailee to show that such loss or damage was not caused by breach of the bailee's obligations.

Often, proprietors of establishments endeavour to reduce their responsibilities by displaying a notice at a cloakroom, purporting to avoid or reduce liability for loss of or damage to deposited goods. Quite apart from questions as to whether the notice is adequate, such a notice can only be valid to the extent that it satisfies the test of reasonableness in section 11 Unfair Contract Terms Act 1977 which, despite its name, is not restricted to bailments arising under a contract. It is for the bailee to demonstrate that the test is satisfied. However, in the case of a bailee for reward it will be difficult to satisfy the test as the purpose of the contract is to ensure the safe keeping of the property.

Property left behind in the room by hotel guests when they book out may still be covered by the strict liability of the hotel proprietor if the establishment is a 'hotel' within Section 1 HPA 1956. This is because the liability lasts until midnight after the guest leaves. Accordingly, a hotel proprietor should ensure that when the room is serviced, the cupboards, drawers etc., are checked to make sure nothing has been left behind before the room is re-let.

If the establishment is not a 'hotel' (and in any event, after the period of strict liability of the hotel proprietor) the proprietor of the establishment is in the position of a gratuitous bailee of any property left behind by a guest, there is no duty to send such property on to the former guest.

If goods are found within the public areas of an hotel or restaurant the question arises as to who is entitled to possession of those goods pending them being claimed by the true owner. If the premises are a hotel (within the meaning of the HPA 1956) then the hotel proprietor is entitled to possession of any goods found within the 'hospitium' of the hotel even if found in public rooms or in the grounds of the hotel. This is because the hotelier is strictly responsible for all guests' property while it is within the 'hospitium' of the hotel. This means that if, for example, a handbag is found in reception, the finder must hand it to the hotel proprietor (or a responsible member of staff of the hotel) and is not entitled to retain it unless and until the true owner can claim it. The position is different where the establishment is not a hotel within the meaning of the HPA 1956. Where something is found in the public part of the establishment, for example in the bar of a public house or in a restaurant, then the finder is entitled to retain possession of those found goods until they are claimed by the true owner. The proprietor of the establishment has no entitlement to possession of the found goods or responsibility for their safety.

If, however, the finder of the lost property hands it to the proprietor, then the proprietor of the establishment will be in the position of a gratuitous bailee of the item and must take prudent care of it until it is claimed.

What happens if the goods in the possession of the proprietor (the bailee) are not claimed by the bailor? The bailee does not have to keep them indefinitely. The Torts (Interference With Goods) Act 1977 gives the proprietor of an establishment a power of sale of such property subject to certain conditions which depend on the circumstances in which the goods came into the possession of the bailee, and whether the identity of the bailor is known or can be discovered. If, for instance, a camera is left behind by a guest in an hotel then the proprietor should write, by recorded delivery, to the former guest telling him or her that the camera can be collected. If it is not collected by a certain date, it will be sold on that date. In the case of very valuable items which are found, left behind or not collected, it would be prudent to use the alternative procedure under the 1977 Act which involves having the sale authorised by the court and the proceeds of sale being paid into the court.

SAFETY OF GUESTS

Common law duty of hoteliers

A proprietor of a hotel within the meaning of the HPA 1956 is under a common law civil duty for the safety of guests. The duty is not one of strict liability, but is a duty to take reasonable care for the safety of guests. The duty is wide as it covers all aspects of safety.

If a guest is attacked while in a hotel, then the hotel proprietor may be liable for the guest's injuries if for example, a violent drunk was not removed from the premises. Under this common law duty, a hotel proprietor can be liable to guests for the safety of food served to guests.

Apart from this duty, the ordinary law of negligence may apply and this will be considered after looking at the duty under statute.

Statutory civil duty of care

The principal Act of Parliament which provides civil remedies to ensure the safety of persons on premises, is the Occupiers' Liability Act 1957 which was considered in some detail in Chapter 3.

Guests in a hotel or guest house have a contract with the hotel proprietor which provides for them to occupy and sleep in accommodation in the hotel or guest house. The duty of care under such a contract is the common duty of care under the Occupiers' Liability Act 1957.

Section 5 Occupiers' Liability Act 1957

(1) Where persons enter or use . . . any premises in exercise of a right conferred by contract with a person occupying or having control of the premises, the duty he owes them in respect of dangers due to the state of the premises or to things done or omitted to be done on them, insofar as the duty depends on a term to be implied in the contract by reason of its conferring that right shall be the common duty of care.

The occupier will not be entitled to restrict or exclude this liability by any provision in the contract for accommodation, because such an attempt is thwarted by section 2(1) Unfair Contract Terms Act 1977 to the extent that it relates to the occupiers' liability for the death of, or personal injury to, the guest.

Negligence

The Occupiers' Liability Act 1957 covers dangers arising from the state of the premises themselves, rather than things done in it. So the Occupiers' Liability Act 1957 covers liability for injuries caused by an accident due to a slippery floor or a broken stair tread. The ordinary law of negligence will be appropriate if, for example, an employee is so careless while using a vacuum cleaner that a hotel guest is knocked over and injured.

The difference between the two sets of liabilities is sometimes referred to as the occupancy duty (OLA 1957) and the activity duty (negligence). The distinction is often difficult to tell. In *Banks v Bury Borough Council 1989*, the plaintiff was severely injured when he dived into the shallow end of a swimming pool which was only 0.9 m deep. The recommendations for the display of signs as to the depth of the pool had not been followed. The appropriate duty arose under The Occupiers' Liability Act 1957 because the state of the swimming pool itself was dangerous due to the lack of clear marking showing the depth.

But what if a hotel swimming pool was quite safe with all markings clearly displayed etc., but the hotel staff were refilling the pool after having cleaned it out, and had taken no steps to warn guests that it was still being filled up? If, in those circumstances, a guest dived into the deep end but the depth of the water was inadequate, would the liability be under the Occupiers' Liability Act 1957 or the common law tort of negligence?

In practice, an injured party will sue alleging a breach of either duty, which are, in fact, identical duties of care.

Intoxicated customers

A licensee of premises may owe a duty of care to a customer not to serve him or her with such an amount of alcohol so that they become incapable of taking care of themselves.

◆ MUNRO v PORTHKERRY PARK HOLIDAY ESTATES LTD (1984)

One weekend three friends went to a cliff top leisure park. They drank a lot in the bar and became boisterous. They were asked to leave the bar. They went out of the bar and one climbed over a fence and fell down a sheer cliff on the other side and was killed.

The deceased's father sued the proprietor of the leisure park, alleging that the deceased was owed a duty not to be served so much alcoholic drink that he became incapable of looking after himself.

The judge decided there was a duty on a licensee of licensed premises to guard against a customer becoming incapable of taking care of himself but, in this case, there was no evidence to suggest that the licensee should come to the conclusion that the deceased was incapable of looking after himself, and, indeed, the deceased had friends with him, and so the claim failed.

This case should be contrasted with *Barrett v Ministry of Defence.*

◆ BARRETT v MINISTRY OF DEFENCE (1995)

The deceased had been a naval airman. One evening at one of the duty free bars at a Royal Navy shore establishment he drank so much that he became unconscious and collapsed. The deceased died from choking on his own vomit. In this case the Ministry of Defence was not responsible for his death through serving the deceased with too much alcohol. The deceased was a responsible adult in an environment where people were expected to exercise self-discipline. However, the Ministry did have a share of responsibility for his death because once the deceased became unconscious he was incapable of looking after himself and the Ministry assumed responsibility for him and should have ensured he was put into such a position and/or watched to avoid what in fact happened.

A licensee may owe a duty to other customers not to serve a person with such an amount of alcohol that he or she becomes a danger to other customers.

◆ CHORDAS V BRYANT (1988)

This was an Australian case but likely to be equally applicable here. A customer was assaulted by another customer in a hotel bar. The customer carrying out the assault had had rather a lot to drink at the bar, but it was not known by the licensee that he would become aggressive. The court decided that although the hotel management should take appropriate steps to protect the safety of its customers, including ejecting any customers who drank too much or who became violent, the facts in this case were that the intoxicated customer had not had so much to drink that a reasonably prudent manager should have ordered him out, or forseen that he might harm other customers. Accordingly, the hotel proprietor was not liable for the injuries to the assaulted customer.

Criminal liability

The Health and Safety at Work etc. Act 1974 places duties on employers. The 1974 Act is a criminal statute and a breach of the duties contained in the Act will result in a prosecution and do not entitle any injured party to sue.

Section 3 Health and Safety at Work etc. Act 1974

(1) It shall be the duty of every employer to conduct his undertaking in such a way as to ensure, so far as is reasonably practicable, that persons not in his employment who may be affected thereby are not exposed to risks to their health or safety.

(2) It shall be the duty of every self-employed person to conduct his undertaking in such a way as to ensure, so far as is reasonably practicable, that he and other persons (not being his employees) who may be affected thereby are not thereby exposed to risks to their health or safety.

The duty is not owed only to guests and customers, it applies to anyone, but the guest at a hotel or the customer in a restaurant may well be at risk from the way a person carries on their business.

Many hotels have swimming or leisure pools. It is under section 3 of the 1974 Act that the hotelier has a duty to ensure as far as reasonably practicable the safety of persons using such pools.

There are no laid down legal standards but to assist compliance with section 3 the Health and Safety Commission and the Sports Council has jointly prepared guidance in a booklet *Safety in Swimming Pools*. The booklet has no legal force but could well be used by courts to assess what is 'reasonably practicable'. The guidance covers all aspects of swimming pool safety including safety signs, maximum numbers of swimmers and pool supervision by lifeguards. The facts may, of course, also give rise to civil liability, so in the case of a hotel guest injured while using the hotel swimming pool, which has been insufficiently filled, the guest may sue (under negligence or Occupiers' Liability Act 1957) as well as the hotel facing a prosecution under the Health and Safety at Work etc. Act 1974.

Accidents and dangerous occurrences

Certain accidents and dangerous occurrences have to be reported to the local authority. This duty is under the Reporting of Injuries, Diseases and Dangerous Occurrences Regulations 1985. These Regulations are looked at in more detail in Chapter 9 in relation to accidents etc., to employees, but the Regulations are equally applicable where the victim is a guest or a customer.

Guests suffering from infectious diseases

Section 29 Public Health (Control of Disease) Act 1984 states that the proprietor of a hotel, guest house etc., who allows a room to be occupied by another guest without having that room and all its contents properly disinfected when he knows that the previous guest was suffering from a notifiable disease, commits a criminal offence.

Notifiable diseases are one of a long list of infectious diseases in or under section 10 of the 1984 Act, which includes cholera, meningitis, diphtheria, dysentery, measles, and a whole host of other diseases.

The disinfection must be carried out to the satisfaction of the local authority.

DISCRIMINATION

The Sex Discrimination Act 1975 (SDA 1975) and the Race Relations Act 1976 (RRA 1976) generally come to mind in the employment context. But the Acts outlaw sex and race discrimination in many other situations where it is likely to be encountered, and one such situation is in the provision of goods, facilities and services as part of a business, such as service in a restaurant and letting of hotel rooms.

The Acts define two types of discrimination which are generally referred to as direct and indirect discrimination. Direct sex discrimination is where a woman or man is treated less favourably because of her or his sex than a person of the opposite gender, and direct racial discrimination arises where a person is treated less favourably on racial grounds than he or she would otherwise be treated.

The expression 'racial grounds' is defined to mean colour, race, nationality or ethnic or national origins. The other type of discrimination, indirect discrimination, does not at first sight create any inequality. Indirect discrimination is where, in order to obtain some benefit, there is a condition or requirement which applies equally to men and women, irrespective of racial grounds, and it is necessary to comply with that condition to obtain that benefit, for example, admittance to a discotheque or use of a swimming pool. However, such a condition or requirement will create indirect discrimination if it satisfies the following criteria

- the proportion of persons of one sex, or members of a racial group, who can comply with the condition or requirement is considerably less than the proportion of persons of the other sex or persons not of that racial group, who can comply with it
- it is to the detriment of the person concerned because he or she cannot comply with the requirement or condition and therefore cannot obtain the benefit, and
- the imposition of the requirement or condition cannot be justified on a non-gender or non-racial basis.

The definition of discrimination is looked at in more detail in Chapter 9 where it will be seen that discrimination against a person because of his or her marriage status is also discrimination in the employment context. However, that type of discrimination does not apply to the provision of goods, facilities and services.

So, having seen what discrimination is, when is discrimination unlawful?

Section 29 Sex Discrimination Act 1975

(1) It is unlawful for any person concerned with the provision (for payment or not) of goods, facilities or services to the public or a section of the public to discriminate against a woman who seeks to obtain or use those goods, facilities or services.

  (a) by refusing or deliberately omitting to provide her with any of them, or

  (b) by refusing or deliberately omitting to provide her with goods, facilities or service of the like quality, in the like manner and on the like terms as are normal in his case in relation to male members of the public or (where she belongs to a section of the public) to male members of that section.

(2) The following are examples of the facilities and services mentioned in subsection (1)-

  (a) access to and use of any place which members of the public or a section of the public are permitted to enter;

  (b) accommodation in an hotel, boarding house or other similar establishment;

  (e) facilities for entertainment, recreation or refreshment;

  (f) facilities for transport or travel;

(3) For the avoidance of doubt it is hereby declared that where a particular skill is commonly exercised in a different way for men and for women it does not contravene subsection (1) for a person who does not normally exercise it for women to insist on exercising it for a woman only in accordance with his normal practice or, if he reasonably considers it impracticable to do that in her case, to refuse or deliberately omit to exercise it.

The SDA 1975 applies equally to discrimination against men.

Section 20 RRA 1976 is almost identical to section 29 SDA 1975 except that in relation to discrimination against a person on racial grounds there is no equivalent to subsection (3).

Before moving on to see what this means in practice, the opportunity will be taken of explaining subsection (3) of section 29 SDA 1975. This covers services such as hairdressers or tailors where a service is supplied for one sex only and the skill necessary to provide the service for persons of the opposite sex is different. In such situations the provider of the service can refuse to provide that service for persons of the other sex.

As can be seen, section 29 SDA 1975 and section 20 RRA 1976 make it unlawful for a person who is providing goods, facilities or services to the public (or a section of the public) to discriminate in the provision of those goods, facilities or services. This obviously covers an outright refusal, provided, in the case of racial discrimination, the refusal is directed against a racial group.

◆ COMMISSION FOR RACIAL EQUALITY V DUTTON (1989)

The licensee of a public house put up a sign at the pub 'sorry, no travellers'. The sign went up in response to some gypsies setting up camp nearby. The question arose whether the refusal to serve gypsies was racial discrimination. The Court of Appeal decided:

1 gypsies were a separate racial group
2 the expression 'traveller' was not another name for gypsies but referred to anyone leading a nomadic way of life; and
3 because most gypsies were nomadic the proportion of gypsies who could comply with the condition was considerably smaller than non-gypsies who could comply.

Accordingly, the 'no travellers' condition amounted to indirect discrimination.

The law as to who are separate racial groupings is not always easy to apply. Sikhs are a separate racial grouping but Rastafarians are not.

Refusal to provide goods, facilities or services is, however, not the only situation in which discrimination can arise.

◆ GILL V EL VINO CO LTD (1983)

The defendants were the proprietors of a popular wine bar in London. It was the defendants' practice not to allow women to drink while standing at the bar but to require women to be seated at one of the tables. Men could buy and consume their drinks at the bar.

Mrs Gill and Miss Coote went into the wine bar and ordered drinks. The barman referred them to the tables and said their drinks would be brought to them at the table.

The practice of requiring women to be seated originated many years earlier because the bar area became so crowded and was so cramped that it was considered it would be preferable for ladies to be served away from the bar so they did not get jostled in a small area while trying to order. The wine bar was still very popular and frequently resembled the inside of a tube station at rush hour. The tables were serviced by a waitress who took orders for drinks, and this avoided having everyone fighting through the crowd to get their drinks at the bar. Orders given at the tables received priority to orders at the bar.

The County Court Judge who dealt with the case decided on these facts that there was no discrimination against women but the Court of Appeal reversed that decision and decided that the refusal to serve women at the bar was sex discrimination. Male customers had a choice whether to sit at the tables or to stand at the bar. Women could only be served at the tables. In other words, women were denied the opportunity of drinking at the bar and mixing with the people at the bar to whom they might wish to talk, and that was treating women less favourably than men.

In the El Vino case the proprietor was not motivated by any discriminatory dislike of women, indeed the original rule was probably inspired by motives of chivalry, but the rule deliberately differentiated between men and women and hence fell foul of the law. But what if the different treatment arises not through the deliberate different treatment of men and women but the application of a rule which has that effect?

◆ JAMES V EASTLEIGH BOROUGH COUNCIL (1990)

Mr and Mrs James went to the Fleming Park Leisure Centre swimming pool in Eastleigh. At the time, both were aged 61 and both were retired. Mr James had to pay 75p for his swim but Mrs James got in free. This was because the Council who ran the centre allowed in free, anyone of State Pension age, namely 60 for women and 65 for men.

Mr James claimed that this was unlawful discrimination, but had Mr James been treated less favourably because of his sex? The case had to go to the House of Lords before it was decided that this was unlawful direct discrimination. The House of Lords decided that the appropriate question to ask was whether Mr James would have been treated more favourably had he been a woman. The answer to that question was obviously 'yes', because his wife had been treated more favourably. In those circumstances there was direct discrimination and the motive for it was irrelevant.

So treating men and women differently or according different treatment to members of a particular racial group in the provision of goods, facilities or services so that one gender or racial group receive less favourable treatment, will amount to unlawful discrimination and the motive for the different treatment is irrelevant. If, however, the discrimination is indirect, that is the imposition of a condition or requirement which has a discriminatory effect, then the motive may be relevant to the question of justification of the appropriate condition or requirement.

Section 29 SDA 1975 and section 20 RRA 1976 both give as examples of situations where discrimination can arise, the provision of accommodation in a hotel, boarding house or similar establishment. Hence, sex or racial discrimination in the provision of such accommodation is unlawful. But these are examples only and the sections cover all provisions of goods, facilities or services to the public or a section of the public. The two Acts do not apply to transactions of a private nature, however, racial discrimination by private clubs and societies may be unlawful, but male or female only private clubs are lawful.

Anyone who knowingly helps or assists another to discriminate unlawfully, commits an unlawful act (section 33 RRA 1976 and section 42 SDA 1975) and this applies to employees who carry out their employer's instructions to discriminate. But what if an employee refuses to carry out discriminatory instructions and is dismissed?

◆ SHOWBOAT ENTERTAINMENT CENTRE LTD v OWENS (1984)

Mr Owens was the white manager of an amusement centre. The proprietors of the centre issued an instruction not to admit young blacks to the centre. Mr Owens was dismissed because he refused to carry out those instructions. At the time of his dismissal, Mr Owens had not been employed by the centre for the necessary qualifying period to permit him to claim unfair dismissal. He therefore claimed he had been unlawfully discriminated against, for which there is no requirement for any qualifying period of employment. The only question for the employment appeal tribunal was whether the proprietor of the centre could unlawfully discriminate against Mr Owens on the ground, not of his race, but someone else's race. The tribunal had some difficulty in deciding that question but eventually decided that the employer could discriminate in this way and therefore Mr Owens had been the subject of unlawful race discrimination.

Unlawful race or sex discrimination is not a criminal offence. It is a civil wrong, which entitles the person discriminated against, to compensation.

Complaints of unlawful discrimination in the provision of goods, facilities and services are dealt with in the County Courts in England and Wales, and the Sheriff's Court in Scotland, and the remedy available is usually damages, but an injunction may be awarded to prevent the discrimination in future in appropriate cases.

In the case of sex discrimination the Equal Opportunities Commission, and for race discrimination the Commission for Racial Equality, may provide assistance to a complainant. Furthermore, both bodies have the right to take court proceedings in respect of discriminatory practices or advertisements.

Also, both bodies can conduct formal investigations, either on an industry basis, or into the practices of a particular person or company.

Non-payment by customers

The contract and the obligation to pay

As already seen, the taking of accommodation at a hotel or the ordering of a meal at a restaurant, creates a contract. The proprietor of the business is one party to the contract and can sue if the other party does not fulfil his or her contractual obligations – to pay for the goods or services.

Hoteliers can avoid some bad debts by requiring payment in advance and the common law duty of hotel proprietors to offer travellers accommodation does not prevent the proprietor requiring payment in advance.

Part payment is not sufficient to discharge the contract, so that if a customer offers only part of the bill in full settlement, the creditor may take what is offered and sue for the balance.

However, if the payment obligation is genuinely disputed, for example, because of poor quality food or dirty accommodation, or even that the amount charged is not the same as the customer agreed to pay in the first place, then the parties may agree to settle the dispute by the creditor accepting a smaller amount and in such a case, he or she will not be entitled to sue for the balance.

The difference between the two situations is that, in the situation where the amount is not in dispute, the creditor gives no consideration for his or her agreement to accept a lower amount and therefore the original agreement is not amended. In the latter situation, that is, where there is a dispute, the creditor is bound by the agreement to accept a lower amount because the amount properly payable is in doubt and the subsequent agreement fixes that amount.

Hotel proprietors' lien

Elsewhere, the strict liability of a hotel proprietor for a guest's property has been considered. The other side of the coin is that the proprietor of a hotel (as defined in section 1 HPA 1956) has a 'lien' on all the guest's property for which he or she would have strict liability. A lien is a right to keep goods until a debt is paid, and the effect is that any luggage or goods of the guest in the possession or under the control of the hotel proprietor, may be retained by the proprietor until the bill for the guest's food and accommodation has been settled. The guest cannot recover those goods by suing the proprietor for unlawfully refusing to hand them over, because until he or she has paid, the proprietor is perfectly entitled to refuse to hand them over.

As a hotel proprietor has no strict liability for damage to or loss of a vehicle, he or she cannot prevent the hotel guest driving off in his or her car, by exercising a lien over it.

The hotel proprietor has no common law right to detain the guest, but might be able to arrest the guest under section 3(4) Theft Act 1978 (see below).

While goods are the subject of the hotel proprietor's lien, the proprietor ceases to be strictly liable for such goods, but instead becomes a bailee of such goods and will therefore be liable to the owner of those goods under the lesser duty of taking prudent care of the goods.

The right of lien is a common law right but the right to sell the goods is statutory under the Innkeepers' Act 1878.

In order for the Innkeepers' Act 1878 to operate, the goods must be with hotel proprietor for six weeks without the bill having been paid. The hotel proprietor then has to give one month's notice in a London (or national) and a local newspaper of the intention to sell the goods. The notice must specify the goods and the name of the guest. If the bill is still unpaid the goods may be sold in a public auction and after payment of the auctioneer's charges the hotelier may pay off his or her bill, but not the cost of storing the goods during the exercise of the lien. Any surplus proceeds of the sale must be paid to the guest on demand.

The power of sale under the 1878 Act is, however, not limited only to a hotel proprietor, because the Act permits a sale (subject to the procedural safeguards already outlined) by the proprietor of any hotel or public house whether or not falling within the definition of section 1 HPA 1956, and the power of sale relates to any 'goods, chattels, carriages, horses, wares or merchandise which may be deposited with him or left in the house he keeps'. The sale must only be to satisfy the customer's debt.

The power of sale of goods held by a hotel proprietor under the common law right of lien, only arises under the Innkeepers' Act 1878 and not under the Torts (Interference with Goods) Act 1977, and so the strict requirements of the 1878 Act cannot be avoided by endeavouring to use the 1977 Act instead.

Criminal liability for non-payment

The Theft Act 1978 provides two criminal offences of assistance to hoteliers and caterers who find their guests or customers have left without settling the bill.

Section 1 Theft Act 1978

(1) A person who by any deception dishonestly obtains services from another shall be guilty of an offence.

'Deception' does not necessarily mean something said.

◆ **DIRECTOR OF PUBLIC PROSECUTIONS v RAY (1973)**

Mr Ray and four other men went into a Chinese restaurant, sat down and ordered a meal. The meal came and they ate it. They then decided to run out without paying and when the waiter went into the kitchen, they all ran out of the restaurant.

Mr Ray was convicted of dishonestly obtaining the meal by deception but he appealed against the decision on the ground that there was no deception. The conviction was upheld on the basis that there was a deception by pretending to be an ordinary customer who had the intention and the means to pay for the meal.

So someone who books into a hotel with the intention of leaving without paying for the accommodation can be convicted of a criminal offence under section 1 Theft Act 1978.

The second criminal offence is to be found in section 3.

Section 3 Theft Act 1978

(1) Subject to subsection (3) below, a person who, knowing that payment on the spot for any goods supplied or service done as required or expected from him, dishonestly makes off without having paid as required or expected and with intent to avoid payment of the amount due shall be guilty of an offence.

(2) For the purposes of this section 'payment on the spot' includes payment at the time of collecting goods on which work has been done or in respect of which service has been provided.

(3) Subsection (1) above shall not apply where the supply of the goods or the doing of the service is contrary to law, or where the service done is such that the payment is not legally enforceable.

(4) Any person may arrest without warrant anyone who is or whom he, with reasonable cause, suspects to be, committing or attempting to commit an offence under this section.

This section covers a variety of situations where the person is required to pay immediately for the goods. An obvious example is where someone drives off without paying for the petrol at a self-service petrol station, but it can also occur with any situation where the customer is expected to pay there and then but who leaves without doing so. The expression 'making off' means leaving the place where the payment should be made.

◆ SELF EXAMINATION QUESTIONS ◆

1 Megabig Hotels require guests at their hotels to sign a registration form on the back of which are numerous printed conditions. These conditions provide, among other things, that the hotel can require guests to move rooms during their stay, that the hotel manager's decision is final as to the standard of any accommodation or service and such decision is binding on guests and that no claim can be made against the hotel or commenced in the courts unless the guest has made a written complaint before the end of his/her stay. Consider the enforceability of these printed conditions.

2 Sally arrives one evening at the Ocean Hotel, Chester-le-Sea without having booked in advance. The hotel has rooms available. The manager tells Sally he is not prepared to let her have a room at the Ocean Hotel but can arrange a room at the nearby Station Hotel owned by the same company. Sally does not want to go to the Station Hotel. The manager still refuses to provide her with a room at the Ocean Hotel. From various things said by the manager and from what she sees of the hotel Sally gets the impression that the manager is not willing to let her have a room because she is a single female. Discuss the potential liability of the proprietor of the Ocean Hotel.

3 Derek has a disastrous stay at the Mountbatten Hotel, Middlehampton. On the first day his wallet is stolen from his room. On the second day he suffers severe bruising when he slips on a wet patch on the marble floor of reception and on the last day he is assaulted by a fellow guest who has had far too much to drink in the hotel bar. What legal liability might the Mountbatten Hotel have over Derek's misfortunes?

See Appendix for suggested answers.

Chapter 6

CONSUMER PROTECTION

CIVIL LIABILITY

The Sale of Goods Act 1979

The seller of goods (including food) in the course of a business is obliged to supply goods which are fit for their purpose and of satisfactory quality (section 14 Sale of Goods Act 1979 as amended by the Sale and Supply of Goods Act 1994) and where the goods are sold by description or by sample, the goods must correspond with the description or the sample (sections 13 and 15 Sale of Goods Act 1979).

These obligations arise because the Sale of Goods Act 1979 (SGA 1979) implies into sale contracts conditions on the part of the seller to that effect. Where the buyer is a consumer, those implied conditions cannot be excluded or restricted (section 6 Unfair Contract Terms Act 1977).

So, where a person buys food or drink in a restaurant or cafe, the restaurateur or cafe proprietor is in breach of contract if the food or drink is not fit to be eaten or drunk. The breach of contract gives rise to absolute liability so that the proprietor is liable even though there was no fault or blame on his or her part.

Negligence

As seen in Chapter 5, usually only a party to a contract can sue for a breach of that contract. However, a consumer may have rights in the tort of negligence despite having no contractual rights.

◆ DONOGHUE v STEVENSON (1932)

A boy and his girlfriend went into a café. The boy bought the girl a bottle of ginger beer. The bottle was made of dark glass and the girl poured out a glass of ginger beer and drank it. When a second glass of ginger beer was poured, a decomposed snail floated out of the bottle into the glass. The girl became very ill. She sued the manufacturers of the ginger beer in tort and succeeded. The court decided that the manufacturers owed a legal duty of care to the consumer to take reasonable care to make sure the ginger beer could not cause injury.

The difference between the rights arising for breach of the implied contract conditions under the SGA 1979 and the rights for breach of the duty of care in the tort of negligence, is that in the former, the supplier is liable without proof of fault, whereas in negligence the injured party has to prove negligence. This distinction was starkly illustrated in *Daniels and Daniels v R White and Sons Ltd and Tarbard (1938)*.

◆ **DANIELS AND DANIELS V R WHITE & SONS LTD AND TARBARD (1938)**

Mrs Tarbard was the licensee of a public house in Battersea. Mr Daniels was a regular customer and on the day in question he took a jug to the public house and bought a jug of beer and a bottle of lemonade. He took them home, which was nearby, and Mr Daniels and his wife had a drink. They immediately both experienced a burning sensation which resulted in them both being ill. The reason for this was because the lemonade contained carbolic acid.

Mr Daniels sued Mrs Tabard for breach of the implied conditions created by the Sale of Goods Act 1893 (the forerunner of the 1979 Act) and he succeeded because there had been a breach of the implied condition as to quality.

Mrs Daniels could not sue Mrs Tabard because she had no contract with her, instead she sued the manufacturers of the lemonade, a company called R. White & Sons Ltd. Mrs Daniels had to prove negligence on the part of the manufacturers. In fact, the manufacturers went to extreme lengths to ensure that all bottles were thoroughly cleaned before use, that the lemonade was a good quality and the bottles covered to protect against tampering. The carbolic acid was present in spite of any lack of negligence by the manufacturers and therefore Mrs Daniels' claim failed.

Part 1 Consumer Protection Act 1987

Part 1 the Consumer Protection Act 1987 (CPA 1987 Part 1) implements EC Directive 85/374, which is generally referred to as the Product Liability Directive. This part of the CPA 1987 avoids the problems of the distinction (as seen above) between liability in contract (which does not require proof of fault) and liability in the tort of negligence (which does require proof of fault).

Under the CPA 1987 Part 1 there is strict liability that is without proof of fault, without the necessity for any contractual relationship if damage is caused by a defective product. A product means goods and therefore includes food. A product is defective if it is not up to the standard generally expected. The damage for which there is redress is death, personal injury, or loss of, or damage to any property for private use.

The person suffering the damage has a number of possible persons to sue

- the producer of the product
- the person whose name or trademark appears on the product
- the importer into the EEC.

If the person who suffers the damage requests the supplier of the product for the identity of at least one of these persons and the supplier fails to give that information, then the supplier is also liable.

Liability is strict, but there are defences set out in section 4, CPA 1987, one defence being that the defect did not exist when the person sued supplied the product to somebody else. Liability under CPA 1987 Part 1 cannot be restricted or excluded (section 7 CPA 1987).

CPA 1897 Part 1 is concerned with the safety of goods, not with goods which are of poor quality. So, a meal which causes food poisoning can be the subject of a claim under the Act, but a meal which is of inferior cuisine, but harmless, cannot be the subject of a claim under the 1987 Act.

There is no upper limit to the amount of damages which can be awarded under CPA 1987 Part 1, but there is a lower threshold, and no damages can be claimed under the 1987 Act if the total loss does not exceed £275. This is intended to cut out minor claims.

The CPA 1987 Part 1 applies only the 'products', it does not cover services.

Civil liability in respect of services

The ordinary law of negligence applies to the provision of services in the same way as it applies to goods, but neither the SGA 1979 nor Part 1 CPA 1987 applies to services.

The Supply of Goods and Services Act 1982 implies certain terms into a contract with the supplier of a service, the main implied term being found in section 13.

Section 13 Supply of Goods and Services Act 1982

In a contract for the supply of a service where the supplier is acting in the course of a business, there is an implied term that the supplier will carry out the service with reasonable care and skill.

The supply of a package holiday or of hotel accommodation comes within section 13 of the 1982 Act but it is important to note that the care and skill to be exercised is qualified by the word 'reasonable'.

◆ **Wilson v Best Travel Ltd (1993)**

The plaintiff while holidaying in Greece fell through a glass patio door. Although not safety glass, the glass met Greek safety standards but not British safety standards. The plaintiff sued the tour operator for compensation for his injuries claiming that the tour operator was in breach of the duty under Section 13 of the 1982 Act. The evidence was that the tour operator had inspected the hotel and checked that local safety regulations had been complied with. Accordingly, the tour operator had exercised reasonable care and skill in selecting that hotel and the plaintiff's claim failed.

Subject to the Unfair Contract Terms Act 1977, the liability arising under the 1982 Act may be excluded or restricted.

There is no equivalent to the CPA 1987 Part 1 covering the supply of services, but the Package Travel, Package Holiday and Package Tour Regulations 1992 create certain civil liability where what is sold is a 'package' as defined in those regulations (see later).

Trade descriptions

The consumer is protected from unscrupulous trading by numerous criminal legislation and probably the best known is the Trade Descriptions Act 1968 (TDA 1968). There are two sections in the TDA 1968 which create general criminal liabilities. The first is section 1, which relates to goods, the second is section 14 which applies to services.

Section 1 Trade Descriptions Act 1968

Any person who, in the course of a trade or business

(a) *applies a false trade description to any goods; or*
(b) *supplies, or offers to supply, any goods to which a false trade description is applied;*

shall . . . be guilty of an offence.

The expression 'trade description' is defined in section 2 TDA 1968.

Section 2 Trade Descriptions Act 1968

(1) A trade description is an indication direct or indirect, and by whatever means given, of any of the following matters with respect to

any goods or parts of goods, that is to say

(a) quantity, size or gauge;

(b) method of manufacture, production, processing or reconditioning;

(c) composition;

(d) fitness for purpose, strength, performance, behaviour or accuracy;

(e) any physical characteristics not included in the preceding paragraphs;

(f) testing by any person and results thereof;

(g) approval by any person or conformity with a type approved by any person;

(h) place, or date of manufacture, production, processing or recondition;

(i) person by whom manufactured, produced, processed or reconditioned;

(j) other history, including previous ownership or use.

A description is false, if it is false to a material degree or if it is misleading. A description may be written or spoken and can be by advertisement.

A restaurant which states on its menu 'fresh vegetables' would run the risk of conviction under section 1 TDA 1968 if any of the vegetables used were frozen. Similarly, if beef was described as 'Scotch beef' it would be a false trade description if, in fact, the beef was not of Scottish origin.

Section 1 TDA 1968 creates a strict liability offence, in other words, the person who applies the false trade description or who supplies the goods with a false trade description commits a criminal offence without fault or blame, however (as will be seen later) there is the due diligence defence to be found in section 24 TDA 1968.

By contrast, section 14 TDA 1968 is not a strict liability offence.

Section 14 Trade Descriptions Act 1968

(1) It shall be an offence for any person in the course of any trade or business

(a) to make a statement which he knows to be false; or

(b) recklessly to make a statement which is false

as to any of the following matters, that is to say

> *(i) the provision in the course of any trade or business of any services, accommodation or facilities;*
> *(ii) the nature of any services, accommodation or facilities provided in the course of any trade or business;*
> *(iii) the time at which, manner in which, or persons by whom any services, accommodation or facilities are so provided;*
> *(iv) the examination, approval or evaluation by any person of any services, accommodation or facilities so provided; or*
> *(v) the location or amenities of any accommodation so provided.*

(2) For the purposes of this section

> *(a) anything (whether or not a statement as to any of the matters specified in the preceding subsection) likely to be taken for such a statement as to any of those matters as would be false and shall be deemed to be a false statement as to that matter; and*
> *(b) a statement made regardless of whether it is true or false shall be deemed to be made recklessly, whether or not the person making it had reasons for believing that it might be false.*

(4) In this section 'false' means false to a material degree.

Section 1 TDA 1968 relates to goods but section 14 is the corresponding criminal offence for the false description of services including accommodation and facilities. So section 14 is the appropriate offence where hotel accommodation is misdescribed in a brochure or advertisement, for example, 100 yards from the sea, AA ***, or rooms en suite. The offence is of making a false or misleading statement as to the matters stated in subsection (1).

◆ BRITISH AIRWAYS V TAYLOR (1975)

Mr Edmunds booked a seat on a particular flight and the airline wrote a letter confirming the booking. The airline's policy was to operate an 'overbooking' system, that is, to make more reservations than there were seats. When Mr Edmunds made his booking, there were seats available, but more reservations were made and when Mr Edmunds arrived at the airport he was told he could not go on that flight because it was overbooked.

The airline was charged with an offence under section 14 TDA 1968, namely that in the letter of confirmation, they had confirmed the booking of flight accommodation. That statement was false in view of the overbooking policy because the place was not reserved for Mr Edmunds. In fact, the overbooking policy meant that no places were bookable at all. Accordingly there was an offence under section 14.

Many of the prosecutions under section 14 arise out of statements made in holiday brochures and a whole series of cases have shown how the courts deal with statements in brochures.

The statement must be false or misleading. If it is correct, but some third party does something outside the control of the accused, then there can be no conviction under section 14.

◆ **SUNAIR HOLIDAYS LTD V DODD (1970)**

A travel agent issued a brochure in which it described rooms in an hotel in Majorca including the statement 'all rooms with terrace overlooking the harbour'. Two couples booked through the agent to go to the hotel, but in both cases were given rooms without a terrace.

The travel agents were prosecuted for an offence under section 14 TDA 1968. In fact, the contract between the travel agents and the hotel was for rooms only with a terrace, and the hotel had been in breach of contract in allocating inferior accommodation.

The travel agents were acquitted, and there was no false statement made because the accommodation which they had booked did have a terrace.

◆ **R V SUNAIR HOLIDAYS LTD (1973)**

A holiday brochure published by the accused described the Hotel Cadi at Celella on the east coast of Spain as having a swimming pool, pushchairs for hire and a modern restaurant with special meals for children.

Mr Bateman booked a holiday for his family at the hotel but when they arrived they found that the swimming pool was not properly completed and was unusable, there were no pushchairs for hire at the hotel nor were there any special meals for children.

Sunair Holidays was charged with offences under section 14 TDA 1968 but it had contracted with the hotel to provide all these facilities. The hotel had been in the course of construction at the time Sunair Holidays contracted with the proprietors of the hotel but it was intended that the hotel would be completed in good time and would have all of these facilities.

As the statement in the brochure was as to services to be provided and which services were genuinely intended to be provided by the date of the holiday, it was not a false statement and therefore Sunair Holidays was acquitted.

But a statement about something to take place in the future can be a false statement of existing fact.

◆ R v AVRO PLC (1993)

A holiday maker booked a flight out and return for a holiday. The return ticket stated it was for 12.55pm from Alicante to Gatwick. On the outward flight he was given replacement return flight tickets for a flight at 12.00 from Alicante to Southend. In fact there never was any flight at 12.55pm from Alicante to Gatwick.

The company was convicted under section 14 TDA 1968 because, although it was a statement as to future services, it was a false statement when made.

So if the statement is as to present incorrect facts, there can be a conviction. The relevant time for testing whether the statement is incorrect, is not when the brochure is published, but instead when it is read and acted on.

◆ WINGS LTD v ELLIS (1984)

Wings was a tour operator. It published a holiday brochure which described a hotel in Sri Lanka as air conditioned. At the time, it believed the statement to be true but subsequently discovered it was false. They then informed travel agents, and customers who had already booked, of the error.

Mr Wade read the brochure and booked a holiday at the hotel but he was not informed when he booked, or before he left on holiday, of the error.

Wings was prosecuted under section 14 TDA 1968. It alleged that when it 'made' the statement they believed it to be true. The court decided that the statement was made when it was read by the customer and the booking made. At that time Wings knew the statement was wrong and it was therefore convicted.

As a result of a statement being made when it is read it is possible for the statement in a brochure to result in more than one conviction.

◆ R v THOMSON HOLIDAYS LTD (1974)

Thomson Holidays sold package holidays and they published a brochure. Mr and Mrs Brown read the brochure and were attracted by the description of the hotel Golden Coast in Greece which was described as a modern hotel with an enormous swimming pool and a children's paddling pool; dining room with terrace overlooking the garden; a bar; ladies' hairdressing salon; a nightclub on the beach outside the hotel and a resident representative of the company. They booked a holiday at the hotel.

The facts were that there was no childrens' paddling pool, the swimming pool was not the hotel's private pool but was used by local residents and all and sundry, and there was no nightclub.

Another holidaymaker suffered exactly the same experience as a result of having read another copy of the same brochure. As a consequence of that other holidaymaker's experience, Thomson Holidays was charged with an offence under section 14 TDA 1968 and was convicted.

When Mr and Mrs Brown returned home from their holiday they complained to the local authority about their experience and another prosecution then commenced against Thomson Holidays. This time Thomson Holidays said it had already been convicted of the offence and could not be convicted again for the same thing.

The court decided that there was a fresh offence each time someone else read the statement in the brochure and Thomson Holidays was therefore convicted twice for the same false statement because it had been communicated to two separate sets of people.

Section 24 TDA 1968 contains the Act's main defence.

Section 24 Trade Descriptions Act 1968

In any proceedings for offences under this Act it shall, . . . be a defence for the person charged to prove

   (a) that the commission of the offence was due to a mistake or to reliance on information supplied to him or to the act or default of another person, an accident or some other cause beyond his control; and

   (b) that he took all reasonable precautions and exercised all due diligence to avoid the commission of such an offence by himself or any person under his control.

(3) In proceedings for an offence under this Act of supplying or offering to supply goods to which a false trade description is applied it shall be a defence for the person charged to prove that he did not know, and could not with reasonable diligence have ascertained, that the goods did not conform to the description or that the description had been applied to the goods.

There are numerous cases dealing with the defence of 'due diligence' and one of the most important is *Tesco Supermarkets v Nattrass 1971* (see Chapter 7).

PACKAGE ARRANGEMENTS

The Package Travel, Package Holidays and Package Tours Regulations 1992 are mainly aimed at package foreign holidays but the regulations have wider effect. The regulations give effect to EC Directive 90/314.

The regulations apply to a 'package' which is defined as any prearranged combination of any two out of three components which are sold/offered for sale at an inclusive price provided that what is offered will last at least 24 hours or includes overnight accommodation. The three components are

- transport
- accommodation
- other tourist services forming a significant part of the package other than services ancillary to the transport or accommodation.

So it can be seen that a foreign package holiday comprising flight and hotel accommodation is a 'package'. But so also is a theatre break consisting of an overnight stay and tickets for a theatre.

The regulations apply to all 'packages' sold or offered for sale in the UK even if the travel or other components are abroad. Where the regulations apply there are a number of very specific requirements.

- Misleading information about a package contract must not be given and if given may lead to compensation having to be paid.
- Brochures for packages must set out the price and adequate information about the matters specified in Schedule 1 to the regulations. Brochure particulars become contract terms and so can lead to an action for breach of a contract if incorrect.
- If the package includes a journey then in good time before setting off the consumer must be supplied with various written information about the journey, any stops and details of any representatives or a contact telephone number.
- Package contracts must be written and contain the relevant items as specified in Schedule 2 to the regulations for example what meals are included in the price.
- If the consumer becomes ill or otherwise cannot take up the package then he/she can transfer the package to someone else who satisfies any

condition applicable to the package provided that reasonable notice is given.

• There are restrictions on price surcharges or other alterations to the terms and conditions of a package contract.

But probably the most important feature of the Package Travel, Package Holidays and Package Tours Regulations are the requirements for security for advance payments to protect against insolvency of the package organisers. There are different ways of doing this

• bonding arrangements (usually with a bank or insurance company)
• insurance
• a trustee who holds all deposits/advance payments.

The consumer must be informed in writing before the contract is made which security method is in use.

The regulations create a mixture of civil and criminal liability. Most infringements will lead to criminal liability enforced by trading standards authorities.

Not only do the Package Travel, Package Holidays and Package Tours Regulations affect those who organise packages but as a result of Regulation 15, suppliers of services forming part of such a package are also indirectly affected. Regulation 15 provides that the person who puts together the package and sells it is liable to the individual customers for the proper performance of all the components of the package even for those components supplied by a third party. So, if a company organises coach tours with overnight hotel stays and lunch stops at selected restaurants the company will be liable to those who buy the tour for the proper performance by the different hotels and restaurants of those parts of the tour.

To cover this situation the company will want some guarantee of performance by the hotels and restaurants and this will be reflected in the contracts between the tour organiser and the hotels and restaurants.

MISLEADING ADVERTISEMENTS

The Control of Misleading Advertisements Regulations 1988 are somewhat unusual because they do not create either civil or criminal liability. What they do is to set up a long-stop protection mechanism against misleading advertisements. The regulations, which give effect to EC Directive 84/450, apply where an advertisement deceives or is likely to do so and as a result is likely to cause economic harm either to customers of the advertiser or to a competitor of the advertiser.

The Director General of Fair Trading (DGFT) can act on a complaint that an advertisement, other than on commercial television or radio, is misleading. However the DGFT will generally only take any action after other appropriate methods of dealing with the complaint have been followed without success. Such other methods are likely to involve a complaint to a self-regulatory body such as the Advertising Standards Authority (ASA).

If the DGFT does take action then such action will be an application to the court for an injunction to prohibit the publication, or further publication, of the offending advertisement. In this way the non-statutory advertising code of practice published by the ASA has some statutory backing.

The Independent Broadcasting Authority carries out a similar function to the DGFT under the 1988 regulations concerning complaints about television and radio advertisements. A court will only grant an injunction if satisfied that an advertisement is misleading and after considering the public interest. Breach of a court injunction is a criminal offence.

FOOD QUALITY AND MISDESCRIPTION

Apart from the safety aspects of food (see Chapter 7) there are various criminal provisions concerning the quality of food and its description.

- Regulation 4 Food Labelling Regulations 1984 specifies that the presentation of food must be such that there is no likelihood that a customer could be misled to a material degree as to the nature, substance or quality of the food.
- Section 1 Trade Descriptions Act 1968 creates the offence of supplying goods (including food) with a false description.
- Part 4 Food Labelling Regulations 1984 prohibits certain claims and misleading descriptions (see below).
- Section 14 Food Safety Act 1990 creates the offence of selling food not of the nature, or substance, or quality requested (see below).
- Section 15 Food Safety Act 1990 enacts the offence of falsely describing or presenting food.

The last three will now be considered in turn.

Particular descriptions

Certain words and descriptions may only be used in the labelling or advertising of food (including on a menu) if they comply with certain conditions. The food and the conditions are set out in Schedule 7 to the Food Labelling Regulations 1984.

- Food described by, or implying that it has the flavour of certain other food, for example, strawberry ice-cream, must have that flavour at least mainly derived from that other food unless it is described as 'flavour'. For example, strawberry flavour ice-cream, when the flavour need not be derived mainly from that other food.
- The words 'fresh' 'garden' or 'green' may not be used for canned or frozen peas which have been dried or soaked before being canned or frozen.
- The word 'milk' must only be used to describe cows' milk unless qualified by the name of the animal, for example, 'goats' milk'.

There are also words and descriptions relating to drinks which are strictly controlled, for example, Scotch whisky (Scotch Whisky Order 1990).

Certain claims for foods are also strictly regulated under the Food Labelling Regulation 1984. By way of example, food and drink can only be claimed to be suitable for diabetics, babies or persons with certain dietary requirements, if certain conditions are met (Schedule 6 Food Labelling Regulations 1984). Similarly, drinks can only be described as 'low alcohol' if they have an alcoholic strength of not more than 1.2 per cent (Food Labelling (Amendment) Regulations 1990).

Section 14 Food Safety Act 1990

The Food Safety Act 1990 (FSA 1990) is largely concerned with the safety of food for human consumption and is dealt with in detail in Chapter 7, but there are two sections dealing with consumer protection where the question of the safety of the food is not necessarily an issue. Section 14 is the first of these two sections.

> ### Section 14 Food Safety Act 1990
>
> *(1) Any person who sells to the purchaser's prejudice any food which is not of the nature or substance or quality demanded by the purchaser shall be guilty of an offence.*
> *(2) In subsection (1) above the reference to sale shall be construed as reference to sale for human consumption; and in proceedings under that subsection it shall not be a defence that the purchaser was not prejudiced because he bought for analysis or examination.*

A person 'sells' food who supplies it in the course of a business and therefore the word has a wider meaning than merely exchange for money (section 1 FSA 1990). The word 'demanded' is rather strong in this context and what it means is either that the purchaser requests the food by reference to its quality etc., or such quality can be reasonably expected by a purchaser. Similarly, the word 'prejudice', means to the purchaser's disadvantage.

The safety of food as indicated above may not be in doubt as illustrated by *Shearer v Rowe and Rowe (1985)* and *Macdonalds Hamburgers v Windle (1987).*

◆ SHEARER V ROWE AND ROWE (1985)

The Rowe brothers sold mince described as minced beef. In fact it contained 10 per cent pork and 10 per cent lamb. They were guilty of an offence of supplying food which was neither of the required nature nor the required substance, because if a purchaser buys food described as minced beef he is entitled to expect the mince is wholly beef and not a mixture of other mince.

◆ MCDONALDS HAMBURGERS V WINDLE (1987)

McDonalds displayed a 'nutrition guide' in one of its restaurants which showed that its ordinary cola contained between 96 and 187 kilocalories per serving but that its diet cola had less than 1 kilocalorie per serving.

On two separate occasions a trading standards officer asked for diet cola but was served with ordinary cola.

McDonalds was convicted of an offence of selling food not of the requested quality.

In neither of these cases was there any suggestion that the food was not safe to consume, but, the food was not what the purchaser was entitled to expect or had requested.

Accordingly, section 14 FSA 1990 will usually be enforced by trading standards officers rather than environmental health officers unless the food in question fails to comply with section 14 because of microbiological contamination or contamination due to mould or because of the presence of some foreign matter in the food. In these events the environmental health officer will instigate any prosecution (Code of Practice No 1 issued under section 40 FSA 1990).

The offence under section 14 is of selling food not of the required nature (something entirely different) or substance (something of a different composition) or quality (description or standard).

So, in the case of quality, what standards are required? For some foods there are regulations which specify standards. The Food Standards (General Provisions) Order 1944 prohibits the sale of any food for which a standard is prescribed unless the food complies with that standard. The number of standards has been reduced by the Food (Miscellaneous Revocations) Regulations 1991 but even so, there are foods for which standards are still laid down. Examples of foods which must comply with legal standards are fishcakes, ice cream, cheese, cream, fruit juices, jam, honey, margarine, meat and fish spreads, salad cream and soft drinks.

If food is sold which fails to meet the prescribed standards the prosecution will be under the 1944 Order. If there is no legal minimum standard then the standard applicable to section 14 FSA 1990 is what the purchaser specifies, or in the absence of such a specification, what the court considers to be reasonable for that food. This is because the law will imply a contract term that the food is to be of reasonable quality.

◆ TONKIN V VICTOR VALUE LTD (1962)

Victor Value Ltd sold 'mock salmon cutlettes'. It was charged for the offence of supplying food not of the substance demanded because it was found that the cutlettes contained only 33 per cent of fish. Although there was no standard for such description of food, it could be compared with a fishcake which had to be of not less than 35 per cent fish.

The public analyst considered that the items in question should have a higher fish content than fishcakes. The expression 'cutlette' indicated a small cut of fish and in those circumstances a conviction was appropriate.

In some cases the seller may make the purchaser aware that the food may not be of an expected quality, for instance, by displaying a notice that the 'cream cakes' contain artificial cream or that the bread was baked the previous day not the same day.

◆ GOLDUP V JOHN MANSON LTD (1981)

A butcher sold two qualities of minced beef, a cheap quality and a more expensive quality. A notice was on display in the shop stating that the cheaper quality contained up to 30 per cent fat. There was no legal maximum percentage of fat for minced beef but the shop was charged with selling food not of the quality demanded, when on analysis the cheaper mince was found to contain 33 per cent fat. The evidence from the experts was that minced meat generally contained no more than 25 per cent fat.

The court decided that the notice displayed in the butcher's shop together with the choice of quality, were deciding factors and the 3 per cent difference was immaterial so that no offence had been committed.

Section 15 Food Safety Act 1990

This is the second consumer protection offence to be found in the FSA 1990 and it is entirely enforced by trading standards officers rather than the environmental health officers, this means that in non-metropolitan counties the enforcement authority is the county council rather than the district council (Food Safety (Enforcement Authority) Order 1990). The offence is of falsely describing food.

Section 15 Food Safety Act 1990

(1) Any person who gives with any food sold by him, or displays with any food offered or exposed by him for sale or in his possession for the purpose of sale, a label, whether or not attached to or printed on the wrapper or container, which

  (a) falsely describes the food; or
  (b) is likely to mislead as to the nature or substance or quality of the food,

shall be guilty of an offence.
(2) Any person who publishes, or is a party to the publication of, an advertisement (not being such a label given or displayed by him as mentioned in subsection (1) above) which

  (a) falsely describes the food; or
  (b) is likely to mislead as to the nature or substance or quality of any food,

shall be guilty of an offence.
(3) Any person who sells, or offers or exposes for sale, or has in his possession for the purpose of sale, any food the presentation of which is likely to mislead as to the nature or substance of the food shall be guilty of an offence.
(4) In proceedings for an offence under subsection (1) or (2) above, the fact that a label or advertisement in respect of which the offence is

> *alleged to have been committed contained an accurate statement of the composition of the food shall not preclude the court from finding that the offence was committed.*
>
> *(5) In this section references to sale shall be construed as references to sale for human consumption.*

There are three separate offences under section 15

- selling food with a false description or one which is likely to mislead as to the nature or substance or quality of the food
- advertising food with a false description or a description likely to mislead as to its nature, substance or quality
- selling or displaying for sale any food which is so presented that it is likely to mislead as to its nature, substance or quality.

The word 'advertisement' is defined in section 53 FSA 1990 and includes almost any method of indicating that food is for sale, including a menu, and therefore if food is misdescribed or misleadingly described in a menu, a prosecution could result.

'Presentation' is also defined in section 53 and includes the shape, appearance, packaging and the way it is arranged and the setting in which it is displayed.

Enforcement

The main enforcement provisions of the Food Safety Act 1990 (other than those dealing with food failing to meet the food safety requirements, and breaches of the hygiene and food processing regulations) also apply to enforcement of the consumer protection provisions of the Food Safety Act 1990.

This means that the rights of enforcement officers to take samples or make test purchases contained in section 29 FSA 1990 apply to sections 14 and 15 FSA 1990 in exactly the same way as they apply to the main food safety offences contained in the 1990 Act. Enforcement is considered in more detail in Chapter 7.

PRICES

Display of accommodation prices

The display of bedroom rates is compulsory in all but the smallest establishments.

Article 3 Tourism (Sleeping Accommodation Price Display) Order 1977

(1) At each hotel there shall be displayed in a prominent position in the reception area or, if none, at the entrance, where it can easily be read by a person seeking to engage sleeping accommodation at the hotel, a legible notice stating the current prices (which, wherever appropriate shall include, and be stated to include, any service charge) payable per night per any such person for sleeping accommodation at the hotel consisting of

(a) a bedroom for occupation by an adult person,
(b) a bedroom for occupation by two adult persons, and
(c) a bed, other than as in (a) or (b) above, for occupation by an adult person and stating also whether it is situate in a dormitory or room to be shared with other guests.

(2) Where Value Added Tax is payable, then either

(a) the price shall include and be stated to include the amount of tax or
(b) the price shall be stated to exclude the amount of tax and that amount shall be stated with equal prominence in money terms as the amount of tax payable in addition to the price.

(3) If the accommodation is only provided inclusive of meals, the price of the accommodation shall be stated to be inclusive thereof and the meals so provided shall be suitably identified.
(4) If the prices in respect of each of the above categories of sleeping accommodation are not standard throughout the hotel it shall be sufficient to state the lowest and highest current price for accommodation of each category (disregarding any bedroom or bed which is normally in the same occupation for more than 21 consecutive nights).
(5) Additional information may be included in the notice provided it does not detract from the prominence to be given to the above information.

The 1977 Order applies to any hotel or other establishment at which sleeping accommodation is provided by way of trade, which has at least four bedrooms or eight beds, but it excludes members' clubs, hotels which provide only lettings for more than three weeks and accommodation in holiday camps.

If a notice is not displayed or does not comply with Article 3 of the 1977 Order, then a criminal offence is committed unless there is reasonable excuse. If the offence is committed by a company but the failure to display the notice is the fault of any director, manager or similar person within the company, then that person (as well as the company) commits a criminal offence.

Display of food and drink prices (consumption on premises)

If food or drink is sold for consumption on the premises then, subject to certain exemptions, the price of the food or drink must be displayed in accordance with the Price Marking (Food and Drink on Premises) Order 1979. The exemptions, that is, the cases in which the prices do not have to be displayed are

- in members clubs, that is, where food or drink is only supplied to club members and their bona fide guests
- staff canteens/restaurants
- college canteens/dining rooms, school dinners and university halls of residence
- hotels, hostels etc., which provide food or drink to residents only
- occasions booked in advance, wedding receptions, meals at conferences etc.
- if the food or drink of that sort is not on the menu but is supplied to comply with a special request, for example because of a particular customer's special dietary needs.

Subject to these exemptions, the 1977 Order specifies both what details must be displayed, and where those details have to be displayed. The details which have to be displayed are as follows.

- The price payable for any food or drink sold for consumption on the premises.
- If the food or drink is sold by quantity or measurement then the price must be shown by reference to the quantity or measurement, for example a price for a portion of chips or per half pint of beer. If the price of multiples of the quantity or measurement is the same multiple of the basic price, for example a double portion of chips costs twice as much, then only the price of the basic quantity or measurement need be given. If there is a price

differential for multiples, for instance if larger portions are supplied at less than if they were supplied as individual portions, then the price of all the quantities and measurements must be displayed.

- The price of a table d'hote meal can be shown as one price and the individual dishes do not have to be individually priced.
- If food is supplied with other food (other than as a table d'hote meal) at one price, then only one price need be shown, but if a meal dish is made up of items sold separately and the price for the meal or dish is the price of the items sold individually, then no price has to be displayed for the finished product. So, for example, at a salad bar either the price of the individual salad items must be shown, or a price has to be displayed per plate of mixed salad. The same applies to drink. A cocktail bar will usually comply with this provision by displaying prices per named cocktail.
- Where there are more than 30 items available to eat or drink then the price of at least 30 items must be displayed. Additionally there are special rules for wine lists.
- All prices must be inclusive of VAT.
- Where there is any service or cover charge then the amount of these must be displayed at least as prominently as the price of the food or drink.
- The strength of alcoholic drinks must also be shown.

The place where the prices must be displayed depends on the type of establishment. In premises where the customer pays for the food or drink and carries the food to the place where it is to be eaten or drunk, for example, a self-service cafeteria, or a carvery, then the prices must be displayed so as to be seen where customers choose the food. Additionally, the prices must be displayed so as to be visible to customers before they enter the premises or they enter the service area unless the prices displayed where the food is chosen can be read easily by customers before they enter the premises or the service area.

In other premises, for instance, a typical restaurant or a hotel dining room, the prices must be displayed at the entrance to the premises or the eating area. Restaurants will usually display prices in the window and the hotel dining room must have a price list on display at the entrance to the dining room.

Display of food and drink prices (Consumption off premises)

The Price Marking Order 1991 requires retailers selling to consumers to show clearly the selling price of goods and the prices must be inclusive of

VAT. How the retailer complies with this is entirely a matter for the retailer but the consumer must be able to identify the items to which the prices apply, either by some sort of label, ticket, or notice near to the goods (including food) in question. If certain food is only available for purchase with other food, then the price of the food must include a statement with equal prominence stating those other foods and their price.

Where there is a change in the rate of VAT then the old price may be used for a period of 14 days provided that there are prominent notices informing consumers of adjustments to marked prices.

This order applies to food and drink for consumption off the premises including take-away meals, meals sold from kiosks or stalls, sandwiches and filled rolls, and the off-sales department of a public house.

Misleading prices

The criminal offence of giving misleading prices is now to be found in Part 3 Consumer Protection Act 1987 (CPA 1987).

> **Section 20 Consumer Protection Act 1987**
>
> *(1) Subject to the following provisions of this part, a person shall be guilty of an offence if, in the course any business of his, he gives (by any means whatever) to any consumers an indication which is misleading as to the price at which any goods, services, accommodation or facilities are available (whether generally or from particular persons).*
> *(2) Subject aforesaid, a person shall be guilty of an offence if*
>
> *(a) in the course of any business of his, he has given an indication to any consumers which, after it was given, has become misleading as mentioned in subsection (1) above; and*
> *(b) some or all of those consumers might reasonably be expected to rely on the indication at a time after it has become misleading; and*
> *(c) he fails to take all steps as are reasonable to prevent those consumers from relying on the indication.*

A price is misleading if the impression given to a consumer is, or a consumer might reasonably believe:

- the price is less than the real price
- the price is not dependent on facts or circumstances, when in fact it is
- the price is inclusive, when it is not
- that the price is about to go up, when it is not
- the price is favourable when compared with prices charged by others or the 'normal price' when the facts or circumstances of those other prices are not comparable.

The CPA 1987 Part 3 applies to prices for food, drink, accommodation or any other goods or services usually supplied by an hotelier or caterer. Misleading prices might appear in advertisements, brochures, price lists, menus and can be written or oral.

A code of practice has been made under section 25 CPA 1987. A contravention of the code is not itself a criminal offence, but in any prosecution, a breach of the code may be relied on for the purpose of showing that a person has given a misleading price. The code is entitled Code of Practice for Traders on Price Indications and it is divided into three parts.

- Price comparisons – these should be accurate. If the comparison is with the trader's own previous prices (for example, '10 per cent off during carnival day') then it should be compared with the price charged for the previous 28 days. If the comparison is with prices elsewhere, then the Code will place difficulties in the way of caterers because of the difficulty of comparing like with like. Reductions for children can be regarded as comparisons ('children meals, half price'). It is important to state any conditions which apply, for example, the reduction only applies if a child is accompanied by an adult.
- Actual prices – all prices should be VAT inclusive and inclusive of any non-optional service charge. An optional service charge should not be suggested or included in the bill, thereby outlawing the percentage added to the bill 'for customer convenience'. Any cover charge or minimum charge should be shown prominently on the price list or menu, but this is already an obligation under the Price Marking (Food and Drink on Premises) Order 1979. Supplements, for example during the high season, should be clearly stated close to the basic price.
- Prices which become misleading – this third part of the Code is particularly relevant to the prices in advertisements, brochures etc., which may be read sometime after they have been published. The Code suggests that prices in daily newspapers should hold good for at least seven days after the date of the newspaper. If brochures/price lists are given to travel or accommodation

agents then reviewed prices should be notified to all such agents before the changes become operative.

The offence of giving a misleading price is a strict offence, that is, no element of fault is necessary for a guilty verdict, so that unintentionally misleading prices can lead to a conviction, but there is a defence of due diligence to be found in section 39 CPA 1987. The onus of proving the due diligence defence (which is a variation of the due diligence defence to be found in section 24 TDA 1968) is on the accused who has to prove that he or she took all reasonable steps and exercised all due diligence to avoid committing the offence.

Increasingly, bookings for hotels and holidays are made through a computer terminal often via a travel or booking agent. The details, including price will be displayed on a screen when the booking is made.

◆ BERKSHIRE COUNTY COUNCIL V OLYMPIC HOLIDAYS LTD **(1994)**

Mr Hollis booked a Greek holiday by going to a travel agent. He had already selected the holiday from a brochure. The agent used a computer terminal. The computer screen showed the details, including price and the booking was made. Mr Hollis was given a computer print-out to confirm the transaction and the price.

Later he received an invoice from Olympic Holidays for payment. The price on the invoice was £182 more than shown on the computer screen and print-out. The invoice price was the same as in the brochure. Olympic Holidays was prosecuted under section 20 Consumer Protection Act 1987 for giving Mr Hollis a misleading price indication. The defence was that Olympic Holidays had thoroughly tested its computer software before and after the incident without the price error happening. It was not possible to explain how the error had occurred.

Olympic Holidays was acquitted because the court was impressed by all that had been done to avoid an error – the company had taken all reasonable steps and exercised all due diligence to avoid giving a misleading price. If it had not been so thorough a conviction would have been the result.

Price indications – resale of tickets

The Price Indications (Resale of Tickets) Regulations 1994 apply where a price is indicated for the resale of tickets to a consumer for admission to entertainment such as theatre, concert, exhibition or sporting event. The regulations do not either prohibit such resale or restrict the resale price, instead they require certain information to be supplied to the buyer before a ticket is resold. The information is:

- the face price of the ticket
- details on the ticket affecting its use (for example performance time)
- the location of the ticket seat/space (if any) and any features of it which could adversely affect the ticket holder's enjoyment of the entertainment such as if the seat only has a restricted view of the performance.

Such information must be in writing except where the sale is over the telephone in which case the information must be given during the telephone conversation.

However, the regulations do not apply where the Package Travel, Package Holiday and Package Tours Regulations 1992 apply, so for example if a hotel sells a package of an overnight stay and a theatre ticket at one inclusive price the 1994 regulations do not apply but instead the 1992 regulations apply (see page 136). But, if a hotel operates a theatre booking service and books theatre (or other event) seats for guests at the hotel the 1994 regulations apply (and not the 1992 regulations) and that is the case whether the hotel resells the tickets at face value or charges a commission or some other higher price.

Price indications – bureaux de change

The Price Indications (Bureaux de Change) Regulations 1992 require any bureau de change to display clearly the rates of exchange for foreign currency and if travellers cheques are exchanged at a different rate then all rates must be displayed.

Customers must be told the details of any proposed transaction when they enquire. Receipts setting out the transaction once concluded must be handed over to the customer.

Hotels etc., who supply a bureau de change service must comply with all the requirements of the regulations.

Differential pricing

For many years, credit card companies incorporated into their contracts with retailers a 'no discrimination' clause under which retailers were required to charge the same price for all purchases made with credit cards as those paid for by cash or other means. Such clauses were abolished in March 1991 by the Credit Cards (Price Discrimination) Order 1990 so that retailers can offer discounts to cash customers or surcharge credit card customers. This is known as differential pricing. The decision whether to apply differential pricing is one for each retailer. However, a credit card company will still be able to limit retailers' price differentials to a maximum of the charge levied on the retailer by the credit card company for the use of the credit card for the transaction.

Hoteliers and caterers who choose to operate differential pricing must make their pricing policy clear to customers. This requirement is explained in detail in the Price Indications (Method of Payment) Regulations 1991 which provides (in outline) where differential pricing applies that the following must be adhered to.

- A statement must be given of any method to which a stated price or prices does/do not apply and any differential payment by that method either as an amount or as a percentage to be deducted or added. Alternatively, separate prices can be given for different methods of payment.
- Where any goods are for sale or services, facilities or accommodation available for purchase by a consumer on any premises, the statement (as above) must be displayed at each public entrance to the premises and at each point where payment is made.
- In the case of kiosks, booths etc., the statement must be displayed at each point where payment is made.
- In the case of a restaurant, bar, hotel dining room etc., where food or drink is available for consumption on the premises the statement must be shown on all menus.
- The statement must be clear, prominent and legible.

In the case of advertisements where differential pricing applies and a price is stated, then it is sufficient to give a method of payment to which the price relates. Failure to display or give the necessary information where differential pricing is in operation, is a criminal offence.

MEASURES OF DRINKS

Beer and cider

The Weights and Measures (Intoxicating Liquor) Order 1988 specifies the measures of alcoholic drinks which are sold for drinking at the time of sale.

Beer and cider may only be sold in quantities of either a third of a pint, or a half or any multiple of half a pint. Where it is for drinking on the premises it must either be served in a marked container (e.g., a pint glass marked to indicate the level for a pint) or be served directly into the glass or mug from which it is to be drunk via measuring equipment stamped in accordance with the Measuring Equipment (Intoxicating Liquor) Regulations 1983, which measuring equipment is situated in a position where it is visible to the customer.

The froth or 'head' of beer forms part of the beer unless excessive.

◆ BENNETT V MARKHAM (1982)

A trading standards officer ordered two pints of beer in a Leeds public house. The barmaid served the drinks in two pint brim measure glasses (that is glasses which when full to the brim hold one pint or 20 fluid ounces). Both glasses were full to the top but each had a half inch 'head' of froth and the actual liquid in each glass was only 18.25 fluid ounces.

The licensee was charged with selling lesser quantity of beer than purported to be sold but was acquitted because the court decided that the 'head' was an integral part of a pint of beer as expected by customers provided the head was not excessive.

Following this case, section 43 of the Weights and Measures Act 1985 was passed to reverse the effect of that case – that is to provide that a pint of beer must be 20 fluid ounces. Section 43 was to come into effect on 1st April 1994 but it did not and that section has since been repealed by the Deregulation and Contracting Out Act 1994. The consequence is that brim measure glasses are still legal for beer and cider but the head of froth must not be excessive. The Brewers Society recommends that a pint of draught beer with a head should be not less than 95 per cent liquid.

The rules as to measures do not apply to mixed drinks such as shandy, nor to bottled drinks.

Spirits

The 1988 Order as amended by both the Weights and Measures (Various Foods) (Amendment) Order 1990 and the Weights and Measures (Intoxicating Liquor) (Amendment) Order 1994 requires gin, rum, vodka, and whisky sold for consumption on premises to be sold

- in an unopened sealed bottle or
- in quantities of either 25 or 35 millilitres, or any multiple of those quantities.

There must be displayed on the premises so as to be readily visible to customers, a statement as to which quantities apply to the spirits offered for sale on those premises.

These rules as to measures of gin, rum, vodka and whisky do not apply where the drink forms part of a mixture of three or more liquids. Accordingly, the rules do apply to gin and tonic but do not apply to gin-based cocktails where at least two other liquids are added to make the cocktail. Other spirits are not covered by rules as to quantities.

Wine

Wine can generally be sold by three methods, namely by the bottle, carafe or glass and there are rules as to all three.

- There are strict rules as to quantities in which wine may be bottled. If wine is sold for consumption on the premises at which it is sold and is sold by unopened bottle then there are no further legal requirements,
- Wine sold by the carafe may only be sold in one of the following quantities, namely 25 centilitres, 50 centilitres, 75 centilitres, or 1 litre,
- Wine sold by the glass (except sparkling wine) may only be sold in quantities of 125 millilitres, or 175 millilitres, or multiples of those quantities.

Where wine is sold by the carafe, and/or by the glass, a statement as to the quantities in which it is sold must either be displayed on the premises so as to be readily seen by the customer, or printed on each wine list/menu.

If a customer orders a drink containing a mixture of liquids, one of which is wine, these rules as to quantities do not apply.

Long pulls

It was an offence, under section 165 Licensing Act 1964, to serve more than the measure of alcoholic drink ordered by the customer. The offence, known as the 'long pull', was introduced in 1921 to prevent pub landlords attracting customers by serving generous measures of draught beer. In December 1995 section 165 LA 1964 was repealed and the long pull offence no longer exists.

FOOD LABELLING

The much amended Food Labelling Regulations 1984 require food for sale/supply to the ultimate consumer or to caterers to be labelled with various details including

- the name of the food
- a list of ingredients (listed in weight order)

- either a 'best before' date or, in the case of highly perishable foods, a 'use by' date (see page 173)
- any special storage or usage instructions
- the manufacturer's name.

But food which is not prepacked and is sold either at a catering establishment or at a hotel to guests at the hotel for immediate consumption there, need not be marked with any of these particulars.

There are, however, certain rules as to labelling which do apply to caterers. First, if food is prepacked and sold as an individual portion to accompany some other food, then it needs to be labelled with its name, for example, individual pre-wrapped sauces.

Second, packaged sandwiches, filled rolls etc., or packaged prepared meals sold by caterers which are sold for immediate consumption on the premises, must be labelled with the name of the food.

Third, sandwiches, filled rolls, take-away meals, hot dogs etc., which are purchased for immediate consumption off the premises, must either be labelled with the name of the food or a notice must be prominently displayed at the point of sale stating the name of the food.

Vending machines selling food must either display the name of the food on the front of the machine, or the machine must be constructed so that the name on the labelling of the food itself is clearly visible, such as through a glass panel in the machine through which an intending purchaser can see the name on the packaging of the food.

Where it is obligatory to label the food with its name, or display the name at the point of sale, then there are certain rules to follow.

- Many types of fish and seafood must be described by their correct name as listed in Schedule 1 to the Food Labelling Regulations 1984. So that, for example, a fish of the species melanogrammus aeglefinus, must be labelled/named 'haddock', and no other fish may be called haddock.
- If a food has a legal name given to it, that name must be used, otherwise the food must be given its customary name or a name or description which is sufficiently precise as to inform the customer of the correct nature of the food.

DISPLAY OF ALCOHOLIC STRENGTHS

The Food Labelling (Amendment) Regulations 1989 amend the Food Labelling Regulations 1984 so as to require the alcoholic strength of drinks (or a representative sample of drinks) to be displayed at bars etc., so that consumers have information about the alcoholic content of the drinks they buy to consume.

Where there is a wine list (or drinks listed on a menu) the alcoholic strength must also be printed alongside the name of the drinks on that list or menu.

The Regulations are complex, but simplified

- they apply to all drinks with an alcoholic strength of more than 1.2 per cent which are served in a glass or carafe
- a notice of alcoholic strength of drinks for sale must be displayed so as to be readily discernable in the 'immediate proximity' of any bar or other point of sale; on any wine list or menu which lists the drinks for sale and in the same place as information is required to be displayed under the Price Marking (Food and Drink on Premises) Order 1979
- the strength must be shown in numbers (not words) to no more than one decimal place and may be preceded by either the word 'alcohol' or the abbreviation 'alc.', and must be followed by 'per cent vol.'
- certain tolerances are permitted to be shown
- the list of drinks may be restricted to 30 provided those listed are a representative sample.

There is no need to display alcoholic strengths for cocktails nor drinks which are usually served in such a way that the alcoholic strength can be seen by the customer.

IRRADIATED FOOD

Prior to the Food Safety Act 1990 coming into force on the 1 January 1991, the irradiation of food was generally prohibited in Great Britain, but section 19 of that Act permits licences to be granted which can permit the irradiation of food.

Irradiation of food is the subjection of the food to ionising radiation in very small doses, in order to preserve the food by killing food poisoning bacteria. It is considered to be a safer way to control bacterial infestation of herbs and spices than the traditional method of using ethylene oxide, but it can be used as a food preservation treatment for a range of other foods and it is claimed that it does not significantly increase the natural radioactivity of the treated food.

The benefits of irradiation are not universally accepted and there is no present test for checking to see if food has been irradiated. Because of public concern about irradiation of food there are two sets of regulations applicable to irradiated food.

The Food (Control of Irradiation) Regulations 1990

The 1990 Regulations prohibit the irradiation of food without a current licence. Licences may only be granted to irradiate certain foods. Importation of irradiated food is strictly controlled so that imported irradiated food must comply with the same requirements.

The sale of irradiated food is made an offence unless it was properly irradiated in Great Britain in accordance with a licence under the Food Safety Act 1990, or the food was imported and complies with the control on imported irradiated food.

If food has been irradiated, then at all times when it is stored or transported it must be accompanied by a statement that the food has been irradiated, and details of by whom it was irradiated, and other prescribed information.

Accordingly, if a caterer purchases any irradiated food then the required documents should accompany the food and be stored with that food.

The Food Labelling (Amendment) (Irradiated Food) Regulations 1990

The purpose of these Regulations is to draw the attention of the consumer to the fact that the food has been irradiated or that it contains ingredients that have (or may have been) irradiated.

In the case of food served in a restaurant, hotel dining room or similar establishment, where the food is for immediate consumption on the premises, and the food has been, or contains an ingredient which has been, irradiated, then a statement must appear on the menu, price list, notice, label or whatever. That statement must identify the food in question, and use the word 'irradiated' or the words 'treated with ionising radiation', or indicate that it does, or may, include ingredients which have been treated.

If the irradiated ingredients only consist of dried herbs and spices, then the menu, price list etc., may contain a general statement that the food sold at that establishment may contain such ingredients, without having to identify particular dishes, but again the word 'irradiated' or the words 'treated with ionising radiation' must be used.

In the case of take-away food, sandwiches, food sold from vending machines etc., for consumption off the premises, and which has been irradiated, or contains irradiated ingredients, then such food must be clearly labelled 'irradiated' or 'treated with ionising radiation'.

─────◆ **SELF EXAMINATION QUESTIONS** ◆─────

1 (a) Outline the distinction between civil consumer protection and criminal consumer protection laws.

 (b) Stephanie and William have a meal in a fish restaurant. They complain about the item described on the menu as scampi. The local authority becomes involved and takes a sample from which it transpires that it is not scampi at all but other cheaper fish shaped to look like scampi.

   Consider the civil and criminal consequences of this incident for the restaurateur.

2 Jill and Trevor book a weekend break at a country hotel from a brochure. The brochure describes the hotel as having five tennis courts and an outside swimming pool.

   When Jill and Trevor arrive they find that the swimming pool is only a mini leisure pool and that the five tennis courts are in poor condition, some overgrown with weeds and uneven and no nets for any of the courts. Consider whether the hotelier has any criminal liability.

3 Justin and Tracey run a small hotel with a licensed restaurant open to non-residents. They make a surcharge for accepting credit cards. Consider what consumer protection notices they need to have on display and where.

See Appendix for suggested answers.

─────────────◆─────────────

Chapter 7

FOOD SAFETY AND HYGIENE

There has been legislation dealing with food safety for very many years. Probably the first major Act of Parliament was the Adulteration of Food or Drink Act 1860 but the first post-war Act tackling the issue was the Food and Drugs Act 1955 and, in Scotland, the Food and Drugs (Scotland) Act 1956. That legislation largely survived intact until the end of the 1980s although in England and Wales the 1955 Act with various minor amendments was replaced by the Food Act 1984.

However, life has changed since 1955, in particular the structure of society has evolved, the food production chain has lengthened and new preservation methods have been introduced. The fact that the food safety legislation failed to keep pace with all these changes became evident from the increasing incidence of food poisoning. The matter came to a head in 1988 and 1989 with a series of food poisoning scares.

The result was the Food Safety Act 1990 (FSA 1990) which is the first major review of the food safety laws since 1955 and has created a change of emphasis by putting responsibility for food safety on each link in the food production chain. In this Chapter it is intended to look at the food safety provisions of the 1990 Act and the various regulations under the Act, in particular the food hygiene regulations.

A point which should be made here is that this Chapter is exclusively concerned with food safety criminal offences. None of the obligations created by the FSA 1990, or the regulations under it, give rise to any civil liability. Consumer protection offences created by the FSA 1990 are looked at in Chapter 6, along with the civil consequences of selling unsafe food.

For the purposes of the FSA 1990, 'food' is strictly not defined so it has its ordinary dictionary definition of nourishment/edible victuals. But the FSA does list things which are included and things which are excluded (section 1 FSA 1990). Included are

- drink (including water)
- things of no nutritional value but used for human consumption
- chewing gum and similar products
- ingredients used in food preparation.

Excluded are

- live animals and birds which are not eaten alive
- animal feeds
- drugs covered by the Misuse of Drugs Act 1971
- licensed medicines.

So almost anything eaten, drunk or chewed by humans is food, except drugs and medicines.

A case under previous legislation also decided that anything else which is supplied as food, even if it is not, is also caught by the food safety legislation.

◆ **Meah v Roberts (1978)**

A family went into an Indian restaurant in Canterbury one lunch-time and ordered a meal and four drinks. The drinks included lemonades for the two children. Unfortunately the drinks were served from a lemonade bottle which contained a caustic soda solution used for cleaning out the draught lager pipes. The lemonade bottle containing the cleaning fluid had been placed in error with the other lemonade bottles containing lemonade. As a result the children suffered severe injuries. The restaurant was prosecuted for selling 'food' unfit for human consumption and one defence which was argued at the court hearing was that the restaurant had not served food because, by no stretch of the imagination, could caustic soda solution be described as food. The court decided that what had been ordered was lemonade, which was food, and the caustic soda had been served as if it was lemonade – the fact that it was something else did not affect the fact that it was served as lemonade, which is food. The restaurant was convicted.

Food safety offences

The FSA 1990 creates criminal offences. Many of the offences are equivalents from previous legislation but the FSA 1990 introduces a new concept which is used throughout the Act, that is, food which fails to comply with food safety requirements.

Food safety requirements

There is no precise definition of the food safety requirements. Instead, section 8(2) FSA 1990 specifies that food fails to comply with the food safety requirements if it

• has had something added to it or something used as an ingredient or something taken out or almost anything else done to it which has made the food injurious to health
• is unfit for human consumption, or
• is contaminated to such an extent that it would be unreasonable to expect it to be eaten or drunk in that condition.

The definition is extended by section 8(3) FSA 1990 because if food is part of a batch, lot or consignment and any part of it fails to meet the food safety requirements then the whole batch, lot or consignment is presumed to fail to meet those requirements, unless and until the contrary is proved.

Food safety offences

There are three criminal offences which result from food failing to meet the food safety requirements (section 8 FSA 1990).

- It is a criminal offence to sell or offer, display or advertise for sale for human consumption, any food which fails to meet the food safety requirements.
- It is an offence for a person to have such food in his or her possession for the purposes of sale, or preparation for sale, for human consumption.
- It is an offence to supply food, which fails to meet food safety requirements, to someone for sale, or preparation for sale, for human consumption.

The FSA 1990 goes on to close any loopholes which could possibly exist in these offences by defining the expression 'sale' and the expression 'food intended for human consumption' in the widest possible terms.

'Sale' (and an offer or display for sale) is given an extended meaning in section 2 FSA 1990 and includes any supply of food in the course of a business such as free tasting or hospitality buffets. Food is treated as offered for sale if it is offered as a prize or given away as part of a business publicity. Furthermore, whether or not as part of a business, food is treated as offered for sale if it is offered as a prize or given away at any public social gathering, amusement, exhibition, performance, game or sporting event. If all that were not enough, there is power to make a statutory instrument to specify anything else as if it were a sale for the purposes of the FSA 1990.

'Food for human consumption' is given similar treatment in section 3 FSA 1990. Any food or ingredient which is usually used for human consumption is presumed to be for that purpose unless and until the contrary is proved. This means that the prosecution does not have to prove that the food was for human consumption, it is for the accused to disprove that it was for human consumption if that is the case.

So what sort of things can make food fail to meet the food safety requirements? Food which is

- contaminated by food poisoning micro-organisms
- chemically contaminated so that it could cause injury to health
- unfit to eat because it is mouldy or contains some foreign material, for example, glass or metal.

But these are examples only and it depends on the severity of the matter. The codes of practice under section 40 FSA 1990 will be looked at later but the above examples are drawn from Code of Practice Number 1 (responsibility for enforcement of the FSA 1990) which in Paragraph 18 recommends prosecution under section 8 for such contamination wherever possible rather than under section 14 (see Chapter 6).

Perhaps the most important thing that can be said about the food safety requirements offences is that they can be committed without any knowledge or 'fault' on the part of the person charged with the offence. This means that if a person is prosecuted under section 8 FSA 1990, the prosecution merely has to prove the facts of the case, for example, that food was sold by the accused and the food failed to meet the food safety requirements. The fact that the food was for human consumption will be presumed by the court (section 3 FSA 1990). The prosecution does not have to prove that the accused knew the food was faulty nor need prove that the food was unsafe due to the fault of the accused. So if the prosecution proves the facts the accused will be convicted unless he or she can establish the due diligence defence, as to which, see later.

Rendering food injurious to health

Section 7 FSA 1990 contains the other food safety offence.

> ### Section 7 Food Safety Act 1990
>
> *Any person who renders any food injurious to health by means of any of the following operations, namely*
>
> a) *adding any article or substance to the food;*
> b) *using any article or substance as an ingredient in the preparation of the food;*
> c) *abstracting any constituent from the food; and*
> d) *subjecting the food to any process or treatment*
>
> *with intent that it shall be sold for human consumption, shall be guilty of an offence.*

Section 7 catches deliberate acts such as deliberate tampering of food and it also catches accidental and non-deliberate acts. It has been suggested that undercooking food, for example, chicken, could be within section 7 especially as the definition of 'treatment' (in section 53 FSA 1990) clearly envisages cooking food. Refreezing de-frosted food could fall within section 7.

Section 7 FSA 1990 goes on to give guidance as to when food is 'injurious to health'. First, regard should be had not only to the probable effect of that food on the health of the person eating (or drinking) it, but also to the probable cumulative effect on a person consuming it in ordinary quantities. Second, 'injury' includes even a temporary impairment.

Cases under previous legislation decided that food can still be regarded as injurious to health even if quite safe for adults but harmful to children or invalids.

The definition of 'food rendered injurious to health' in section 7 FSA 1990 is the same as the first head of food failing to meet the food safety requirements in section 8 FSA 1990. This means that if food has been rendered injurious to health it also fails to meet the food safety requirements. If a manufacturer of food manufactures a batch of food and does something to it so as to render all or some of it injurious to health, and a caterer purchases that food and supplies it to customers, then

- the manufacturer commits an offence under section 7
- the caterer commits an offence under section 8
- the prosecution does not need to prove that either knew that the food was injurious to health or that they were in any way at fault
- the court will accept evidence that any part of the same batch was injurious to health, as evidence that the part the caterer bought failed to meet the food safety requirements.

The difference between section 8 and section 7 is that the latter is aimed at the culprit for making the food dangerous to health in the first place, while section 8 catches anyone who in any way deals with that food. So in the case of a section 7 prosecution, the prosecutor has to prove that it was the accused who made the food injurious to health.

Food product safety

In addition to the Food Safety Act, the General Product Safety Regulations 1994 create a criminal offence of placing a product (including food) on the market which is not safe. The 1994 regulations are mainly aimed at large-scale producers of food products and include various powers requiring food to be taken off the market and public warnings advertised where appropriate. Together with the Food (Lot Marking) Regulations 1992 there exists a mechanism for removing unsafe food from the market.

Food hygiene

The laws concerning food hygiene in catering premises are in the Food Safety (General Food Hygiene) Regulations 1995 which give effect to EC directive 93/43. The Regulations came into effect on 15 September 1995 and replace the previous food hygiene regulations except for those provisions relating to food temperatures. The 1995 Regulations apply to most food businesses whether public or private and whether or not carried on for profit.

There are two general duties on the proprietors of food businesses.

- to carry out all food activities (preparation, storing, transporting etc.) in a hygienic way
- to identify any steps in the activities of the food business which are critical for food safety and to ensure adequate safety procedures are implemented, maintained and reviewed to deal with those critical points.

The hygiene rules

The hygiene rules themselves are set out in ten 'chapters' in schedule 1 to the 1995 Regulations which are a repeat of the annex to the European Directive. It is the duty of the proprietor of a food business to ensure compliance.

Some of the hygiene rules are qualified by one of two expressions, either 'where appropriate' or 'where necessary'. These expressions mean where appropriate or necessary as the case may be for the safety and wholesomeness of the food. The rules in the ten chapters are as follows.

Chapter 1 (General requirements for all food premises other than those in Chapter 3)

(1) Food premises must be clean and in good repair and condition.
(2) The design layout construction etc., of the premises must be such that they are capable of being adequately cleaned and/or disinfected without either accumulation of dirt or formation of condensation or mould and allow good food hygiene practices, including protection against cross contamination.
(3) An adequate number of both wash hand basins and flush lavatories must be available and the lavatories must not lead directly into food rooms.
(4) Wash hand basins must have hot and cold water and facilities for cleaning

and drying hands. Where necessary, food washing and hand washing facilities must be separate.

(5) There must be suitable natural or mechanical ventilation and if mechanical must not draw air from a contaminated area. Ventilation filters etc., must be readily accessible for cleaning.

(6) Sanitary conveniences must have adequate natural or mechanical ventilation.

(7) Food premises must have adequate natural or artificial lighting.

(8) There must be adequate drainage facilities designed to avoid contamination risks.

(9) Where necessary clothes changing facilities must be provided.

Chapter 2 (Specific requirements in food preparation etc. rooms (other than dining rooms and premises in Chapter 3))

1   In food preparation rooms other than dining rooms.
   (a) floors must be sound and easy to clean and, where necessary, disinfect. Where appropriate floors must have adequate surface drainage;
   (b) walls must be sound, easy to clean and where necessary disinfect. Unless inappropriate this will require a smooth surface up to an appropriate height;
   (c) ceilings etc., must be constructed so as to prevent accumulation of dirt and reduce condensation and the growth of undesirable moulds;
   (d) windows which open to the outside must, where necessary, be fitted with insect-proof screens which can be removed for cleaning. If open windows would result in contamination of food, they should remain closed during food production;
   (e) doors must be easy to clean and, where necessary, disinfect;
   (f) work surfaces and surfaces of equipment must be sound and easy to clean and, where necessary, disinfect;

2   Where necessary, there must be adequate facilities for cleaning and disinfecting work tools and equipment.

3   There must be adequate food washing facilities, where appropriate. Any sink should be kept clean and have an adequate supply of hot and/or cold water.

It should be noted that both floors and walls should be of impervious, non-absorbent, washable and non-toxic materials unless the food authority is satisfied that other materials are appropriate.

Chapter 3 (Applicable to moveable and/or temporary premises (such as a marquee, market stalls, mobile sales vehicles), premises used primarily as a private dwelling house, premises used occasionally for catering purposes and vending machines)

1   Premises and vending machines must be silted, designed, constructed and kept clean and in good condition so as to avoid the risk of food contamination and the harbouring of pests, so far as reasonably practicable.
2   In particular and, where necessary
    (a)   there must be appropriate facilities to maintain personal hygiene including for washing hands;
    (b)   surfaces in contact with food must be sound, easy to clean and, where necessary, disinfect. This will mean such surfaces must be of smooth, washable and non-toxic materials unless the food authority is satisfied that other materials are appropriate;
    (c)   adequate provision must be made for cleaning and, where necessary, disinfecting work utensils and equipment;
    (d)   there must be provision for cleaning food
    (e)   there must be an adequate supply of hot and/or cold water;
    (f)   adequate arrangements and/or facilities must be made for the hygienic storage and disposal of hazardous and/or inedible substances and waste;
    (g)   food temperature monitoring arrangements must be adequate;
    (h)   foodstuffs must be kept in such places so as to avoid contamination risks, so far as reasonably practicable.

Chapter 4 (Transport)

1   Vehicles and containers for transporting food must be clean, in good condition, able to protect the food from contamination and, where necessary, be designed to permit adequate cleaning and/or disinfection.
2   Containers must not be used for anything other than food where this may result in contamination and should be marked 'for foodstuffs only'.
3   Where vehicles and/or containers are used for transporting other items there must be effective separation of products, where necessary, to protect against contamination risks.

4   Effective cleaning must be carried out between loads to avoid contamination risks where vehicles and/or containers have been used for transporting non-food items.

5   Food in vehicles and/or containers must be positioned so as to minimise contamination risks.

6   Where necessary, vehicles and containers must be capable of maintaining food at appropriate temperatures.

Chapter 5 (Equipment requirements)

All equipment must be clean and

(a)   be constructed and of such materials and in such condition as to minimise food contamination risks;

(b)   be capable of being thoroughly cleaned and, where necessary, disinfected unless they are non-reusable containers; and

(c)   be installed so as to allow adequate cleaning of the surrounding area.

Chapter 6 (Food waste)

1   Food and other waste must not be allowed to accumulate in food rooms except to the extent it is unavoidable for the proper functioning of the business.

2   Food and other waste must be kept in closable containers unless the proprietor of the food business satisfies the food authority that other types of containers are appropriate. Containers must be of sound condition and, where necessary, easy to clean and disinfect.

3   There must be adequate provision for the removal and storage of food waste and refuse stores must be kept clean and managed so as to protect against access by pests and contamination.

Chapter 7 (Water supply)

1   There must be an adequate supply of drinking water which must be used whenever necessary to make sure the food is not contaminated.

2   Where appropriate, ice must be made from drinking water which ice

must be used whenever necessary to ensure foodstuffs are not contaminated and it must be handled and stored under conditions to protect against contamination.

3   Steam used in contact with food must not contain anything presenting a health hazard.

4   Water unfit for drinking must be kept in a separate system with no connection with the drinking water system. Such system must be readily identifiable.

Chapter 8 (Personal hygiene)

1   Every person working in a food handling area must maintain a high degree of personal cleanliness and wear suitable clean and, where appropriate, protective clothing.

2   Suspected carriers of food poisoning bacteria must not work in any food handling area.

Chapter 9 (Provisions applicable to foodstuffs)

1   Foodstuffs known or believed to be contaminated with parasites, pathogenic micro-organisms or other matters which will not be rendered harmless by the food process must not be accepted by a food business.

2   Raw materials and ingredients must be stored in appropriate conditions designed to prevent harmful deterioration and protection against contamination. Similarly those afflicted with infected wounds, skin infections, sores or diarrhoea must not work in any food handling area while there is a likelihood of food contamination.

3   Stored food must be protected to minimise against risk of contamination and adequate procedures must be in place to ensure pest control.

4   Hazardous and/or inedible substances must be adequately labelled and stored in separate secure containers.

Chapter 10 (Training)

Food business proprietors must make sure that food handlers in the food business are supervised and instructed and/or trained in food hygiene matters appropriate to their tasks.

Food handlers suffering from certain medical conditions

If a food handler knows or believes that he or she is suffering from or is a carrier of a disease likely to be transmitted through food or has an infected wound, skin infection, sores, diarrhoea or any analogous medical condition and there is a likelihood of direct or indirect contamination of food then he or she must report that fact to the food business proprietor. It is a criminal offence for a food handler not to report those matters to the food business proprietor.

The food business proprietor must not permit a food handler known or suspected to be suffering from any of the above matters to work in any food handling area where there is any likelihood of direct or indirect food contamination. This means that either the food handler must be suspended from work or moved to other duties.

Previously, under Regulation 13 of the Food Hygiene (General) Regulations 1970, the food business proprietor was required to notify the local authority of any food handlers suffering from certain infections but the 1995 Regulations have dropped that requirement. However, where a food handler is suspected of being a carrier of food poisoning bacteria a local authority has power to require the food handler to be suspended from any work connected with food (section 20 Public Health (Control of Disease) Act 1984 and schedule 4 Public Health (Infectious Diseases) Regulations 1988).

Industry guides to good hygiene practice

The European Directive places considerable reliance on the preparation of industry guides to good hygiene practice as methods for giving guidance on compliance with the hygiene rules on an industry-by-industry basis. The catering industry guide to good hygiene practice is in preparation at the time of writing and should be available late 1995.

The Food Safety (General Food Hygiene) Regulations 1995 provide that when an enforcement officer enforces the hygiene rules he or she must give due consideration to whether the food business proprietor has followed any relevant guide.

FOOD TEMPERATURE CONTROLS

There are two main sets of temperature controls for food which affect caterers.

- The hot and cold holding temperatures for a range of foods which are susceptible to micro-organism multiplication unless temperature controlled. These are covered by the Food Safety (Temperature Control) Regulations 1995.
- Quick-frozen foods (the Quick-Frozen Foodstuffs Regulations 1990 as amended).

These regulations provide temperature controls for foods. If a breach occurs of those controls, that in itself is an offence, even though the food does not necessarily, as a result, become unsafe to eat.

There are other foods where cold storage is desirable although not obligatory, but in any event, whether food is subjected to regulation or not and whether or not those regulations have been adhered to, it is only food which complies with the food safety requirements which should be retained for sale for human consumption. Therefore it is an offence to be in possession of any food for sale for human consumption which does not comply with the food safety requirements even though such food may have been held at the correct temperature.

Food Safety (Temperature Control) Regulations 1995

The Food Safety (Temperature Control) Regulations 1995 set out minimum and maximum holding temperature laws for food. There is an overall requirement under those regulations for any food, whether raw materials/ ingredients right through to finished products, which is likely to support the growth of pathogenic micro-organisms or the formation of toxins, not to be kept at a temperature which would give rise to a risk to health. The exception being, consistent with food safety, that limited periods outside temperature control is allowed for preparation, storage, display etc. Subject to that overall requirement there is one set of temperature control rules for England and Wales and another set for Scotland. The rules for England and Wales are somewhat complex.

England and Wales

1 There is a chill holding maximum of 8°C for any food which is stored, being prepared, offered etc., for sale and which is likely to support the growth of pathogenic micro-organisms or the formation of toxins.

However, there are certain foods to which the 8°C does not apply at all and certain situations where the 8°C maximum is relaxed.

2 The 8°C maximum does not apply at all for

- food which is subject to the hot holding minimum rules which are explained later
- food supplied by mail order subject to a separate set of conditions
- food which may be kept outside temperature controls without any risk to health
- processed food (e.g. dehydrated or canned) to prevent decay which is kept as such
- food which needs to ripen or mature at normal temperature but only during that ripening/ maturing process
- raw food which will be cooked or otherwise processed so as to make it safe for human consumption
- food which the manufacturer advises (for instance on the label) that it can be kept at a particular temperature higher than 8°C for its shelf life (generally up to its use by or best before date) provided the food is not kept at a higher temperature than the manufacturer recommended maximum.

3 The 8°C maximum is relaxed for

- food for service or display for sale for less than four hours which has not previously been kept for service or display above 8°C
- food being transferred to or from a vehicle
- unavoidable reasons (such as temporary breakdown of equipment, defrosting or the practicalities of food preparation) but for a limited period consistent with food safety.

4 There is a hot holding minimum temperature of 63°C for cooked or reheated food which is for service or on display for service and which needs to be kept hot so as to control the growth of pathogenic micro-organisms or the formation of toxins. But this temperature control is relaxed so that hot food can be kept for service or on display for sale for less than two hours provided it has not previously been so kept.

5 Finally, following cooking or preparation, any food which needs to be kept cold must be cooled as quickly as possible to the appropriate cold holding temperature.

Scotland

The rules for Scotland are not quite so complex.

1 Food which is stored, being prepared, offered etc., for sale on any food

premises must be kept either above 63°C or in a refrigerator, refrigerating chamber or a cool ventilated place.

2 However, this rule does not apply to food

- which is being prepared for sale
- on display for sale to a consumer
- following cooking or final preparation which is being cooled under hygienic conditions as quickly as possible to a safe temperature
- which for convenience for sale it is reasonable to keep outside temperature controls
- which does not need to be kept at such temperatures in order to be safe during its shelf life.

3 Food which has been heated once (e.g. cooked) and which is to be reheated prior to eating must be reheated to not less than 82°C unless that would cause deterioration of food quality.
4 Gelatine for use in bakers' confectionery filling, meat products or fish products must be boiled immediately before use or brought to at least 71°C for 30 minutes and any gelatine left over must either be thrown away or cooled as quickly as reasonably practicable and then kept in a refrigerator, refrigerating chamber or a cool ventilated place.

In General

Unlike the temperature control laws for England and Wales which the 1995 regulations replace, there is no list of foods which are subject to these temperature control laws. Instead there will be guidance issued by the Government and also guidance through the industry guides to good hygiene practice (see page 169). The Food Safety (Temperature Control) Regulations 1995 provide that when an enforcement officer enforces the temperature control laws they must give due consideration to whether the food business proprietor has followed any relevant guide to good hygiene practice made under the EC Directive 93/43 (Hygiene of Foodstuffs Directive).

Quick-Frozen Foodstuffs Regulations 1990

The Quick-Frozen Foodstuffs Regulations 1990 as amended by the Quick-Frozen Foodstuffs (Amendment) Regulations 1994 require quick-frozen foodstuffs (other than ice cream) to be stored at a temperature of −18°C or lower. Additionally, all quick-frozen foods are required to be labelled as such and to give storage information. The 1990 Regulations (as amended) are made to comply with European directives.

USE BY AND BEST BEFORE DATES

The European Food Labelling Directive (EC Directive 79/112 as amended by EC Directive 89/395) requires prepacked foods to have either a 'use by' date or a 'best before' date. In England and Wales this requirement is given effect in the Food Labelling Regulations 1984 as amended by The Food Labelling (Amendment) Regulations 1990. In Scotland the Food Labelling (Scotland) Regulations 1984 as similarly amended have the same effect.

Some food does not need to be marked with either date. Fresh fruit and vegetables, alcoholic drinks with an alcoholic strength of at least 10 per cent, bread and cakes normally eaten within 24 hours of being baked, vinegar and salt all do not need any date marking.

Prepacked food which is from the microbiological aspect highly perishable, and in consequence likely after a short period to be an immediate danger to human health, must display a 'use by' date.

There is no further legal definition of when food must carry a 'use by' date but the Ministry of Agriculture Fisheries and Food has issued guidelines as to the appropriate foods to have a 'use by' date. Those guidelines indicate that all foods which are subject to cold holding temperature controls should carry such a date as well as some other perishable foods including uncooked products comprising or containing meat or fish.

All other prepacked foods must have a 'best before' date.

The difference between use by dates and best before dates is that the latter is concerned with food retaining its optimum condition, for example, not becoming stale. In contrast 'use by' dates are all about the safety of food.

A use by date must have the words 'use by' followed by a day and month (and, possibly, year) up to which the food, if properly stored, is recommended for use. A best before date is the words 'best before' followed by the day, month and year to which, if properly stored, the food can be expected to retain its specific properties except if that period is

- less than three months – only a day and month need be shown
- between 3 and 18 months – the words 'best before end' followed by a month and year
- more than 18 months – the words 'best before end' followed by either a month and year or a year only.

It is an offence to sell any food marked with a 'use by' date after that date but it is not an offence to sell food after its best before date. It is an offence to alter either date although it is lawful to make such an alteration with the written authorisation of the person who was originally responsible for date marking that food.

DEFENCES

The FSA 1990 is a criminal statute. It creates criminal offences. The general rule of criminal liability is that to be convicted of a crime, the accused must not only commit the prohibited act, but must also have the guilty state of mind. By way of example consider the crime of theft – to be convicted, not only must someone take goods not belonging to them, but also it must be done dishonestly with the intention of keeping the goods. So even though someone does the prohibited act, for example, taking a coat from a cloakroom which does not belong to them, they will not commit an offence if they did not have the criminal intent, for example, they mistakenly believed the coat was their own.

Sometimes, however, criminal offences are created which only require the prohibited act to be proved for a conviction to result so that the prosecution does not have to prove any dishonest intention or fault on the part of the accused. These criminal offences are generally referred to as 'strict offences'. It has already been seen that the offences under section 8 (the food safety requirement offences) are offences of strict liability, that is, that the prosecution does not have to prove any blame, fault or dishonesty on the part of the accused. The same is also true of section 7 offences as well as the offences under sections 14 and 15 which are discussed in the previous Chapter. There are also numerous offences created under regulations which are strict liability offences.

The reason for the strict liability is to endeavour to ensure that each link in the food production chain is responsible for the safety of the food supplied. The end consumer is entitled to expect that the food he or she eats or drinks is safe to consume. But it is also the purpose of the criminal law to punish crimes and punishment should only be meted out where there is some element of blame or fault. Hence, there has to be some balance between the legitimate expectations of the public for safe food and the undesirability of punishment without fault.

This is where the due diligence defence makes its entrance because the purpose of the due diligence defence is to strike that balance. The defence will be found in section 21 FSA 1990. There are two heads of the defence, namely the general due diligence defence to be found in subsection (1) and third party fault defences in subsections (2) to (4).

The main due diligence defence

> ### Section 21(1) Food Safety Act 1990
>
> *In any proceedings for an offence under any of the preceding provisions of this part (of this Act) it shall be a defence for the person charged to prove that he took all reasonable precautions and exercised all due diligence to avoid the commission of the offence by himself or by a person under his control.*

This defence is usually referred to as the 'due diligence defence' and is found in identical, or near identical form, in other consumer protection criminal legislation. As such, there is already considerable guidance from cases on that legislation even though this due diligence defence is relatively new to food safety law.

The defence applies to all criminal offences in the preceding sections of the FSA 1990 and also to almost all regulations made or effective under the Act including the hygiene regulations – the Food Safety Act 1990 (Consequential Modification) (England and Wales) Order 1990.

The task of proving the defence falls on the accused and he or she must prove that they took all 'reasonable precautions' and exercised all 'due diligence' to avoid the offence being committed by themselves or their staff. What does that mean?

'Reasonable precautions' means a system or routine for dealing with the points at which risks can occur or problems be discovered. Obvious points are checking food on delivery, ensuring stock is used within storage times, checking refrigerated temperatures daily, setting up a cleaning and inspection routine for premises etc.

'Due diligence' means monitoring or a system of supervision to try and ensure that the systems set up do work and to take appropriate action if necessary. For instance, the periodic stocktaking may be an opportunity to check that the stock rotation records agree with the stored stock, and managers may be required to make periodic returns/reports to check that the correct procedures are followed and the correct records kept.

The fact that the offence was committed is not evidence of a failure to exercise all due diligence. So in *R v Bow Street Magistrates Court ex parte Cow and Gate Nutrition plc 1994*, a magistrate misunderstood the defence when he decided that the accused could not have exercised all due diligence because otherwise the piece of bone would not be in the jar of baby food. The point of the defence is that something can go wrong despite the exercise of all due diligence and if so then that is a defence to a prosecution.

In rare circumstances an accused can rely on the actions of a third party to satisfy the due diligence defence. In *Hurley v Martinez & Co Ltd 1990*, a wine merchant in this country was entitled to rely on the checks carried out by the German wine producer and in *Carrick District Council v Taunton Vale Meat Traders Ltd 1994*, a slaughterhouse charged with an offence under section 8 of the Food Safety Act 1990 was able to rely on the checks carried out by the local authority meat inspector and did not have to duplicate those checks to show the exercise of all due diligence.

Staff and due diligence

What happens if the systems are set up, the monitoring in place and all staff trained to operate them, but a staff member fails to do his or her job properly or just disobeys instructions with the result that an offence is committed. That was the question raised in the House of Lords case of *Tesco Supermarkets v Nattrass 1971*.

◆ **TESCO SUPERMARKETS V NATTRASS (1971)**

Tesco Supermarkets were prosecuted for an offence under section 11 Trade Descriptions Act 1968 of advertising goods at a lower price than the price to be paid. The case involved packets of washing powder which Tesco had on special offer and were advertising by means of large posters displayed in all their store windows. The system for dealing with special offers was for all the existing stock to be removed from display and new stock put out marked with the lower (special offer) price. At the Northwich Tesco store this procedure was followed but the offer was such a success that all the special offer packs were sold. A shop assistant then went to the storeroom and took more packets of washing powder to put on display but unfortunately she took the packets that had previously been removed, that is, those which were already marked with the higher price. She did not tell the store manager. The store manager was responsible for checking all stock every day and filling in a daily return for his Head Office. He marked his daily return 'all special offers OK' despite the fact that the washing powder was incorrectly priced. A customer, attracted by the advertisement in the window, went into the store, picked up a packet of washing powder from the display shelves and was charged the higher price at the check-out.

Initially, Tesco was convicted, because the courts considered that the store manager's fault meant that Tesco had not exercised all due diligence. Tesco appealed all the way to the House of Lords. In the House of Lords it was decided that, although acts and defaults of some senior managers and executives can be the acts and defaults of the company, this is only true of the most senior level of executives who are effectively in control of the company and decide company policy. Such executives are the 'controlling mind' of the company. The store manager at Northwich did not come into that category and therefore his default was not his employer's default. The manager had not done his job as instructed, but apart from that, Tesco had an adequate system and monitoring controls which should have avoided the offence being committed. Accordingly, Tesco was entitled to rely on the due diligence defence and was acquitted.

If, therefore, the organisation has in place its systems and controls in order to comply with the due diligence defence the fact that a member of staff does something which results in an offence being committed does not necessarily mean that the business is criminally liable. However, the fact that a staff member does do something which results in an offence being committed may, in itself, be evidence that there are insufficient controls and systems in place.

If a staff member does do something which causes an offence to be committed, that staff member can be prosecuted personally, whether or not his or her employer is also prosecuted (section 20 FSA 1990).

Likewise, if the senior managers or executives of a company who decide that company's policy, set the company on a course which results in the company committing an offence, then those managers and executives can be prosecuted as well as the company (section 36 FSA 1990).

The third party due diligence defences

Bolted on to the general due diligence defence in section 21(1) FSA 1990 are two third party fault defences to be found in the following subsections of that section. These are important, because if either is proved by the accused, then he or she will be presumed to have satisfied the due diligence defence.

There are four preconditions which must apply before either of the third party fault defences can be applicable. Third party fault defences can only apply:

- To offences under sections 8, 14 or 15 FSA 1990 and to offences under most Regulations under the FSA 1990.
- Provided the accused did not prepare the food in question. 'Prepare' is defined in section 53 and has also been the subject of case law. For example, cooking meat or making a gateau counts as preparation, but merely slicing or cutting up bought-in cooked meat or gateau is not preparation (*Leeds City Council v J H Dewhurst Ltd (1990)*).
- Provided the accused did not import the food into Great Britain. Buying

and importing wine direct from the producer in France means the caterer cannot rely on either of the third party fault defences if the wine happens to be defective.

- If the offence was committed due to the act or default of another person (other than one of the employees of the accused) or to reliance on information supplied by such a person.

If these four preconditions apply then there are two third party fault defences.

The first is often referred to as the brand name third party fault defence, and it applies if the sale (or intended sale) was not under the accused's name or mark, and the accused did not know, and could not reasonably have been expected to know, that he or she was committing an offence.

The second third party fault defence is the non-brand name defence and applies if two conditions are satisfied

- the accused carried out such checks on the food in question as was reasonable in the circumstances or the accused reasonably relied on checks carried out by his or her supplier, and
- he or she did not know and had no reason to suspect that he or she was committing an offence.

These third party fault defences are unique to food safety laws and it can be seen that the brand name defence is easier to prove than the non-brand name defence because it requires no checks to be carried out by the caterer.

In every case where either of the third party fault defences is to be used, or if the accused intends to plead the main due diligence defence and that defence involves alleging the offence was committed due to someone else's fault, or due to reliance on information given by them then the accused has to give written notice to the prosecutor of that fact within a strict timetable prior to the court hearing. The notice must also identify, or help to identify, the other party at fault.

ENFORCEMENT

Enforcement authorities

The FSA 1990 contains offences which are enforced both by local environmental health officers and by local trading standards officers. Sections 5 and 6 define the enforcement authorities and those sections are supplemented by the Food Safety (Enforcement Authority) Order 1990 which sets out the division of responsibility for enforcing the Act in non-metropolitan counties of England and Wales. In such counties the environmental health officers are employed in district councils and the trading standards officers are within the County Councils. The 1990 Order is itself supplemented by Code of Practice Number 1 – 'Responsibility for Enforcement of the Food Safety Act 1990' issued under section 40 FSA 1990.

Section 15 FSA 1990 is entirely a trading standards matter but sections 7, 8 and 14 are the joint responsibility of the enforcement authorities. However, as very much a generalisation, it can be said that food safety (which is the concern of this Chapter) is an environmental health matter, whereas food standards (considered in the previous Chapter) are for the trading standards officers to enforce.

It is the duty of the relevant enforcement authorities to enforce the provisions of the FSA 1990 (section 6(2) FSA 1990) and in doing so, they must have regard to any relevant provisions of a code of practice issued under section 40 FSA 1990, and comply with any directions given under that section. There are 17 codes of practice which are published by the Ministry of Agriculture Fisheries and Food and the Department of Health jointly.

The purposes of these codes of practice is to try and achieve consistent standards of enforcement throughout the country. They do this by giving guidance to enforcement authorities either generally, such as in relation to inspection of food, use of improvement notices and enforcement of the food premises registration requirements, or in relation to specific matters such as the food safety aspects of fishery products. The codes do not give guidance to those running a food business and should not be confused with the various industry guides to good hygiene practice which guides support the food hygiene regulations.

Enforcement authorities are required by section 27 FSA 1990 to appoint a public analyst for their area who must be a qualified person not involved in any food business in that area (Food Safety (Sampling and Qualifications) Regulations 1990). A deputy may also be appointed. The public can submit suspect food to the public analyst to be analysed (section 30 FSA 1990).

Enforcement officers

An officer of an enforcement authority who is authorised by that authority to carry out functions under the FSA 1990 (in section 5 FSA 1990 and also here referred to as an 'authorised officer') has certain powers which include

- to make test purchases (section 29 FSA 1990)
- to take samples of any food which has been sold, or is for sale for human consumption (section 29 FSA 1990)

- on production, if requested, of some official identification, to enter any premises to see if there has been any contravention of the FSA 1990 or any regulations or order made under the Act, and for certain other purposes (section 32 FSA 1990).

Obstruction of an authorised officer is a criminal offence punishable by fine and/or imprisonment for up to three months (sections 33 and 35 FSA 1990). If entry to any premises is refused, or a refusal is expected, then a warrant to force an entry may be obtained on application to a magistrate and the warrant is valid for one month (section 32 FSA 1990).

If an authorised officer obtains a sample (whether or not by a test purchase) which he or she considers should be analysed to determine the composition of that food, then the sample must be divided into three parts unless not readily practicable to do so. One part must be left with the owner of the food, one part submitted for analysis and one part retained so that if necessary it can later be sent to the Government analyst. If a sample obtained by an authorised officer is to be sent to a food examiner (rather than an analyst) for microbiological examination then it does not have to be divided into parts.

The rules about taking samples are to be found in the Food Safety (Sampling and Qualifications) Regulations 1990 as supplemented by Code of Practice Number 7. The food analyst or examiner must analyse or examine the sample sent to him or her and issue a certificate showing the result of that analysis or examination, and the certificate can be used as evidence in court.

Generally, any authorised officer or other officer of a food authority is immune from any court action for anything done in connection with the FSA 1990, provided they acted in the honest belief that they were doing their duty under that Act (section 44 FSA 1990).

Registration of food premises

Under the Food Premises (Registration) Regulations 1991 it is a criminal offence for a caterer to use any premises for the purposes of business unless those premises are registered. There are some exceptions the main ones being

- premises used less than five times in any period of five weeks
- premises where no food is kept (e.g. the head office of an hotel group)
- bed and breakfast run from the proprietor's home using not more than three letting bedrooms.

Moveable premises, such as ice cream vans, delivery vehicles and mobile kitchens do not have to be registered but the place where they are normally kept or garaged must be registered.

If a food business is carried on in a market then the market controller must register but only if the stalls are supplied by him or her. If the market trader provides the stall (for example a hamburger stand) then the market trader is responsible for registration.

Contract caterers are responsible for registering any canteens or staff restaurants which they operate.

There is no fee for registration which is with the district council but application for registration has to be made at least 28 days before the premises are opened. Renewal of registration is not necessary but a change of proprietor or changes in the nature of the business do have to be notified.

The purpose of registration is so that the enforcement authorities have details of the premises in their area which are subject to the FSA 1990 which information will enable hygiene inspections to be organised efficiently.

Inspection and seizure of suspect food

Section 9 FSA 1990 is designed to ensure that food which fails to comply with the food safety requirements is removed from the food production chain as soon as possible.

An authorised officer (who would generally be an environmental health officer) is entitled to inspect any food for human consumption which has been sold, or is for sale, or is in someone's possession for sale, or preparation for sale, and if the officer believes that the food fails to comply with the food safety requirements (as defined in section 8 FSA 1990) he or she may either remove the food, or require it to be detained pending further investigation. Any food which is removed must be taken before a magistrate, and if it is believed (after hearing any appropriate evidence) that the food fails to meet the food safety requirements, the food must be destroyed.

Section 9 is supplemented by Code of Practice Number 4 made under section 40 FSA 1990.

Improvement notices

Improvement notices may be served on a caterer if there are reasonable grounds for believing that he or she is failing to comply with either the hygiene regulations, or any of the food processing regulations, (as to which refer to code of Practice Number 6). Improvement notices must be in a prescribed form, and require the caterer to do certain things within a stated period, so as to comply with the appropriate regulations. Failure to comply with an improvement notice is itself an offence (section 10 FSA 1990) and an appeal against an improvement notice may be made to a court (section 37

FSA 1990). The court can cancel, confirm or make alterations to an improvement notice (section 39 FSA 1990). If an appeal is made against an improvement notice then the notice is suspended pending the outcome of that appeal.

Prohibition orders

If a caterer is convicted of an offence under the hygiene regulations and the court considers one of the preconditions in Table 7.1 applies, then the court must, by order, make an appropriate prohibition as shown in Table 7.1. Such an order is known as a prohibition order (section 11 FSA 1990). The first three prohibitions shown in Table 7.1 also apply if the caterer breaches any of the regulations relating to food preparation and processing.

TABLE 7.1

Preconditions	Appropriate prohibition
1 If any process or treatment used in a food business gives rise to a risk of injury to health.	1. Prohibition on the use of the process or treatment for the purposes of that business.
2. Either the premises themselves or the use of a piece of equipment used in a food business involves a risk of injury to health.	2. Prohibition on the use of those premises or that equipment either for that business or any other food business of the same type.
3. The state or condition of any any premises or equipment used for business purposes involves a risk of injury to health.	3. Prohibition on the use of those premises or equipment in any food business.
4. The court thinks it proper to ban the proprietor or manager from being involved in any food business.	4. Prohibition on the proprietor or manager of a food business being involved in the management of any food business or any particular type of food business.

It is important to note that in the expression 'risk of injury to health', the words 'injury to health' have the same meaning as in section 7 FSA 1990 (rendering food injurious to health) so that injury need not be permanent.

If a court makes a prohibition order then it must be served on the proprietor of a business and in the case of one of the first three, a copy of the order conspicuously displayed on the relevant premises. It is an offence to contravene a prohibition order.

Only a court can lift a prohibition order on a proprietor or manager, and not earlier than six months after it was made. In the case of any other prohibition order, that is, any of the first three in the table above, the enforcement authority can lift the prohibition if it is satisfied that the proprietor has taken sufficient measures so that the precondition no longer applies. Unless a prohibition order is lifted by one of these methods it remains in force indefinitely.

Emergency prohibition notices and orders

Sometimes things are so bad that emergency action is needed to close down a business, or prevent equipment being used, or food being prepared. In such a situation an emergency prohibition notice may be issued.

If an authorised officer believes that there is an imminent risk of injury to health, due to any food processing or treatment, or the state of the food premises or any food equipment, he or she may issue an emergency prohibition notice (section 12 FSA 1990).

An emergency prohibition notice must be on a prescribed form and it prohibits with immediate effect the use of the offending process, treatment, premises or piece of equipment. The notice must be served on the proprietor of the business and a copy affixed by an authorised officer in a conspicuous place on the relevant premises. The unauthorised removal of such a notice is in itself a criminal offence under section 1 Criminal Damage Act 1971 or section 78 Criminal Justice (Scotland) Act 1980.

Because emergency prohibition notices are such powerful weapons in the armoury of the enforcement authorities and there is no appeals procedure there are certain safeguards

- guidance is given to the enforcement authorities as to the use of emergency prohibition notices in Code of Practice Number 6, and in exercising their powers the authorities must take notice of that guidance
- such a notice expires after three days unless, within that period, the authority makes an application for a court order or (in Scotland) submits the case to the Procurator Fiscal
- full compensation is payable to the proprietor of the business, unless both an application is made to the court for an order before the emergency prohibition notice expires and the court considers the service of the notice was justified.

From this it can be seen that an emergency prohibition notice is a short-term emergency measure designed to have immediate effect until it can be superseded by a court order. Such a court order is known as an emergency prohibition order.

On an application for an emergency prohibition order the question for the court is the same, namely, whether due to some food process or treatment, or the state or condition of food premises or any food equipment, there is an imminent risk of injury to health. If so, the court must make an emergency prohibition order prohibiting the use of the process or treatment, or premises or equipment for the purposes of that food business, or any food business.

It is also important to note here that there does not have to be a conviction before an emergency prohibition order can be made. An emergency prohibition order is not a criminal conviction, it is a court order prohibiting certain activities, but breach of an order is a criminal offence.

An emergency prohibition order must be served on the proprietor and displayed on the relevant premises. It ceases to have effect if the relevant enforcement authority issues a certificate, following remedial action by the proprietor of the business, that they are satisfied the imminent risk to health no longer exists. Until such a certificate is issued, an emergency prohibition order continues in force.

Prosecution and penalties

Prosecution for most offences in the Food Safety Act 1990 and the regulations under the Act must be commenced within three years of the commission of the offence, or (if earlier) one year from its discovery by the prosecutor. These are time limits beyond which the offender is safe from prosecution (section 34 FSA 1990).

For most offences there are maximum fines and imprisonment, but in some cases the court has power to impose unlimited fines (section 35 FSA 1990). Most regulations under the FSA 1990 specify the level of punishment applicable to the offences they create.

————————◆ **SELF EXAMINATION QUESTIONS** ◆————————

1   Rita is the manager of a popular salad bar. She is visited by the local environmental health officer (EHO) who informs her that a number of her customers have complained of food poisoning symptoms after eating the previous day at the salad bar.

   The EHO inspects and finds that one of Rita's refrigerators has an intermittent fault and is not keeping the food at the correct temperature. Rita checks refrigerator temperatures every other day and keeps records of those checks.

Consider

- What criminal offences Rita may be charged with as a result of this incident?
- What defence could be put forward to such prosecutions?
- What legal consequences might follow if Rita is convicted?

2 Rita obtains some of her supplies from a catering supplier, in particular scotch eggs and quiches. These are supplied individually wrapped, each date marked. Unfortunately for Rita the sharp-eyed EHO notices that some of the scotch eggs in the salad bar are past their use by date.

Consider the consequences for Rita.

3 On inspection of Rita's kitchen the EHO discovers that there are no flyscreens covering the windows, there is a toilet leading directly off the kitchen and the bin for food waste has no lid. The EHO serves an improvement notice in respect of these matters.

   Rita's boss Nerys, who is the proprietor of the salad bar, considers that none of these matters require correction and she wants to challenge the improvement notice. Advise what Nerys should do.

See Appendix for suggested answers.

Chapter 8

DRINK LICENSING

INTRODUCTION

The need for a licence

The retail sale of alcoholic drinks is strictly controlled by a licensing system under the Licensing Act 1964 (LA 1964) as amended by the Licensing Act 1988 (LA 1988).

Section 160 Licensing Act 1964

(1) If any person

(a) sells or exposes for sale by retail any intoxicating liquor without holding a justices' licence . . . authorising that sale . . . or

(b) holding a justices' licence . . . sells or exposes for sale by retail any intoxicating liquor except at the place for which their licence authorises that sale

he shall be guilty of an offence.

So, it is the person who is licensed to sell alcoholic drinks, but only at the premises authorised by that licence.

It is also only retail sales which require a justices' licence. Retail sales are defined in section 201 LA 1964, as amended by the Licensing (Retail Sales) Act 1988, and is the sale of alcoholic drinks to the public but not in large quantities, which in the case of spirits or wine means 9 litres or one case, and in the case of beer or cider means 20 litres or two cases.

The LA 1964 uses the expression 'intoxicating liquor'. The corresponding Scottish legislation uses the expression 'alcoholic liquor', but in this book the expression 'alcoholic drink' will be used instead. The definition of 'intoxicating liquor' is spirits, wines, beer, cider, and any fermented, distilled or spirit drink, but the definition does not include drinks which do not have an alcoholic strength at the time of sale exceeding 0.5 per cent. This definition of intoxicating liquor excludes low alcohol beer and wines (Licensing (Low Alcohol Drinks) Act 1990).

There are certain situations where a justices' licence is not needed to sell alcoholic drinks. The principal exemptions are listed in section 199 LA 1964, and include the sale of alcoholic drinks to railway passengers in a buffet car of a railway train. As will be seen later, a members' club may have a registration certificate instead of a licence.

The licensing system

The licensing of retail sale of alcoholic drinks is controlled by local licensing justices who grant licences at either the annual licensing sessions held in February each year, or at any of the transfer sessions which are held throughout the year.

In the case of new towns designated under the New Towns Act 1981 there is an additional layer of control, because in addition to the normal licensing system there is a Licensing Committee which carries out licensing planning functions. The procedure in new towns is that any application for a new on-licence can only be granted by the licensing justices if the Licensing Committee has first considered the matter and has no objection to the grant of the licence.

Display of name of licensee

Section 183 Licensing Act 1964

(1) . . . the holder of a justices' licence, other than a residential licence, shall keep painted on or affixed to the licensed premises in a conspicuous place, and in such form and manner as the licensing justices may direct, his name, and after the word 'licensed' followed by words sufficient to express the business for which the licence is granted, and in particular

   (a) words expressing whether the licence is an on-licence or an off-licence;

So, on all licensed premises the name of the licensee together with whether or not it is an on-or off-licence must be stated, and if the licence is restricted to certain categories of drink for example, beer, cider and wine only, then that also should be stated.

If the licence is a restaurant licence then it is sufficient to indicate that the licence permits sales for consumption on the premises with meals.

Scotland

The licensing system described in this book is the system which operates in England and Wales. The law in Scotland is different and is governed by the Licensing (Scotland) Act 1976. The principle of the Scottish law is the same, namely that retail sales of alcoholic drinks may only take place under a licence. The practice is slightly different and the various licences go under different names.

TYPES OF LICENCES

Licences are broadly divided into those which permit the alcoholic drink to be consumed on the premises where it is bought, for example a public house, and those where the drink is to be taken away before being drunk, for example a supermarket. These licences are known respectively as 'on-licences' and 'off-licences'.

The typical on-licence will permit off-sales as well, so that a public house will usually be able to sell drinks for drinking on the premises as well as selling bottled drinks to be taken away.

Off-licences are usually held by supermarkets, corner shops and specialist off-licence shops. They are, therefore, not of great relevance to the hotel and catering industry. A guest house or small hotel which neither has a bar nor serves alcoholic drinks with meals, might want an off-licence so as to provide small bottles of wine with packed lunches, but apart from this example it is difficult to imagine any catering establishment having only an off-licence. For this reason, this Chapter considers first the different rules which apply to off-licences and then concentrates on on-licences.

Off-licences

Apart from the fact that an off-licence only permits the sale of alcoholic drinks for drinking off the premises, an off-licence differs from an on-licence in a number of ways. First, there are only two categories of off-licence whereas there are five categories of on-licence. The two categories of off-licence are those which authorise the sale of

- beer, cider and wine
- all descriptions of alcoholic drinks.

Various conditions may be imposed on an on-licence (indeed it is possible for a condition to be imposed banning off-sales) but no conditions at all may be imposed on an off-licence. So, for instance, an off-licence to sell wine only cannot be created by putting a condition on the licence to that effect.

The hours during which alcoholic drinks may be sold from an off-licence are longer than the permitted hours for an on-licence. During weekdays (other than Good Friday) off-licensed premises may be open for business from

8am to 11pm. The permitted hours for off-licensed premises on Sundays are from 10am to 10.30pm and on Good Friday from 8am to 10.30pm. Because of the longer permitted hours, it is possible (in suitable cases) for on-licensed premises also to have the equivalent of an off-licence which will then permit sales for consumption off the premises outside the on-licence permitted hours but within the off-licence permitted hours (section 86 LA 1964).

The final distinction between on- and off-licences is the rules concerning conduct of business. There are numerous rules concerning the conduct of business in on-licensed premises, some of which apply to off-licences, for example no sales to persons under the age of 18, but the following distinctions apply.

- Wine and spirits may only be sold in off-licences in bottles or other sealed containers.
- Persons under 18 may be employed in off-licensed premises, but any sales of alcoholic drinks by them must be specifically approved by the licensee or another employee who is aged 18 or over.
- Sales from off-licensed premises may be by credit, for example by credit card.
- It is an offence if a customer, with the consent or connivance of the off-licensee, buys alcoholic drink and consumes it on the premises, or on adjoining or nearby premises owned or controlled by the licensee, or on the adjoining highway. This offence is committed by the licensee who effectively operates a public house or a restaurant but with only an off-licence, so that a licensee with an off-licence only, could not keep a garden next to the off-licensed premises with picnic tables where people may sit and drink drinks bought at his or her off-licence.

On-licences

A full on-licence permits the licensee to sell alcoholic drinks for consumption on or off the premises and with or without meals. On-licences are divided into five categories according to the type of alcoholic drinks which are licensed to be sold

- wine only
- cider only
- beer and cider only
- beer, cider and wine only
- all descriptions of alcoholic drinks.

So, premises which wish to sell spirits for drinking on the premises must apply for the last category of licence. It is not possible to create other varieties of licence by imposing conditions. In *R v Inner London Crown Court ex parte Sitki* (1993) a 'no beer' condition made the whole licence invalid.

Part IV of the LA 1964 makes provision for variants of on-licences which are distinguished only by conditions on the licence and the premises for which they are granted. These are known as 'Part IV licences' and there are three types – a restaurant licence, a residential licence and a combined residential and restaurant licence. The advantages of a Part IV licence are

- there are only limited grounds for refusing an application for a Part IV licence
- only limited conditions may be imposed on the Part IV licence
- the permitted hours for a Part IV licence are or can be longer.

Restaurant licences

A variety of on-licence is a restaurant licence.

> ### Section 94 Licensing Act 1964
>
> *(1) In this Act 'restaurant licence' means a Part IV licence which*
>
> > *(a) is granted for premises structurally adapted and are bona fide used or intended to be used for the purpose of habitually providing the customary main meal at mid-day or in the evening or both, for the accommodation of persons frequenting the premises; and*
> >
> > *(b) is subject to the condition that intoxicating liquor shall not be sold or supplied on the premises otherwise than to persons taking table meals there and for consumption by such a person as ancillary to his meal.*

So, a restaurant licence is an on-licence with a condition imposed that drinks may only be served to diners taking table meals for consumption ancillary to the meal. The meals served must include lunch or dinner.

Restaurant licences have certain advantages.

- Such licences are easier to obtain than full on-licences because there is no need to prove a need for the premises and the only grounds on which an application for such a licence may be refused are those set out in section 98 LA 1964. If a person wants to open a licensed restaurant, a licence can usually be obtained if he or she is 18 or over and a fit and proper person to hold a licence and provided the premises are suitable.

- The general discretion to impose conditions under section 4 LA 1964 does not apply to restaurant licences and only the conditions in section 93 LA 1964 may be imposed.
- A licensee under a restaurant licence can generally obtain a supper hour certificate which will extend the permitted hours by one hour per day.

An important restriction on a restaurant licence is that alcoholic drinks may only be served to those taking 'table meals' and the drink must be 'ancillary' to those meals. That raises two questions.

- What are 'table meals'? The LA 1964 defines table meals as 'meals eaten whilst seated at a table or some other counter or structure serving as a table which is not used for any other purpose'. So finger buffets, eaten while standing, are not table meals, nor are meals to be taken away, so that a restaurant licence does not allow sales of alcoholic drinks to those waiting for a take-away meal. Bar meals are also not table meals because the bars or tables in the bar are not used exclusively for table meals,
- When is drink 'ancillary' to the meal? Drinks served at the same time as a meal, which drinks are not predominant, are ancillary. So a drink of wine with a three course meal is ancillary. A pint of beer with a bag of crisps is not, indeed the crisps are probably ancillary to the beer! It is possible that an aperitif beforehand, while making the choice from the menu, and liqueur afterwards are ancillary even though not consumed at a table, for example in a lounge area.

Every restaurant licence has a condition that suitable non-alcoholic beverages, including water, must be available for consumption with meals, and this means that a licensee must be prepared to supply non-alcoholic drinks, including water to diners.

Off-sales are *not* permitted under a restaurant licence.

Residential licences

Another variety of on-licence is a residential licence.

> **Section 94 Licensing Act 1964**
>
> (2) In this Act 'residential licence' means a Part IV licence which
>
>   (a) is granted for premises bona fide used or intended to be used

> *for the purpose of habitually providing for reward board and lodging including breakfast and one other at least of the customary main meals; and*
>
> (b) *is subject to the condition that intoxicating liquor shall not be sold or supplied on the premises otherwise than to persons residing there or their private friends bona fide entertained by them at their expense and for consumption by such a person or his private friend so entertained by him either on the premises or with a meal supplied at but to be consumed off the premises.*

So, a residential licence is for hotels and guest houses etc., which provide bed, breakfast and at least one other main meal. Such a licence only allows alcoholic drinks to be served to residents and their friends. The drinks are to be supplied either for consumption on the premises, or as part of a meal for consumption off the premises, for example as part of a packed lunch. Off-sales otherwise than with a meal for a resident and friends are prohibited. Only residents are permitted to buy the drinks but they may buy the drinks for their friends.

Residential licences have considerable advantages.

* If the applicant for a residential licence is over 18 years and is a fit and proper person and provided the premises are suitable, then a residential licence will normally be granted.
* The conditions which may be imposed on the grant of a residential licence are limited to those set out in section 93 LA 1964 and hence, the wide discretion of licensing justices under section 4 LA 1964 to impose conditions does not apply to residential licences.
* The normal permitted hours do not apply, so that residents may buy and consume alcoholic drinks at any time of the day or night. Many hotels take advantage of this provision by providing refrigerated vending facilities in residents' rooms so that residents may purchase and consume a variety of alcoholic drinks at any time. The drink does not have to accompany meals unless it is for consumption off the premises.

There are two important restrictions on a residential licence.

* Such a licence can only be granted to an establishment which provides not only accommodation but also breakfast and at least one other main meal. The price does not have to be inclusive, so that a holiday camp with an on-site restaurant which serves breakfast and another main meal at a separate

194 ◆ Essential Law for Caterers

price, could obtain a residential licence, but a motel which supplies sleeping accommodation only or a bed and breakfast establishment which does not do any other meals, cannot obtain a residential licence,

- Alcoholic drinks may only be bought by a 'person residing on the premises'. Such a restriction means that hotel guests can buy and consume alcoholic drinks and even residents in an hotel annexe are considered to be 'persons residing on the premises'. The difficulty occurs with holiday camps as to whether persons occupying chalets or caravans can be described as 'persons residing on the premises'.

There are certain conditions which will apply to a residential licence.

- The first condition will be that there must be available a lounge or sitting room with adequate seating which is neither used as a dining room restaurant or bar nor used for consumption of alcoholic drinks. This is the coffee lounge or reading room from which alcoholic drinks are banned and such a condition will apply unless the applicant for a residential licence persuades the licensing justices that the condition need not apply.
- A condition which always applies, is that suitable non-alcoholic beverages including drinking water must be just as available as alcoholic drinks with meals. There is no requirement for such drinks to be available to those not taking meals.

Residential and restaurant licences (combined licences)

A further variety of on-licence is the residential and restaurant licence often known as the combined licence. It is simply a combination of a residential licence and a restaurant licence and therefore suited to a hotel operating a restaurant open to non-residents.

The various conditions and restrictions applicable to a restaurant licence and a residential licence will operate to a combined licence. This can cause some difficulties in operation, for instance, if the dining room is operated for both residents and non-residents, different rules will apply to different diners.

If a hotel also wants to operate a public bar then a combined licence is inappropriate because the public will only be able to buy drinks if those drinks are ancillary to a meal, so to operate a public bar a full on-licence is required.

Occasional licences

An occasional licence is granted to a person who has an existing on-licence (other than a residential or club licence) and it allows him or her to sell drinks somewhere other than his or her licensed premises. An occasional licence can be granted for a maximum period of three weeks.

Such a licence is useful for a licensee to run a bar or a refreshment marquee at a show or exhibition but it will also cover one day events, for example a dance in a hall.

An occasional licence will only be granted to the holder of a restaurant licence (or a combined licence) if the sale of alcoholic drinks will be ancillary to the provision of substantial refreshment (section 180 LA 1964). Therefore under an occasional licence, a restaurant licensee cannot run a bar only, but can organise a wedding reception with alcoholic drinks in a place other than his or her restaurant.

If the licensee only has a licence to sell a limited category of drinks, for example beer, cider and wine only, he or she can only sell the same category of drinks under an occasional licence.

A use which has been made of occasional licences is to enable drinks to continue to be served in premises where, inadvertently, the licence has lapsed.

◆ R v BOW STREET JUSTICES EX PARTE COMMISSIONER OF THE METROPOLITAN POLICE (1983)

Mr Paul was the licensee of two premises in London. One of them was Tokyo Joe's in Piccadilly. Unfortunately Mr Paul forgot to apply for a renewal of the licence of Tokyo Joe's with the result that the licence expired on the 4 April 1982. Mr Paul continued to run Tokyo Joe's not appreciating that the licence had expired. In May, two police officers visited the premises and at that stage Mr Paul realised what had happened. He immediately applied for a late renewal, but to cover the period up to the next licensing sessions he also applied for an occasional licence for Tokyo Joe's.

The police objected to the occasional licence for Tokyo Joe's on the basis that an occasional licence can only be granted for some 'occasion' i.e. an event or function such as a sports meeting or festival and did not cover the situation here. It was decided on appeal that an occasional licence to cover such a situation could be granted.

Occasional licences are not available on Christmas Day, Good Friday or any other day appointed for public fast or thanksgiving. The time during which drinks may be sold under an occasional licence will be specified in the licence itself.

Occasional permissions

Occasional permissions are not licences under the LA 1964. Instead they are a special variety of permission granted by the licensing justices and governed by the Licensing (Occasional Permissions) Act 1983.

Occasional permissions enable non-profit making organisations to run a bar at a fund raising event without having to get a licensee to run the bar (under an occasional licence). In this way the bar profits can swell the funds raised.

An occasional permission may be granted on the application of an officer of an organisation which is not carried on for private gain, and, if granted, permits the organisation to sell alcoholic drinks for the period specified in the permission, which period cannot be longer than 24 hours. The function for which the permission is wanted must be specified on the application form together with the place where it is to be held, and the permission, when granted, will be for that function and at that place.

An organisation cannot obtain more than four occasional permissions in any period of 12 months, except that each branch of an organisation is treated individually, for example the Round Table Club in one town is a separate organisation from the Round Table Club in another town.

It is the organisation which must not be for private gain but the funds may be raised for a particular beneficiary, for example a person needing a particular operation or to provide a guide dog for a blind person.

An occasional permission can only be granted if the justices are satisfied that the place where the function is to be held is suitable and that the applicant is a fit and proper person.

The permission may be granted on such conditions as the licensing justices think fit including the start and end times. The 1983 Act sets out the various offences which may be committed, for example selling alcoholic drinks to anyone under 18.

PERMITTED HOURS

General licensing hours

The general permitted hours for on-licensed premises are

- Sundays and Good Friday – 12 noon to 10.30pm
- other days – 11am to 11pm

The Sunday afternoon break in the permitted hours was removed by the Licensing (Sunday Hours) Act 1995.

The permitted hours for off-licence premises have already been considered and there are special rules concerning on-licences in vineyards. The hours for the district, whether the permitted hours as above, or as modified are known as the 'general licensing hours'.

In Wales there are special provisions about the sale of alcoholic drinks on Sundays and these are to be found in section 66 LA 1964. The law is that there are no permitted hours on Sundays in any local government district in Wales unless the local electorate have voted in favour of Sunday opening. Most districts in Wales do have Sunday permitted hours but there are a few districts which still are 'dry' on Sundays.

It is an offence to sell or supply alcoholic drinks on licensed premises outside the permitted hours.

Licensing Act 1964 section 59

(1) . . . no person shall, except during the permitted hours

    (a) himself or his servant or agent sell or supply to any person in licensed premises or in premises of which a club is registered any intoxicating liquor whether to be consumed on or off the premises; or

    (b) consume in or take from such premises any intoxicating liquor.

As can be seen, a customer also commits an offence if he or she drinks alcoholic drinks on licensed premises outside the permitted hours. The permitted hours may be modified by the licensing justices for their area for weekdays only (excluding Christmas Day and Good Friday) by an order that the permitted hours commence earlier than 11am but not earlier than 10am.

A licensee is not obliged to keep the premises (or bar) open throughout the permitted hours (section 90 LA 1964). Indeed many public houses close during the afternoon due to lack of demand outside the lunchtime and evening periods and many restaurants are open evenings only. However, if fully on-licensed premises are often closed or keep only very restricted opening hours it may be grounds for non-renewal of the licence on the basis that the licensed premises are not meeting the need in the area, or that there is no need for such premises.

A licensee is not obliged to close premises outside the general licensing hours but must not sell alcoholic liquors. So, a cafe which does not have a supper licence (see later) can remain open after 11pm on weekdays but must not serve any more alcoholic drinks.

There are various exceptions to, and methods of extending the general licensing hours in particular circumstances.

Exceptions to the general licensing hours

The general licensing hours are the hours during which licensees of on-licensed premises in the area may sell alcoholic drinks, but there are various exceptions.

- Both occasional licences and occasional permissions have their own 'permitted hours' which are specified in the licence or permission, and in the case of the latter the period cannot exceed 24 hours.
- Drinks may be served to a resident of premises at any time and the resident may also buy drinks for a friend. So a hotel which has a full on-licence may operate a bar for the public during normal permitted hours and then keep it open for residents outside those hours.
- Other exceptions include supplies to employees at the employer's expense for consumption on the premises.

General orders of exemption

Under section 74(1) LA 1964 the local magistrates can grant a general order of exemption to the licensee of on-licensed premises and the effect of this is to add to the permitted hours for those premises as specified in the order on a continuing basis. Such an order can specify additional hours every day or for certain days of the week, month or whatever.

However, a general order of exemption can only be made if the premises are in the 'immediate neighbourhood' of a public market or some place where people trade or carry on business and the magistrates decide that there is a need for such an order in view of the number of people attending the market or carrying out their trade or business.

◆ **HUNTER V SOUTH WARWICKSHIRE JUSTICES (1992)**

The licensee of a Stratford-upon-Avon hotel applied for a general order of exemption as the hotel was in the immediate area of two theatres employing 475 people. The application was refused due to the inability to predict the need from the theatre staff.

If a general order of exemption is granted, then a notice stating the effect of the order, including the days on which it applies, must be conspicuously displayed on the premises (section 89 LA 1964).

Special orders of exemption (extensions)

Special orders of exemption are similar to general orders of exemption in that they extend the permitted hours but, as their name implies, they are only for 'special occasions' rather than continuous or recurring events. Such orders are generally referred to as extensions.

Under section 74(4) LA 1964, local magistrates can grant a special order of exemption to the licensee of on-licensed premises (including premises with a restaurant licence) which order will add to the permitted hours on a particular day or days as specified in the order for the purpose of a special occasion.

The order is therefore for a specific event or occasion but the event or occasion has to be 'special' and the question whether or not an event is special can often create difficulties. The annual dinner/dance of a local organisation, or the home match of particular significance for the local football team, can be 'special occasions', however, if the licensee organises a dance which is unconnected with any local or national event, that is, just to increase business, or the local publican seeks an order for each Sunday evening after matches the local hockey team is playing, then the event is not special and the frequency of the events means that they cease to be special and therefore will not qualify for special orders of exemption.

◆ PAULSON V OXFORD CITY MAGISTRATES COURT **(1989)**

The Oxford Union held weekly debates finishing at 12.30am and 1.00am. Although such a debate could be a special occasion the fact that they were weekly meant that each occasion was not 'special'. Accordingly an application for eight special orders of exemption was refused.

The magistrates have complete discretion whether or not to grant a special order of exemption but in the case of a private function, for example a private dinner/dance, the magistrates will usually wish to be satisfied that the extension will only benefit that private function and not the public bars.

Supper hour certificate

The licensee of on-licensed premises can apply for a supper hour certificate under section 68 LA 1964 to serve drinks with meals for an extra period after the permitted hours on a continuing basis, that is not just for a particular day.

There are some conditions which have to be satisfied before a supper hour certificate can be granted

- the premises must be used (or, in the case of new premises or business, intended to be used) on a regular basis for serving substantial refreshment
- the premises must be appropriately constructed or adapted for the service of meals and the premises, or a part of them, must normally be exclusively used for table meals, and
- the sale or supply of alcoholic drinks must be ancillary to the meals.

So, in practice, a supper hour certificate can only be granted to a restaurant, or if there is a restaurant or dining area of a hotel, public house etc. A supper hour certificate cannot be granted for bar meals in a public house which are consumed in the bar area.

If granted, a supper hour certificate will add one hour at the end of the permitted hours for the part of the premises used for table meals, that is usually up until midnight.

The holder of a supper hour certificate must display a notice on the premises, in a conspicuous place, stating the effect of the certificate (section 89 LA 1964). A supper hour certificate does not need renewal but it can be surrendered or withdrawn.

Extended hours order

If the premises qualify for the extra hour under a supper hour certificate then it is possible to extend the permitted hours for the premises even longer by having 'live' musical or other entertainment.

In such a case, an extended hours order may be granted which will extend the permitted hours for the premises until 1am the following day. The order operates on a continuing basis, that is not just for one day, but only when the entertainment is provided.

The conditions for the grant of an extended hours order are set out in section 70 LA 1964 and are that

- the premises qualify for a supper hour certificate to extend the permitted hours
- the premises are appropriate for the provision of live musical or other entertainment in addition to substantial refreshment, for example there is a stage
- the premises are genuinely used (or, in the case of new premises or business, intended to be used) for live musical or other entertainment in addition to refreshment
- the sale or supply of alcoholic drinks is ancillary to the refreshment and entertainment, and

- the entertainment is provided regularly each week, not necessarily every day, for at least 50 weeks of the year.

A typical example of premises which would qualify for an extended hours order is a cabaret club where patrons sit at tables, have a meal and watch a variety show, however, a restaurant with a palm court orchestra might qualify.

The effect of the extended hours certificate is to continue the permitted hours while both the refreshment and entertainment is provided, but no later than 1am or an earlier time as specified in the order.

An important condition is that the entertainment must be live (the Act uses the expression 'by persons actually present and performing'), so neither televised entertainment nor recorded music will do.

One important constraint in an extended hours order is that alcoholic drinks must not be served to any person who enters the premises after midnight or less than half an hour before the entertainment is due to end.

The holder of an extended hours order is required to display a notice on the premises in a conspicuous place stating the effect of the notice and the days it operates (unless that is every day). An extended hours order does not need to be renewed.

Special hours certificate

If, in addition to substantial refreshment, there is also music and dancing, then the licensing justices can grant a special hours certificate to extend the permitted hours for the premises, into the early hours of the morning.

The conditions for the grant of a special hours certificate are that

- the premises have an entertainment licence from the local authority
- the premises are appropriate for the provision of music and dancing in addition to substantial refreshment, for example there is an adequate dance floor
- the sale or supply of alcoholic drinks is ancillary to the refreshment and dancing
- the premises are genuinely used (or, in the case of new premises or business, intended to be used) for music and dancing with refreshments, and
- the music and opportunity for dancing must be provided regularly every week for at least 50 weeks of the year, but not necessarily every day of the week.

This type of certificate is appropriate to a nightclub – it is not necessary for there to be table meals but the refreshment which is available must be substantial.

The effect of a special hours certificate is to extend the permitted hours to 2am the following morning (3am in certain parts of central London) except on Sundays, that is into Monday mornings, but a draft deregulation order under the Deregulation and Contracting Out Act 1994 is expected to amend the LA 1964 to allow special hours certificates to permit sale of alcohol on Sunday evenings on the same basis as weekday evenings.

But alcoholic drinks may not be served

- after midnight if the music and dancing ends on or before midnight
- after the music and dancing stops if it stops after midnight.

Even though a public entertainment licence is a prerequisite for a special hours certificate, such a certificate is not limited to public events but can also allow late drinking in a private function with music.

The licensing justices have a very wide discretion whether or not to grant a special hours certificate, they can also impose various conditions on a certificate so as to specify an earlier closing time or limited to certain days of the week or periods of the year.

Where a special hours certificate is in force, a notice must be displayed on the premises stating the effect of the certificate (section 89 LA 1964). Such a certificate does not have to be renewed but the entertainment licence from the local authority must be renewed annually.

Drinking up time

At the end of the permitted hours there is further 'drinking up' time permitted, during which time alcoholic drinks which have been purchased before the end of the permitted hours may be consumed.

There are two drinking up times. The shorter period is 20 minutes and applies in public houses and hotel bars where the drink is not accompanying a meal. There is a longer period of 30 minutes drinking up time for drinks being consumed as ancillary to a meal. So the drinking up time in a restaurant or hotel dining room is 30 minutes for late diners (section 63 LA 1964).

The drinking up time applies at the end of the period when drinks may lawfully be sold on the premises. So, if a restaurant has a supper hour certificate which adds an extra hour in the evening, a customer in such a restaurant will be able to order a drink at any time up to midnight on weekdays and continue to drink it up to half an hour after midnight.

Restriction Orders

Prior to the LA 1988, the permitted hours for full on-licences had a break in the afternoon. The LA 1988 did away with the weekday afternoon break in permitted hours and the Licensing (Sunday Hours) Act 1995 abolished the Sunday afternoon break. However, the justices have power to make orders to apply to particular on-licensed premises to impose a break of up to three hours between the lunchtime and evening hours. Such orders are known as restriction orders and cannot apply to off-licences.

A restriction order may be applied for by a variety of people including local residents and grounds for an application are set out in section 67A(7) LA 1964 (which was inserted by the LA 1988).

Section 67A Licensing Act 1964

(7) A Restriction Order may be made

(a) on the ground that it is desirable to avoid or reduce any disturbance of or annoyance to

(i)   persons living or working in the neighbourhood,
(ii)   customers or clients of any business in the neighbourhood or,
(iii) persons attending, or in charge of persons attending, any educational establishment in the neighbourhood.

due to the use of the premises or part of the premises; or
(b) on the ground that it is desirable to avoid or reduce the occurrence of disorderly conduct in the premises or part of the premises or the occurrence in the vicinity of the premises of disorderly conduct on the part of persons resorting to the premises or part of the premises.

The justices may impose a restriction order for any period but not earlier than 2.30pm and not later than 5.30pm from a specified date for a maximum period of 12 months. The order can specify different days of the week on which it is to be effective or a variety of other conditions.

The effect of the restriction order is to remove from the permitted hours, for the affected premises, the period mentioned in the restriction order.

Where a restriction order has been made, the licensee must display a notice on the premises of the effect of the order on the permitted hours for those premises (section 67D LA 1964).

Licensing procedure

Licensing Justices

The licensing system for the sale or supply of alcoholic drinks is administered on a local basis by the licensing justices who are appointed from the local magistrates. The licensing justices conduct their proceedings in public in the local magistrates' courtroom.

They hold an annual meeting in the first two weeks each February which is often referred to as the 'Brewster Sessions'. They also hold at least four other meetings during the year which are called 'Transfer Sessions'.

Prior to the LA 1988, licences had to be renewed annually and this was done at the annual Brewster Sessions. Since then licences have had a life of three years, all expiring at the same time, and this means that every third Brewster Sessions renewals are considered.

In some restricted cases the local magistrates' court deals with licensing matters, for example applications for special orders of exemption (extensions) are made to the magistrates rather than the licensing justices.

Many of the applications under the LA 1964 require not only notice to the licensing justices but also to the police and sometimes the local fire service.

New licences

The application for any type of justices' licence involves a procedure of giving notice and advertising the application prior to consideration of the application by the justices. In every case a licence can only be granted if the applicant is a 'fit and proper person to hold a licence'. This is a question for the justices to decide, but

- anyone with a previous criminal record may find that they are not considered to be a fit and proper person, however, a conviction which is 'spent' under the Rehabilitation of Offenders Act 1974 (see Chapter 9) will not normally be taken into account
- knowledge of the law as to the conduct of licensed premises would be expected
- previous experience in the licensed trade, not necessarily as a licensee, is usually an advantage.

The justices will usually expect the applicant (or one of them in the case of a joint application) to exercise day-to-day control of the premises and so applications by a head office official or an area manager on his or her own will often not find favour. In addition, in every case, premises must be suitable for the type of licence proposed and usually the justices will wish to see a plan of the premises and might wish to visit the premises. Licences cannot be granted to motorway service areas.

Except in the case of a Part IV licence, the justices will need to be satisfied that there is a need for additional licensed premises. They have a complete discretion whether or not to grant a licence after consideration of the application except in the case of an application for a Part IV licence, when the justices may only refuse to grant a licence on the grounds for refusal set out in section 98 LA 1964. These grounds for refusal of a Part IV licence are

- the applicant is under 18 or is not a fit and proper person
- the premises are unsuitable for the intended use (including the requirement for a dry room)
- that in the past 12 months, an on-licence for the premises has been forfeited, the premises ill-conducted or the conditions for a dry room, and availability of soft drinks with meals have been generally ignored
- in the case of a restaurant licence, that the business carried on is not essentially a restaurant business
- the sale of alcoholic drinks is by self-service
- customers are generally unaccompanied under 18s
- the police, fire officer or local authority have been unable to inspect the premises despite reasonable attempts to do so.

If a Part IV licence is refused, the licensing justices must give written reasons for refusal.

Licence conditions

On the grant of an on-licence, other than a Part IV licence, (or one for the sale of wine only) the justices have a wide discretion to impose conditions.

Section 4 Licensing Act 1964

Subject to the provisions of Part IV of this Act, licensing justices granting a new justices' on-licence other than a licence for the sale of wine alone may attach to it such conditions governing the tenure of the licence and any other matters as they think proper in the interests of the public.

There are also certain conditions which can be imposed at the request of the applicant

- section 64 LA 1964 – no permitted hours during certain periods of the year (a seasonal licence)
- section 65(1)(a) LA 1964 – that Sunday is not included in the permitted hours (a six-day licence)
- section 65(1)(b) LA 1964 – that the permitted hours end an hour earlier in the evenings (early closing licence)
- section 86 LA 1964 – that part of the premises be used for off-sales only, for example public houses having a 'jug and bottle' sales area in which case the permitted hours for off-licences apply to that part of the premises.

The wide powers to impose conditions in section 4 LA 1964 do not apply to Part IV licences. Instead, the conditions which must, or can, be imposed in respect of Part IV licences are set out in section 93 LA 1964. Restaurant licences must have a condition to the effect that alcoholic drinks may only be served to customers having table meals and as ancillary to those meals. For residential licenses there must be a condition that alcoholic drinks can only be sold to residents for consumption by the resident or a friend on the premises, or for consumption with meals eaten off the premises, for example, a packed lunch.

A combined licence is subject to the conditions appropriate to both a restaurant licence and a residential licence. Additionally, in the case of a residential licence (or combined licence), section 96 provides that there has to be a condition on the licence that there must be a 'dry room' that is, a room (other than a bedroom) where no alcohol is served or drunk, for instance, a coffee lounge. This condition can be left off the licence if the licensing justices think that there is a good reason for doing so.

Every Part IV licence is subject to an implied condition that suitable non-alcoholic drinks, including drinking water, must be available with meals.

Provisional licences

As seen, a licence can only be granted once the licensing justices are satisfied that the premises are suitable. But what if the premises need conversion, for example a shop which needs to be converted into a restaurant, or have not even been built, for example a new hotel? An entrepreneur is likely to be reluctant to spend a great deal of money converting or building premises for a particular purpose and then find that he or she cannot use it for that purpose because he or she cannot get a licence.

In such circumstances a provisional licence may be applied for under section 6 LA 1964. Such a licence does not permit the sale of drink but what it does do, is to limit the powers of the licensing justices to refuse an application for the licence when the premises are ready.

> ### Section 6 Licensing Act 1964
>
> *(1) Where licensing justices are satisfied on application made by a person interested in any premises which are*
>
> > *(a) about to be constructed or in the course of construction for the purpose of being used as a house for the sale of intoxicating liquor (whether for consumption on or off the premises); or*
> >
> > *(b) about to be altered or extended or in the course of alteration or extension for that purpose (whether or not they are already used for that purpose)*
>
> *that the premises, if completed in accordance with plans deposited under this Act would be such that they would have granted a justices' on-licence or a justices' off-licence for the premises they may make a provisional grant of such a licence for those premises.*

If the premises are completed as shown on the deposited plans, and provided the justices are satisfied that the applicant is a fit and proper person, then the licence will be made final, that is, no longer provisional and as from that date the premises will be licensed.

Renewal of licences

All justices' licences expire every three years starting from the 4 April 1989, so that the next expiry dates are 4 April 1998, 4 April 2001, etc. The three-year periods are known as licensing periods and applications for renewal of licences must be made at the last annual licensing session of each licensing period.

There is no set procedure for applying for renewal. In some licensing districts the clerk to the licensing justices sends out renewal application forms, but an application in person at the annual licensing session is sufficient. Objection to renewal may be made at the licensing sessions.

For historical reasons the licensing justices have only restricted powers to refuse to renew an on-licence which has been renewed in respect of the same premises without a break continuously since 15 August 1904. The limited grounds for refusal are set out in detail in section 12 LA 1964.

Additionally, there are some licences known as 'old beer house licences' which are licences for the sale only of beer and cider with or without meals, which have been continuously renewed since the 1 May 1869, and there are also only limited grounds on which renewal of such a licence can be refused.

Subject to those two exceptions the licensing justices have a complete discretion as to whether or not to renew a licence, but if there are no objections (including objections by the justices themselves) the licence must be renewed.

If there was some valid reason why a licensee did not apply for renewal at an annual licensing meeting the licensing justices can renew the licence at the next transfer sessions (section 7 LA 1964).

Revocation of licences

Because licences only come up for renewal every three years, there is power for a licence to be revoked by the licensing justices on any ground on which the justices might refuse to renew a licence, and that revocation can be at any licensing sessions during the licensing period. This power is found in section 20A LA 1964 which was inserted into the 1964 Act by the LA 1988.

Transfers

A transfer is the process by which a licence for premises is transferred from the licensee to another person. It usually happens on the sale of the premises or due to the death, ill-health or retirement of the licensee. The circumstances in which a transfer can take place are set out in section 8 LA 1964.

The procedure for a transfer is similar to the application for the grant of a licence but the only issue is whether the incoming licensee is a 'fit and proper person'. The application must be made at any sessions of the licensing justices either at the annual licensing sessions or at any other sessions.

Protection orders

Because there can be quite a wait between licensing sessions (only five must be held every year) and because the need for transfer may arise urgently, there is a procedure for temporary transfers, known as 'protection orders' (section 10 LA 1964).

An application for a protection order is made to the local magistrate's court. Usually seven days notice is required of an application for a protection order so that the police may check the applicant's background.

A protection order can only be granted if the applicant intends to apply for the transfer of the licence into his or her name. The effect of such an order is to licence the incoming licensee on a temporary basis, namely, until the second licensing sessions after it is made, unless it is replaced by a full transfer before then.

Removal of licences

A removal is a process by which a licence for certain premises is transferred from those premises to other premises. A removal is suitable for the situation where the business has outgrown its existing premises and needs to move the business to larger premises but a removal cannot be granted for a Part IV licence. The licensing justices will be concerned to ensure that the new premises are suitable (section 5 LA 1964).

Surrender of licences

There are no provisions in the LA 1964 for the surrender of a justices' licence but the case of *Drury and Samuel Smith Old Brewery (Tadcaster) v Scunthorpe Licensing Justices (1993)*, has established that a licence can be surrendered in two situations

- where the existing licence is subject to a condition which the licensee wants to have removed
- the licensee wants to open new licensed premises and is prepared to offer to surrender the licence of the existing premises.

In both situations the licensing justices can accept the surrender of the existing licence at the time of the grant of the new licence and in the first situation the new licence can omit the condition.

The only other situation in which a licence may be surrendered is if alterations are carried out without the prior approval of the licensing justices.

Alteration of premises

> **Section 20 Licensing Act 1964**
>
> *(1) No alteration shall be made to premises for which a justices' on-licence is in force if the alteration*
>
> > *(a) gives increased facilities for drinking in a public or common part of the premises or*
> > *(b) conceals from observation a public or common part of the premises used for drinking; or*

> *(c) affects the communication between the public part of the premises where intoxicating liquor is sold and the remainder of the premises or any street or other public way;*
>
> *unless the licensing justices have consented to the alteration or the alteration is required by order of some lawful authority.*
> *(3) If subsection (1) of this section is contravened a magistrate's court may by order . . . declare the licence to be forfeited or direct that within a time fixed by the order the premises shall be restored to their original condition.*

What cannot be granted is consent for the alterations after they have been carried out.

◆ R v Croydon Crown Court ex parte Bromley Licensing Justices (1988)

The proprietor of a restaurant in Bromley had an on-licence and he decided to increase the dining area of the restaurant. To do this he had to remove the part then used for the sale of take-away food. No consent under section 20 LA 1964 was requested and instead the work was carried out during the winter months.

In February, the licence came up for renewal but by that time the alterations were almost finished. It then came to light that the alterations had been done without consent.

The proprietor promptly applied for consent under section 20 but the application was refused. The proprietor appealed and it was decided that the consent could not be granted because there was no power under the LA 1964 to grant consent after the alterations had been carried out.

The result of the case was that the licensee either had to restore the premises or surrender the licence and apply for a new licence for the altered premises.

Mention should also be made of section 19 LA 1964 which gives the licensing justices certain powers to order structural alterations to be carried out and section 20 Local Government (Miscellaneous Provisions) Act 1976 which empowers a district council to require the owner or occupier of any place where food or drink is served to the public for consumption on the premises, to provide and/or maintain suitable toilets for customers. These latter powers apply whether or not the premises are licensed.

Conduct of licensed premises

The enforcement of licensing laws and the good conduct of licensed premises is achieved by a mixture of the criminal law and control of licenses by the licensing justices with the ultimate threat that the licence may be revoked or not renewed.

As already seen, the sale and supply of alcoholic drinks outside the permitted hours for the premises is a criminal offence (section 59 LA 1964). A customer commits an offence if he or she is still drinking after drinking up time (section 59 LA 1964) and the licensee can be guilty of an offence of permitting drinking to continue beyond that time.

Various conditions may be imposed on a licence and generally breach of such conditions does not mean that a criminal offence has been committed. Instead, the fact that the licensee has broken a licence condition will be taken into account by the licensing justices when the licence comes up for renewal (or there is an application to revoke the licence). But there are some circumstances in which the breach of a licence condition will be a criminal offence.

Section 161 Licensing Act 1964

(1) If the holder of a justices' on-licence knowingly sells or supplies intoxicating liquor to persons to whom he is not permitted by the conditions of the licence to sell or supply it he shall be guilty of an offence under this section.
(2) If the holder of a Part IV licence knowingly permits intoxicating liquor sold in pursuance of the licence to be consumed on the licensed premises by persons for whose consumption there he is not permitted by the conditions of the licence to sell it he shall be guilty of an offence under this section.

So, if the licence conditions restrict the type of customers to whom alcoholic drink may be served, and that condition is broken, then the licensee commits a criminal offence.

Credit sales

Section 166 LA 1964 makes it a criminal offence to sell or supply alcoholic drinks for consumption on the premises unless paid for at the time of the sale or supply. There are two exceptions. First, if drinks are supplied with a meal, and the total, inclusive of drinks is paid for together, then the sale can be on credit. Second, if the drink is sold or supplied to a resident and is paid for together with the accommodation, then again the total bill may be on credit.

Children prohibited from bars

Children under 14 are prohibited from being in a bar unless a children's certificate is in force. A licensee who permits such a child to be in a bar during the permitted hours without a certificate commits a criminal offence (section 168 LA 1964).

A bar is a place which is only (or mainly) used for the sale and drinking of alcoholic drinks, but not somewhere where only drinks are served to those taking table meals. So, while 13 years-olds are not allowed into a public house they can be in the bar of a restaurant if that bar only serves customers taking meals in the restaurant.

Section 19 of the Deregulation and Contracting Out Act 1994 amended the LA 1964 to allow licensing justices to grant children's certificates if

- the bar is suitable for children under 14
- meals and non-alcoholic drinks are served.

Children under 14 are allowed in a bar when a children's certificate is in force but only if in the company of someone aged at least 18. A children's certificate can be subject to conditions including the time it is operational. A notice must be displayed in the bar stating that a children's certificate is in force and the effect of any conditions. Children's certificates remain in force until revoked.

Sales to (or for) children

It is a criminal offence for a licensee or employee to sell alcoholic drinks to anyone aged under 18 whether for drinking on or off the premises (section 169 LA 1964). It is also an offence to allow an under-18-year-old to drink such drinks in a bar and it is an offence for a person under 18 to buy, or attempt to buy, alcoholic drinks in licensed premises.

To complete the picture, it is also an offence for anyone aged 18 or over to buy drinks in licensed premises, and for a person under 18 to drink in a bar.

The offence of selling alcoholic drinks to someone under 18 is a strict offence, but a licensee has a defence if he or she exercised all due diligence to avoid the offence. If in doubt, evidence (such as a birth certificate) should be requested, or service refused. It is a sensible precaution for licensees to display a notice in the bar stating that sales to persons under 18 are not allowed.

Drinking by a person under 18 is allowed outside the bar area although there is an overall prohibition in the Children and Young Persons Act 1933, which prohibits giving a child under five years of age any alcoholic drink. This latter prohibition applies anywhere (not just on licensed premises) even at home. It is not therefore an offence for a person aged 18 or over to buy a drink in a public house for a person aged 5 to 17 years to drink outside the bar.

Those aged 16 or over can buy beer, porter, cider or perry for drinking with a meal in a restaurant, or in the restaurant part of on-licensed premises other than in a bar.

Employees under 18 in bars

A licensee commits a criminal offence if he or she employs a person under 18 in a bar at a time when it is open. 'Bar' means a place which is only (or mainly) used for selling and drinking alcoholic drinks, except a bar serving only diners who are taking table meals. Therefore, while it is an offence to have an under-age barman or barmaid in a public house or in a hotel bar, it is not an offence to have an under-age waiter or waitress in a licensed restaurant.

Drunkenness and disorderly behaviour

Section 172 Licensing Act 1964

(1) The holder of a justices' licence shall not permit drunkenness or any violent, quarrelsome or riotous conduct to take place in the licensed premises.
(2) If the holder of a justices' licence is charged under subsection (1) of this section with permitting drunkenness and it is proved that any person was drunk in the licensed premises the burden of proving that the licence holder and the persons employed by him took all reasonable steps for preventing drunkenness in the premises shall lie upon him.
(3) The holder of a justices' licence shall not sell intoxicating liquor to a drunken person.

The offence of selling drink to a drunk is an absolute offence, that is, there is no need for the prosecution to prove any blame in the sense that the bar staff knew that the customer was drunk. There is a separate offence committed under section 173 which is committed by a sober (not drunk) customer who buys a drink for someone who is drunk.

Excluding people from licensed premises

A licensee is entitled to refuse anyone admission to the licensed premises and is also entitled to require someone to leave. A person who enters (or refuses to leave) despite such a request does not commit a criminal offence but can be sued in the tort of trespass.

There are certain circumstances where it may be a criminal offence to be on licensed premises despite being told not to be there. These circumstances are to be found in section 174 LA 1964 which entitles a licensee to refuse admission to, or eject, anyone who is drunk, violent, quarrelsome or disorderly or whose presence in the licensed premises would involve the licence holder in criminal liability. If the person concerned fails to leave the premises when requested to do so, then that person commits a criminal offence.

There is also a separate Act of Parliament – the Licensed Premises (Exclusion of Certain Persons) Act 1980 – which allows a court when dealing with a person convicted of violence in on-licensed premises, to impose on the convicted person, an exclusion order (in addition to any other penalty) which order prohibits for a period, not exceeding two years, that person entering certain specified licensed premises.

◆ R v Grady (1990)

In addition to a six months' suspended sentence, a one year exclusion order was imposed on a 31-year-old woman who pushed and punched the landlady of a public house after an argument while she was with a party drinking in the public house.

The effect of an exclusion order is that it is a criminal offence for that person to enter those premises within that period without the licensee's consent. If an on-licensee believes that a person on his or her premises is there in breach of an exclusion order, he or she can evict him or her and the police, if they are of the same belief, must assist him or her to remove that person from the premises.

Prostitutes on licensed premises

There are two specific offences relating to prostitutes under the LA 1964. Under section 175 it is an offence for a licensee to allow the licensed premises to be used as a 'habitual resort or place of meeting of reputed prostitutes'.

Section 176 provides that it is an offence for a licensee to allow licensed premises to be used as a brothel.

Gaming on licensed premises

As seen in Chapter 4, gaming is considered to be an activity which should be controlled. There are many forms of gaming and much of it is harmless, such as gaming amusements at charitable fêtes.

Dominoes and cribbage may be played in any on-licensed premises (other than premises with a Part IV licence) and any other non-banker games authorised for particular premises by the licensing justices (section 6 Gaming Act 1968) subject to such restrictions as the licensing justices may impose.

The Gaming Board has issued an advisory memorandum as to the operation of section 6. The overall policy should be that gaming in public houses must be ancillary entertainment for those attending rather than the principal reason for being on the premises.

Games of pure skill do not come within the definition of gaming so that darts, chess, bar billiards and skittles do not need a permit under the Gaming Act 1968.

Gaming machines are subject to control under Part 3 of the Gaming Act 1968 and a permit under that Act is necessary. The number of machines on any premises will be limited by the permit and usually the limitation is two machines per premises.

Police on licensed premises

A licensee commits an offence if he or she allows a police constable on duty to remain on licensed premises if he or she is not there on police business. A licensee also commits an offence if he or she serves drink to a police constable on duty (section 178 LA 1964).

A licensee is obliged to produce his or her licence on demand by a police officer (section 185 LA 1964) and the police also have rights to enter licensed premises, in particular to make sure the licensing laws are being observed (section 186 LA 1964).

Forfeiture of licences

Licences may be forfeited (terminated automatically) in certain circumstances. These include if a licensee is convicted on a second occasion within five years of selling drinks without a licence, for example from premises not covered by a licence or by an occasional licence and, as already seen, if a licensee makes alterations to the premises in breach of section 20 LA 1964 (which includes enlarging the drinking area without consent). If a licensee is convicted of permitting the licensed premises to be used as a brothel the licence is forfeited.

Section 9(3) LA 1964 provides that if a licensee has his or her licence forfeited, and within two years thereafter another licensee of the same premises also has his licence forfeited, then the premises are disqualified from being licensed for one year after the second forfeiture.

Clubs

There are two types of clubs so far as licensing laws for alcoholic drinks are concerned

- members' clubs
- proprietary clubs.

The difference between them is who owns/controls the club. In the case of members' clubs the members themselves run the club under a constitution which provides that members have equal voting rights and are eligible for election to the various offices within the club. Typically these are sports, social or community clubs.

A proprietary club is one owned and run by someone. Sometimes, the difference is blurred, for instance, a company may have a sports and social club for its employees and there may be a committee, but the company will probably control various aspects of the running of the club including who can be members, or who can be on the committee, and hence it will be a proprietary club and not a members' club.

There are different licensing provisions for both types of clubs.

Registered clubs

A members' club can be registered under section 40 LA 1964, in which case it does not need a separate justices' licence to serve members with drinks.

There are various conditions which must be satisfied before a registration certificate can be issued (section 41 LA 1964)

- there must be at least 25 members
- the club rules must provide for two days before a person nominated for membership may be entitled to the privileges of membership (including using the bar)

- the constitution of the club must satisfy Schedule 7 LA 1964
- the purchase of alcoholic drinks by the club must be either by the club as a whole or by an elected committee of members
- no person must receive any commission for club purchases of drinks.

Provided the various conditions are satisfied and the club has suitable club premises, then the club may apply for a registration certificate. Once a registration certificate has been issued, the club may operate a bar in its premises but

- only members may purchase drinks unless the club rules/constitution incorporates a provision under section 49 LA 1964 which allows guests to purchase drinks
- off-sales may only be made to members personally.

Many of the provisions relating to licensed premises apply also to registered clubs including as to the permitted hours.

Application for a club registration certificate is made to the magistrates and the first registration certificate is for one year but may be renewed for a further one year, and thereafter can be renewed for up to ten years at a time.

Alterations of the club's rules must be notified to the police and local authority.

Proprietary clubs

Proprietary clubs may be licensed by means of a licence under section 55 LA 1964. There will usually be conditions either prohibiting or placing restrictions on the sale of alcoholic drinks to non-members.

To all other intents and purposes, a proprietary club licensed under section 55 is in no different position to any other licensed premises.

◆ SELF EXAMINATION QUESTIONS ◆

---

1 John and Marie own and run a small hotel in a tourist area used by families with children. The hotel has a residential licence. There is a dining room and bar both for residents. John and Marie wish to turn the dining room into a restaurant for both residents and non-residents and to make the bar into a family room with bar snacks and hot and cold non-alcoholic drinks. Consider the licensing implications of such changes.

2 Cecil is the proprietor of the Bon Appetit bar/restaurant. Lunch time and early evening the trade is mainly from local office workers who often only want a drink and a chat. Evening trade is mainly theatre goers having a meal. Cecil has

a full on-licence for the premises and finds he needs to expand and provide adequate facilities for both types of customer. He acquires the next door premises and starts alterations to knock the two premises into one. When the alterations are nearly finished he applies for a licence for the next door premises.

Consider what problems arise, how they could have been avoided and how to overcome those problems now.

3 Margaret has a full on-licence for her busy hotel. She receives enquiries from

- Mr and Mrs Jones who want to hold their daughter's wedding reception one Saturday afternoon at the hotel with champagne when guests arrive and wine during the meal.
- The local twinning association wishing to have a cash bar at a disco to be held at the local village hall one evening for visitors from the twin town.
- The local rotary club wanting to hold their annual President's Night dinner dance at the hotel with the bar open until 12.30am.

Consider what, if any, special licensing arrangement Margaret needs to comply with those enquiries.

See Appendix for suggested answers.

Chapter

STAFF

Who are employees?

This Chapter is all about staff employed in an hotel or catering business. Sometimes the relevant law applies not only to employees, but also to other workers for example self-employed or casual staff. The discrimination laws (both sex and race discrimination) cover more than employees. Similarly the Health and Safety at Work etc. Act 1974 imposes duties to persons other than employees. Another area where employment law is widened out to include workers generally, in particular self-employed, is the Wages Act 1986.

Apart from those this Chapter is restricted to considering the employment relationship and matters arising from that relationship. But who are employees? That may sound a simple question. The classic example is the difference between a chauffeur (an employee) and a taxi driver (an independent contractor). The distinction in that example is obvious, but why? The answer is that the distinction lies in the contract, whether written or oral, and the test is whether it is a contract of employment or a contract for a specific service.

There are no hard and fast rules to answer that question. Both types of contract will have an employer and a worker with the former providing work and the latter doing it. To decide if the worker is an employee the courts will look to see who controls the work, who takes the financial risks and benefits, whether the worker provides his or her own tools and materials and how far the worker is integrated into the business.

Sometimes the distinction between an employee and an independent contractor is difficult to see.

◆ O'Kelly and Others v Trust House Forte plc (1983)

Trust House Forte ran a banqueting business at the Grosvenor House Hotel. Because of the nature of this business, especially its seasonal nature, there were only 34 permanent staff. In addition there were some 300 to 400 casual staff of whom 104 were 'regular casual staff'. The regular casual staff were 44 wine butlers and 60 food waiters and waitresses. These regular casual staff could expect to be called on first for a function and were expected to attend. To the customer the casual staff were indistinguishable from the permanent staff because all were supplied with uniforms by Trust House Forte. The casual staff were only required to work when there were functions in the banqueting rooms but for the regular casual workers this meant almost full-time employment during the season and many had no other jobs. The work was rostered on a weekly basis. The regular casual workers were paid each Thursday the same as the weekly paid permanent staff and Tax and National Insurance Contributions were deducted. They also received holiday pay. All casual staff worked under the direct supervision and control of the head waiters or head barmen.

Some of the regular casual staff felt they should be classified as permanent staff and pressed, through their union, for that status to be recognised. They were dismissed. They complained to an Industrial Tribunal that they had been unfairly dismissed but as unfair dismissal can only be claimed by a dismissed employee the first question to be decided was whether the dismissed regular casual staff had been employees. The Industrial Tribunal decided that they were not, on the basis of the whole relationship including that if there was no work available, the casual staff were not given any work and not paid.

Because a self-employed contractor will not be entitled to protection under the employment legislation, the tribunals and courts will tend to favour a finding that a person is an employee in a borderline case.

APPOINTMENT

Children

There are restrictions on employment of children, that is those who have not attained 16 years of age. Generally there is an absolute bar on the employment of a child until he or she is 13 years old. Thereafter until the age of 16 there are restrictions on the hours which may be worked by a child. These vary according to the days worked

- school days – the child may only be employed for a maximum of 2 hours per day but not before 7am, during school hours or after 7pm
- Sundays – the child may not be employed before 7am or after 7pm and not more than two hours in total
- other days (i.e. school holidays and Saturdays) – the child may not be employed before 7am and not after 7pm.

Previous criminal convictions

Central to the operation of the Rehabilitation of Offenders Act 1974 is the concept that after a period of time criminal convictions become 'spent'. The length of time is known as the rehabilitation period and the length of that period depends on the sentence imposed on the convicted person. Rehabilitation periods range from six months up to ten years.

Sentences for life or for a period exceeding 30 months can never be treated as being spent.

Once a conviction is spent then (unless applying for certain jobs not relevant here) the rehabilitated person does not have to disclose such conviction either on a job application form or in response to a question at interview.

If an applicant for a job does not reveal a spent conviction, and is employed, but the employer subsequently finds out about the previous conviction, it is not a valid reason to dismiss the employee.

A person who has previously been the proprietor or manager of a food business may have been convicted of offences under Food Hygiene or Food Processing Regulations and if so, that person may be the subject of a Prohibition Order under section 11 Food Safety Act 1990. In that case, he or she should not be employed in any managerial position within a food business covered by the Prohibition Order until the Order has been lifted. An employer who takes on a person knowing that the new job will be in breach of a Prohibition Order commits a criminal offence.

Disabled persons

At present there are two sets of provisions about disabled people. Disabled persons may be registered as such under the Disabled Persons (Employment) Act 1944 and certain jobs are reserved for registered disabled persons. The jobs are as a car park attendant and as a passenger lift operator and it is unlawful to employ a person who is not registered disabled for such a job without a permit. A permit will usually only be granted if an unsuccessful attempt to employ a disabled person has first been made.

The second provision is the quota system. This system affects every employer with at least 20 employees. Each such employer is required to ensure that at least 3 per cent of the workforce are registered disabled persons. There is again a permit system for an employer who is unable to fill his quota.

The Disability Discrimination Act 1995 will come into effect in late 1996 and will then replace the above provisions with new disability discrimination laws similar to race and sex discrimination laws.

Work permits

Nationals of EU member states do not need work permits to take up jobs in the UK (Article 48 EC Treaty and EC Regulation 1612/68).

Nationals of other countries (subject to certain exceptions, in particular for certain Commonwealth countries) must have a work permit before they can be employed in the UK. Work permits are only granted to certain categories of workers. These categories include skilled and experienced workers for senior posts in hotel and catering work who have had a minimum of two years training abroad and key workers with a scarce qualification.

Contract of employment

The relationship between the employer and employee is contractual, that is the employer agrees to employ the employee, and the employee agrees to work for the employer. The contract can be written, oral, or a mixture of the two.

There are some terms and conditions of all contracts which are implied.

- The common law implies some basic terms which are necessary for the employer/employee relationship. These include duties by the employee to be honest, obedient and work competently and a general duty by the employer to be reasonably considerate to the employee, but the extent of the employer's duty is still evolving through court decisions.
- The Equal Pay Act 1970 implies an equality clause in every contract of employment where there is not one. An equality clause is a clause whereby a woman is to be treated equally with any man in the same employment or doing work of equal value and vice versa.

There are numerous situations where legislation prevents the parties to a contract of employment agreeing that statutory rights and duties do not apply. The main example of this is section 140 Employment Protection (Consolidation) Act 1978 (EP(C)A 1978) which prevents (subject to limited exceptions) an employer and employee agreeing that the unfair dismissal provisions of the 1978 Act will not apply.

Written particulars of employment

Although the contract of employment itself does not have to be in writing, every employer (subject to certain very limited exceptions) must give each employee a written statement containing certain particulars of the employment. This right is created by section 1 EP(C)A 1978). A new section 1 was inserted into that Act by the Trade Union Reform and Employment Rights Act 1993.

Section 1 Employment Protection (Consolidation) Act 1978

(1) Not later than two months after the beginning of an employee's employment with an employer, the employer shall give to the employee a written statement which may, subject to subsection (3) of section 2,

be given in instalments before the end of that period.
(2) The statement shall contain particulars of

   (a) the names of the employer and employee;
   (b) the date when the employment began; and
   *(c) the date on which the employee's period of continuous
employment began (taking into account any employment
with a previous employer which counts towards that period).*

*(3) The statement shall also contain particulars, as at a specified
date not more than seven days before the statement or instalment of
the statement containing them is given of*

   *(a) the scale or rate of remuneration or the method of calculating
remuneration;*
   *(b) the intervals at which remuneration is paid (that is, weekly,
monthly or other specified intervals);*
   *(c) any terms and conditions relating to hours of work
(including any terms and conditions relating to normal
working hours);*
   (d) any terms and conditions relating to any of the following –
     *(i) entitlement to holidays, including public holidays, and
holiday pay (the particulars given being sufficient to enable
the employee's entitlement, including any entitlement to
accrued holiday pay on the termination of employment, to be
precisely calculated).*
     *(ii) incapacity for work due to sickness or injury, including
any provision for sick pay, and*
     (iii) pensions and pension schemes;
   *(e) the length of notice which the employee is obliged to give and
entitled to receive to terminate his contract of employment;*
   *(f) the title of the job which the employee is employed to do or a
brief description of the work for which the employee is employed;*
   *(g) where the employment is not intended to be permanent, the
period for which it is expected to continue or, if it is for a
fixed term, the date when it is to end;*
   *(h) either the place of work or, where the employee is required or
permitted to work at various places, an indication of that
and of the address of the employer;*
   (i) any collective agreements which directly affect the terms

> *and conditions of the employment including, where the*
> *employer is not a party, the persons by whom they were made;*
> *and*
> (k) *where the employee is required to work outside the United*
> *Kingdom for a period of more than one month*
> (i) *the period for which he is to work outside the United*
> *Kingdom,*
> (ii) *the currency in which remuneration is to be paid while*
> *he is working outside the United Kingdom,*
> (iii) *any additional remuneration payable to him, and any*
> *benefits to be provided to or in respect of him, by reason of his*
> *being required to work outside the United Kingdom, and*
> (iv) *any terms and conditions relating to his return to the*
> *United Kingdom.*

The statement will also have to include either details of the employer's disciplinary rules (including appeals procedures) and of any grievance procedure or information as to where such details can be read or obtained by the employee. The written statement must be given to each employee within two months of the start of the employment.

It is not a criminal offence to fail to give the written particulars within the two months, but the following must be noted.

• An employee who is not supplied with written particulars may complain to an industrial tribunal.
• The tribunal can say what the particulars are which ought to have been given. This does not mean that the tribunal can invent the particulars, but only that the tribunal must try and decide what the parties have agreed and then say what those particulars are. The difficulty arises if the parties did not agree anything at all on a particular matter, for example if nothing was written or said about holidays. In those circumstances the tribunal might have to invent something on the basis of what they think is normal.

There are certain other points to be noted about this requirement to give written particulars

• where there are no particulars relating to any of the items specified in section 1 then the written particulars should say so, for example if there is no sickness pay scheme, then the written particulars should state that fact
• no written particulars of disciplinary procedures need to be given if, when

the employee commenced employment, there were less than 20 employees including him or herself
- the statement should also say whether or not there is a contracting-out certificate for pension contributions.

Pay

Wages councils

For many years the hotel and catering industry was affected by Wages Councils namely

- – the Licensed Non-residential Establishment Wages Council (public houses etc.)
- the Licensed Residential Establishment and Licensed Restaurant Wages Council (licensed hotels, restaurants etc.)
- the Unlicensed Places of Refreshment Wages Council (unlicensed restaurants etc.).

Wages Councils made orders fixing

- minimum rates of pay
- overtime rates
- maximum amounts which could be deducted for living accommodation.

Wages Councils have now been abolished (section 35 Trade Union Reform and Employment Rights Act 1993). Consequently there are no statutory minimum rates of pay for catering staff.

Reduction of and deductions from pay

In certain circumstances an employer may be entitled to pay less than would otherwise be the case. First, if an employee is on strike, the employer does not have to pay the employee at all. The rule is 'no work, no pay'.

But what if the employee is working but not as he or she should, for instance, a work to rule or a go slow? In those circumstances it may depend on how the employer reacts to the situation.

◆ **Wiluszynski v London Borough of Tower Hamlets (1988)**

As part of a campaign of industrial action, the employee, who was a housing officer in the local authority, refused to answer councillors' enquiries although he carried out the remainder of his duties normally. The employee was notified in writing by his employer that the employer was not prepared to accept only partial performance of the duties, and that unless he worked normally he would receive no pay. The employee sued for his wages but failed.

◆ **MILES V WAKEFIELD METROPOLITAN DISTRICT COUNCIL (1985)**

A registrar of births, deaths and marriages refused to perform marriages on Saturday mornings. This represented 3 hours out of his total working week of 37 hours. He performed his other duties on Saturday morning. The employer reduced his pay by 3/37 and the House of Lords decided that they were entitled to do so.

So, in the case of a work to rule/go slow the employer will be entitled either, to notify the employee that it is all or nothing and refuse to pay him or her anything if he or she fails to carry out all duties, or reduce the pay by a fair proportion.

An employee can only be suspended on less than full pay if the contract of employment gives the employer such a power. Such a suspension may be used as a short disciplinary measure in appropriate circumstances.

Deductions from wages come in many guises. Examples are PAYE, employees' National Insurance Contributions and Superannuation/Pension contributions. Other deductions are covered by the Wages Act 1986 (WA 1986).

Wages Act 1986 section 1

(1) An employer shall not make any deduction from any wages of any worker employed by him unless the deduction satisfies one of the following conditions, namely

(a) it is required or authorised to be made by virtue of any statutory provision or any relevant provision of the worker's contract; or

(b) the worker has previously signified in writing his agreement or consent to the making of it.

The definition of 'worker' is given in section 8 WA 1986 and is wide enough to include certain self-employed persons.

There are special rules about deductions from wages of workers in retail employment which are in section 2 WA 1986. Subject to the employer having the power to make deductions from wages (that is section 1 is satisfied) then if the worker is employed in the sale of goods or supply of services directly to members of the public, for example bar staff, the employer may not deduct from the worker's wages any amount for cash shortages or stock deficiencies of more than 10 per cent of the worker's gross wages on any one pay day. If the 10 per cent is not sufficient to cover the shortage or deficiency then a deduction may be made the next pay day, but again limited to 10 per cent of the gross wages and so on until the total is recovered.

It must be emphasised that section 2 is supplementary to section 1 so that no deduction at all may be made unless either provided for in the contract of employment or the employee has agreed to the deduction. The restriction to 10 per cent of the gross wage does not apply to the employee's final wages, that is, when the employee is leaving that employment.

Section 1 WA 1986 applies to 'any deduction' from 'any wages'. In fact 'any deduction' includes a complete non-payment and the expression 'any wages' is wide enough to include a whole host of payments including bonuses, holiday pay, commission and statutory sick and maternity pay. The WA 1986 does not apply to expenses, pensions, redundancy pay or pay in lieu of notice.

A breach of the WA 1986 is not a criminal offence. The aggrieved worker may complain to an industrial tribunal within three months of the date of the unlawful deduction, and, if the tribunal decides that the deduction was in breach of the WA 1986 it will order the employer to pay the amount unlawfully deducted, to the worker.

Payslips

An employer is obliged to give each employee each pay day, an itemised pay statement usually referred to as a payslip – (section 8 EP(C)A 1978). Payslips must set out the following

- the gross amount of the pay
- the amount of all deductions and what they are for, for example tax, superannuation, union dues etc.
- the net amount paid.

Where there are fixed deductions, then, to save setting them out each time, for example Christmas club contributions or union subscriptions, it is possible for the employer to give the employee a statement of the fixed deductions, and if he or she does this, then the payslip does not have to repeat all of the fixed deductions each time, but can show them as a total figure. Such a statement of fixed deductions only holds good for 12 months, and then needs to be renewed.

Failure to supply a written payslip, when one should be supplied, is not a criminal offence but enables the employee to make a complaint to an industrial tribunal.

Sick pay

Statutory Sick Pay (SSP) is the minimum level of pay which an employer must pay to any employee who is off work due to illness. SSP is not payable to any employee who

- earns insufficient to pay National Insurance Contributions
- is aged over 65
- is getting statutory maternity pay.

The period of illness must be for at least four consecutive days (whether or not work days) but SSP is not payable for the first three days off work. Thereafter SSP is payable until the employee is no longer away ill but subject to a maximum period of 28 weeks.

If there are intermittent spells of sickness each of at least four days but separated by eight weeks or less the periods may be linked together so that for the second and subsequent periods the employee does not have to wait three days before getting any SSP, but the 28 week maximum is calculated by adding the periods together.

There are two rates of SSP, a higher and a lower rate depending on earnings. These rates are reviewed every year, but the Government has announced that it intends to abolish the lower rate of SSP.

Many employers operate their own sick pay schemes, such schemes must not pay less than SSP.

Unlike Statutory Maternity Pay, employers cannot claim back from Government funds any SSP paid to employees unless the total amount of SSP paid in a tax month exceeds 13 per cent of the total employers and employees National Insurance contributions paid in the same tax month, in which case the SSP paid in excess of 13 per cent of the National Insurance contributions can be recovered by deduction from the National Insurance contributions paid to the Inland Revenue.

Accordingly every employer has to bear all the cost of SSP up to 13 per cent of the total National Insurance bill of the business but after that the Government bears the cost. In this way employers have a safety net should their business be hit by unusually high sickness costs, e.g. because of an epidemic or an accident affecting a number of employees.

For an employer there are various forms to be completed (including for staff who leave) and records to be kept.

An employer may require an employee who is unable to work due to illness, to obtain a medical certificate, but only after seven days of illness. Prior to the eighth day it is usual to require employees to complete a self-certification form to confirm that they are incapacitated for work.

The law on SSP is to be found in the Social Security Contributions and Benefits Act 1992 as amended by the Statutory Sick Pay Act 1994 and various Regulations made under those Acts in particular the Statutory Sick Pay Percentage Threshold Order 1995.

Maternity pay

Statutory Maternity Pay (SMP) is a payment calculated on a weekly basis made by employers to women employees absent from work due to pregnancy. An employee qualifies for SMP if

- she was employed by the employer for at least 26 weeks prior to week 15 before the week the baby is due
- she earned enough to pay National Insurance Contributions
- she ceased working because of the pregnancy
- she gave notice of her intention to stop working to have a baby and gave the employer a maternity certificate.

SMP is payable for the maternity pay period, which is a maximum period of 18 weeks starting not earlier than the 11 weeks before the baby is due and not later than when the baby is born. SMP does not depend on the woman intending to return to work after having had her baby.

SMP is payable at the same time as the employee would otherwise have been paid. The amount is reviewed each year and is 90 per cent of the employee's average weekly earnings for the first six weeks of the maternity pay period, and then at a weekly rate equivalent to the higher rate of SSP.

The employer is able to recoup 92 per cent of SMP paid to an employee by deducting the amounts from the monthly National Insurance Contributions paid to the Inland Revenue. For small employers (defined in the same way as for SSP) the recoupment rate is 104 per cent, the extra 4 per cent representing the employer's National Insurance contributions on SMP.

The provisions concerning SMP are to be found mainly in the Social Security Contributions and Benefits Act 1992 and regulations made under that Act.

Tips

The hotel and catering industry is one of the service industries where tips are normally given and quite often expected. Tips are not wages for the purpose of being detailed on a payslip.

The tax treatment of tips is somewhat complex. The rules are to be found in the Income Tax (Employments) Regulations 1993 and can be summarised as follows.

- If the employer levies a service charge (in lieu of tips) the service charge belongs to the employer and there is no obligation to pay it to the employee. If all or part of the service charge is divided among the staff, it is liable to income tax and the employer must deduct PAYE.
- Non-cash tips such as additions to a cheque or credit card voucher also belong to the employer (*Nerva and others v R L & G Ltd 1994*). If the amount added is paid out to the staff it is treated as additional pay (in exactly the same way as a service charge divided up among staff) and the employer must deduct PAYE.
- If tips are given to individual employees directly by customers and retained by such staff, then the staff are liable to declare such tips to the tax authorities and will be liable to tax on them.
- If tips given to staff are handed to the employer to operate a pool, then the employer must deduct PAYE when the tips are shared out among the staff.
- If tips are pooled between the staff themselves (an arrangement known as a 'tronc') then the person who organises the tronc (known as the 'tronc master') is responsible for deducting PAYE from the distribution of tips including his or her own share, and must account to the Inland Revenue for the tax so deducted. (Regulation 5 of the Income Tax (Employments) Regulations 1993). When a tronc system comes into operation the employer should notify the Inland Revenue together with the name of the tronc master.

Sometimes it is difficult to tell whether or not a tronc is in operation.

◆ FIGAEL V FOX (INSPECTOR OF TAXES) (1990)

A system was in operation in a restaurant owned by a company whereby the tips were pooled each day and then at the end of each week the director of the company who was in charge of the running of that restaurant divided the tips up among all of the staff. No tax was deducted and no records kept of the amounts involved.

The Inland Revenue assessed the company to £32,000 uncollected PAYE. The company contended that it was not responsible for the tax because there was a tronc in existence, in other words, the company alleged that its director who had divided up the money was the tronc master and it was he who was responsible for payment of the tax and not the company.

The decision was that the company (through the director) was sharing out the tips to the employees and the company was therefore liable to pay the PAYE.

Equal pay

The legislation on equal pay is unsatisfactorily divided. The UK legislation is principally the Equal Pay Act 1970 (EqPA 1970) as subsequently amended. In addition there is Article 119 of the Treaty of Rome.

EC Treaty Article 119

Each member state shall ensure the application of the principle that men and women should receive equal pay for equal work. For the purpose of this Article 'pay' means the ordinary, basic or minimum wage or salary and any other consideration whether in cash or in kind which the worker receives directly or indirectly in respect of his employment from his employer.

As already seen (in Chapter 1), Article 119 has direct effect and can therefore be relied on by individuals in their national courts (*Defrenne v Sabena 1976*).

The EqPA 1970 is designed to eliminate discrimination as between men and women as to the terms and conditions of their contract of employment. The EqPA 1970 is *not* concerned merely with equality of pay but also with equal treatment as regards other employment conditions, for example holidays and working hours. The Act gives male workers the same rights as female workers and therefore references in the remainder of this section to 'equal pay' and 'women' should accordingly be read as references to equal terms and conditions, and as equally applicable to men.

What the EqPA 1970 does is to insert into every woman's contract of employment an 'equality clause'. The clause operates where a woman does work which is

- the same work or broadly similar work to that done by a man (referred to as 'like work')
- different from that done by a man but which either has been rated as equivalent under a proper job evaluation scheme, or is of equal value in terms of the demands of the job.

Where the equality clause operates, the woman is entitled to be paid the same as the man and her contract of employment is treated as amended accordingly. Similarly where the equality clause operates, if a woman has longer paid holidays, the man will be entitled to equivalent paid holidays. It is, however, necessary to use as a comparator, a person of the opposite sex, so that a woman cannot claim equal pay with another woman.

The key to the operation of the EqPA 1970 is the circumstances in which the equality clause applies. This is in three circumstances.

- Like work – under this heading, the work of the man and woman has to be the same for example waiter and waitress or broadly similar work and any differences being of no practical importance. In one case a woman cook who prepared lunches for the directors was able to claim her work was like work with male chefs who cooked meals and snacks for employees eating in the works canteen.
- Work evaluated as equivalent – this only applies where an objective job evaluation exercise has been carried out, which has rated the woman's job as equivalent to a man's in which case the woman can claim pay equal to the man.
- Equal value – this section was added into the EqPA 1970 by the Equal Pay (Amendment) Regulations 1983 and it applies where the woman's job is neither 'like work' nor been rated as equivalent, but it is of equal value in terms of the demands of the job, for instance, in relation to the effort, skill and decision making within the job. Under this heading a female cook employed in a canteen was able to claim equal pay with a joiner, a painter and an insulation engineer.

A woman may choose as a comparator any male employee of the same employer, either at the same workplace as herself, or at any of the other establishments run by the same employer. This means that a woman employed at one hotel may claim parity with a man employed at another hotel operated by the same company, or indeed another company within the same group of companies.

Even though a woman may be employed on like work, or work evaluated as equivalent, or work of equal value with that of a male employee who is paid more (or has more beneficial terms and conditions of employment) her claim for parity will not succeed if the difference is genuinely due to a material factor other than the difference of sex. For instance, the difference may be due to experience or qualification of one employee over another, or the difference may be because of the different place or circumstance in which the work is performed, for example, if the male comparator works at night and the female during the day or the male is given a London weighting but the female works outside the area qualifying for that weighting, then there may be a genuine material factor resulting in the equality clause not creating parity.

Claims for equal pay under the EqPA 1970 are made to an industrial tribunal and special procedures operate for such claims because of their complicated nature. If the claim succeeds, the woman will be entitled to the same pay (or conditions) as the man in the future, and up to two years arrears of pay (or cash value of equivalent conditions).

The other legislation on equal pay is Article 119 EC Treaty which applies only to 'pay', but pay is widely defined. If the EqPA 1970 does not provide a remedy then the aggrieved person can rely on Article 119. This has happened in a number of cases concerning pensions because pensions fall within the definition of pay under Article 119 but the EqPA 1970 does not apply to terms and conditions relating to death or retirement.

During employment

Vicarious liability

An employer is liable to a third party for the torts (usually negligence) of his or her employees in the course of their employment. This is known as 'vicarious liability'.

An example is a van driver who injures someone by careless driving – the injured person will be able to sue the van driver's employer.

But if the employee goes outside the scope of his or her duties on some activity of his or her own then the employer will not be liable. For example, a night club 'bouncer' who assaults a customer out of personal animosity is not acting in the course of the employment and the employer will not be liable for the customer's injuries.

Vicarious liability is limited to the actions of employees and does not extend to independent contractors.

Additionally there is a statutory version of vicarious liability under section 32 of the Race Relations Act 1976 and section 41 of the Sex Discrimination Act 1975. The effect is that anything done by an employee during employment which would be unlawful discrimination if done by the employer will be treated as done by the employer. For instance a supervisor who detrimentally treats an employee because of that employee's gender or race will cause the employer to be in breach of the relevant anti-discrimination law. An employer who has taken reasonably practicable steps to prevent the employee doing what he or she did has a defence.

Holidays

There is no law giving a right to holidays, paid holidays, or pay in lieu of holidays and accordingly, this is a matter entirely for the contract of employment.

The contractual provisions as to holidays should be detailed in the written statement given to the employee under section 1 EP(C)A 1978. A woman (or man) who has less holiday entitlement than a comparable employee of the opposite sex may be able to claim equal holiday entitlement under the EqPA 1970.

The law concerning holidays and holiday pay may change when (and if) the European Directive on Working Time (93/104/EC) is implemented (see later).

Sickness

Staff who are engaged in handling food must notify the proprietor of the business immediately the employee becomes aware that he or she is suffering from, or is a carrier of, certain infectious diseases. The proprietor must then remove such staff from the food handling area.

The Access to Medical Reports Act 1988 gives employees certain rights to see and vet medical reports which are supplied for employment purposes.

Maternity rights

There are three rights of pregnant employees which will be considered here. First, the right to time off for ante-natal care, second, the right to maternity leave and third the right to return to work after childbirth. Maternity pay has already been considered and the right not to be dismissed as a result of pregnancy is looked at later.

A pregnant employee is entitled to paid time off to attend an antenatal clinic appointment, but the employee must be able to produce (except for the first appointment) a certificate of pregnancy and an appointment card.

For part-time employees the right is restricted to those appointments which cannot be arranged outside the employee's working hours.

The statutory right to maternity leave and the statutory right to return to work following maternity absence are two separate rights. Both are contained in the EP(C)A 1978 but the right to maternity leave was inserted into that Act by the Trade Union Reform and Employment Rights Act 1993. The right to maternity leave was created to implement European Directive 92/85/EEC (the Pregnant Workers' Directive).

The statutory right to maternity leave applies to all pregnant employees irrespective of length of service or hours of work. The right is to 14 weeks unpaid leave starting when the pregnant employee gives notice to take such leave but the leave cannot start earlier than 11 weeks before the week the baby is due. During the leave period, the employee may be entitled to statutory maternity pay and is entitled to other non-pay benefits for example the continued use of her company car. There are provisions to deal both with the situation where the employee has to start maternity leave without having the opportunity of giving advance notice and with the situation where the baby is born late. At the end of the maternity leave period the employee should return to work.

The statutory right to return to work following a pregnancy or childbirth is sometimes referred to as maternity absence and it applies if certain conditions are satisfied before the right arises

- the employee must be employed until 11 weeks before the week her baby is due and by that time she must have been continuously employed for not less than two years, and
- she must write to her employer at least 21 days before her absence begins (if possible) stating that she will be away from work due to having a baby, when the baby is due and that she intends to return to work afterwards.

She can then return to work before the end of 29 weeks beginning with the week the baby is born, and she must be offered her original job on terms which she would have had (including pay rises) had she not been absent. If it is not practicable for her to be offered her original job back, then she should be offered a suitable alternative position on the same or similar terms as would have been appropriate if she had returned to her old job.

The employer is entitled to confirmation that she still intends to return to work, and the date, and so she must give written notice to her employer of the date she intends to return to work, not later than 21 days beforehand.

There are certain rights for the employer to delay the start date by up to four weeks and the employee has a similar right on production of a medical certificate.

If the employer does not permit her to return to work, then he/she will be treated as having dismissed her on the day she intends to return with the possibility that such dismissal will be an unfair dismissal.

The distinction between maternity leave and maternity absence is important. All pregnant employees will qualify for maternity leave but only certain longer serving women will qualify for the longer period of maternity absence. During the period of maternity leave the woman will continue to be an employee although off work. If a woman takes the longer maternity absence then, while the position is not clear, it seems she may cease to be an employee after the maternity leave period but will be entitled to be re-employed at the end of her maternity absence period.

The taking of maternity leave/going on maternity absence is voluntary – it is for the woman to decide if she wants to have the time off. But there is a compulsory leave period of two weeks after the birth of the child. A woman must take those two weeks as maternity leave and it is an offence for an employer to allow her to work those two weeks (Maternity (Compulsory Leave) Regulations 1994).

Working hours

The hours to be worked are a matter for the employer and employee to agree as part of the contract of employment. The terms and conditions of hours of work must be set out in the written particulars of employment given to the employee within two months of starting work. As a general rule there are no limits on what can be agreed but children under 13 cannot be employed and for young people aged 13 to 16 there are restrictions on the hours which can be worked (Children and Young Persons Act 1933 section 18 – considered previously).

However, European Directive 93/104 (the Working Time Directive) does require new laws to be made to impose a maximum 48 hour working week, minimum 4 weeks paid holiday and minimum rest periods. The directive does not have to be implemented until November 1996 and even then there are transitional provisions to allow phasing in of requirements. The UK Government has commenced proceedings in the European Court of Justice to challenge the validity of the Working Time Directive and so one way or another the directive is unlikely to have much impact for a while.

The Sunday Trading Act 1994 (which relaxes restrictions on Sunday shop opening) gives shop workers certain rights to decline to work on Sundays together with employment protection provisions to protect employees who do not want to work on Sundays for whatever reason. The Sunday Trading

Act 1994 has no application to catering premises (whether licensed or not and whether food is for immediate consumption or taking away) nor do the shop worker rights apply to catering staff.

Time off

An employer is obliged to give an employee time off during normal working hours

- to carry out official trade union duties provided the employee is an official of a trade union recognised by the employer
- to carry out public duties as a magistrate, councillor, school governor and certain other public positions
- for an employee who has been given a redundancy notice to look for a new job or make arrangements for training, but this right only arises once the employee has been employed for two years and the time off must be reasonable in all the circumstances and the time off is paid by the employer
- for safety representatives to perform their duties and to be trained in health and safety matters.

Change of employer

The Transfer of Undertakings (Protection of Employment) Regulations 1981 (TUPE) deal with what happens to existing employees when the business in which they are employed is transferred.

The most important consequence of TUPE is that on the transfer of a business as a going concern, the employees who are employed in that business immediately before the transfer, automatically transfer with the business so that the buyer of the business becomes their employer. If an employee informs his or her employer that he or she objects to becoming employed by the transferee of the business then the transfer of the business terminates his or her employment but that is not treated as a dismissal.

Apart from the change of employer, there is no other change, and the staff transfer on their existing terms and conditions of employment and with all their existing rights including such matters as accrued holiday rights. Furthermore, the continuity of service is preserved so that for employment rights which depend on a certain length of service (for example unfair dismissal) the period of service is treated as continuous throughout and does not start again on the transfer of the undertaking.

The regulations (TUPE) were amended by the Trade Union Reform and Employment Rights Act 1993, and were made to implement in the UK a

European directive namely directive 77/187 – the Acquired Rights Directive. Other European member countries also have laws to implement the directive in those countries and cases which reach the European Court of Justice on those laws are useful in showing how TUPE also operates. One such case started out in the Danish courts.

◆ RASK AND CHRISTENSEN V ISS KANTINESERVICE A/S (1993)

A large company decided to contract out the running of its staff canteen to contract caterers. The arrangement was that the caterers would be paid a fixed management fee and in return would run the canteen with their own staff. The company would provide the premises, kitchen equipment, electricity etc. for running the canteen.

The kitchen staff who had been employed by the company were taken on by the contract caterers but on different terms and conditions of employment, in particular the pay day was changed and laundry allowances were stopped. Two of the workers complained about these changes.

The contract caterers claimed to be entitled to make the changes because, they said, the taking over of the management of the canteen did not involve a transfer of undertaking and therefore they could offer new terms and conditions of employment to the staff. The caterers said it was not their business because the company still owned the undertaking and the caterers were merely managing it for the benefit of the owners.

The European Court of Justice decided that the caterers argument failed and that the circumstances were capable of being a transfer of an undertaking.

So it can be seen that a transfer of an undertaking can occur on the 'contracting out' of a staff canteen. Furthermore subsequent cases have decided that TUPE can also apply on the change of a canteen caterer or a change of a restaurant franchise.

A simple test is whether the incoming proprietor steps into the shoes of the outgoing proprietor so as to continue the existing operation.

It should be emphasised that the Rask and Christensen case does not decide that terms and conditions of employment cannot be changed – the case decided that the contract caterers did not have a clean sheet of paper on which to write their own terms and conditions but had to take the existing staff on their existing terms and conditions and could only change those terms and conditions to the same extent as they could be changed before the transfer.

TUPE does not apply to the transfer of a business by the transfer of the shares in the company which runs the business, because, in that situation, the staff throughout are employed by the company and it is only the ownership of the company which has changed hands. As to dismissal because of a transfer of a business, see later.

DISCRIMINATION

Discrimination in employment is unlawful in certain circumstances. Outside those situations there is no law against discrimination. For instance, there is no law which prevents an employer discriminating against smokers so it is quite alright to have a policy of recruitment of non-smokers only but not to recruit men only.

In Great Britain there are laws concerning discrimination on grounds of sex, marital status, race and union membership. The Disability Discrimination Act 1995 comes into effect in late 1996 and will introduce new discrimination laws where a person has a physical or mental impairment which has a substantial and long-term adverse effect on his or her ability to do normal day-to-day activities. In Northern Ireland, race discrimination is replaced by religious discrimination laws. It could be said that the Rehabilitation of offenders Act 1974 is also anti-discrimination law but it is not generally referred to in this context.

Additionally the Trade Union Reform and Labour Relations Act 1993 created yet another right which is of an anti-discrimination nature. An employee must not be subjected to any detriment just because he or she is carrying out duties as a safety representative or member of a safety committee or reacted to certain health and safety situations or shortcomings. This right is in section 22A EP(C)A 1978 (inserted by the 1993 Act) and the remedy is a complaint to an industrial tribunal in much the same way as for sex and race discrimination.

Race and sex discrimination is unlawful, not only in employment, but also in the provision of goods, services and accommodation.

Trade union membership/non-membership

Under the Trade Union and Labour Relations (Consolidation) Act 1992 it is unlawful to refuse someone employment because they are a member of a trade union, or because they are not a trade union member. Similarly, it is unlawful to turn down an applicant for a job because he or she will not become a member of, or leave, a trade union.

Section 152, Trade Union and Labour Relations (Consolidation) Act 1992 makes certain dismissals of employees unfair dismissals. The dismissals are those made because the employee was, or was not, a member of a trade union, or had taken part in trade union activities.

As will be seen later when considering unfair dismissal, the importance about section 152 is threefold

- the dismissals are automatically unfair so that, if the reason for the dismissal is established, the tribunal does not then have to consider whether or not the dismissal was unfair
- the level of compensation is higher than a normal unfair dismissal case
- the employee does not have to have been employed for at least two years before being able to bring a claim for unfair dismissal in such circumstances.

Section 146 Trade Union and Labour Relations (Consolidation) Act 1992 makes unlawful any action by an employer stopping short of actual dismissal but aimed at either preventing or compelling membership by an employee of a trade union, or preventing him or her taking part in union activities. The remedy is compensation.

Sex discrimination

Discrimination on the basis of sex or marital status in employment is unlawful. The law is mainly contained in the Sex Discrimination Act 1975 (SDA 1975) as amended but it covers not only the employees but also certain self-employed persons who perform personal services, for example the casual waiting staff in the case of *O'Kelly v Trust House Forte plc (1983)*.

Sex discrimination is prohibited in the employment relationship from beginning to end. Accordingly, it is unlawful to discriminate at the recruitment stage and once the person is employed it is unlawful to discriminate against that person in relation to promotion, transfer or training of that person or denying them access to other employment benefits. It is also unlawful to dismiss on the grounds of the sex or marital status of the employee.

But what is 'discrimination'? There are two types:

- direct discrimination is treating a woman less favourably than a man or vice versa, or a married person less favourably than a single person
- indirect discrimination is applying a requirement or condition to both men and women but which in practice a significantly smaller proportion of men, women or married persons can comply with as compared with persons of the opposite sex or single persons (as the case may be) and which is to his or her detriment and cannot be justified.

It is direct discrimination, for example, to refuse to employ a woman, or promote a woman because of her sex. The motive of the employer is irrelevant – the test is whether the person concerned would have been treated the same had he or she been of the opposite sex or single.

Indirect discrimination is more difficult both to understand and to identify. The first thing is that there must be some condition or requirement, which need not be obviously discriminatory, and is applied equally to men and women, for example, an upper age limit of 28. The condition must be applied equally to men and women and yet considerably more people of one sex must be unable to comply with the condition than persons of the other sex and to their detriment.

◆ PRICE V CIVIL SERVICE COMMISSION (1977)

A post of executive officer in the Civil Service Commission was advertised with a specified age range for applicants of between 17 and a half and 28 years. Mrs Price, aged 36, complained that this was indirect discrimination because, in practice, many women within that age group would be out of the job market due to family commitments and hence the number of women within the age range who could comply would be significantly less than men. The case was proved.

But it is not enough to show that there is a discriminatory condition or requirement, it must also be shown that it works to the disadvantage of the person in question. In the case of Mrs Price the age range requirement was to her disadvantage because she was older.

If, however, the need for the condition or requirement can be justified for example because of the operational requirements of the employer's business, then it cannot amount to indirect unlawful discrimination. So, if a job requirement is that the job applicant is at least six feet tall, that will be a discriminatory condition (because significantly fewer women could comply with that requirement than men) but if the nature of the job is such that it needs someone that tall to do the job, then that will not be unlawful indirect discrimination.

The question of justification is only relevant to indirect discrimination, not direct discrimination; in other words, it is never possible to justify direct discrimination. For example, only short-listing men for a job as a restaurant manager is direct discrimination and cannot be justified even if all the restaurant staff are female who have said they will not work under a female boss.

There are, however, circumstances in which direct or indirect discrimination is not unlawful, if it can be properly claimed that the job can only be done by men or by women as the case may be. This is in section 7 SDA 1975 and is known as the 'genuine occupational qualification'.

If, due to one of the eight genuine occupational qualifications the job can only be performed by a man or a woman, as the case may be, then an employer can legitimately discriminate in the way the job is filled or by denying an existing employee promotional transfer to that job or training for that job.

Of the eight occupational qualifications only a few are likely to be relevant to the hotel and catering industry.

- The job needs to be held by a man or a woman to preserve decency or privacy because the job involves physical contact with men or women in circumstances where they might object to someone of the opposite sex, or because the persons involved are in a state of undress or using sanitary facilities. An example would be a lavatory attendant.
- The establishment is a hospital, prison or other establishment, for men or women as the case may be, providing special care, supervision or attention and the job should reasonably be held by someone of that sex.
- The job holder provides personal, welfare, educational or similar services which can most effectively be provided by a man or a woman. An example might be a beauty therapist.
- The job is likely to involve duties in countries whose laws or customs require the job to be done by a man or as the case may be, a woman.
- The job is one of two to be held by a married couple, such as a married couple required as club stewards.

There are also certain exceptions to the sex discrimination laws, but the only relevant exceptions are as follows.

- Communal accommodation – if an employer provides living accommodation for employees which is only suited to one sex, e.g. because of communal washing or sanitary facilities, then the employer may discriminate by excluding one sex from that accommodation if reasonable to do so. The question of whether it is reasonable includes whether it would be reasonable to adapt the accommodation e.g. by putting in separate toilets. However, staff of the excluded sex must be compensated in some other way. For example, if a hotel in a particular location can only get staff by providing accommodation and cannot get planning permission to convert the living accommodation to provide separate male and female facilities then it would be reasonable to limit the accommodation, say to female staff, and to pay the male staff a living out and travel to work allowance.

- Positive discrimination – discrimination is referred to as positive where it aims to promote the employment prospects of one sex rather than the other. An employer can legitimately provide training exclusively for either men or women if in the previous 12 months there have been no, or comparatively few, persons of that sex doing a particular job. The employer can also encourage people of that sex to apply for jobs but may not discriminate by preferring such applicants when considering who to promote or appoint.

A person who considers that he or she has been unlawfully discriminated against may apply to an industrial tribunal and compensation may be ordered to be paid if the tribunal considers the complaint is proved. However, discrimination is not always easy to prove even if it is recognised in the first place, and often employees may be unwilling to consider taking action against an employer. This situation can be tackled by the Equal Opportunities Commission (EOC) which is an organisation created under the SDA 1975.

The EOC has various duties under the SDA 1975 including promoting equality of opportunity generally, but additionally there are specific powers which should be noted.

A discriminatory practice is conduct which constitutes indirect discrimination and if there is a belief that an employer may be operating a discriminatory practice then the EOC can carry out a formal investigation and issue a report. Furthermore, the EOC can issue a non-discrimination notice which may require an employer to change his or her practices to avoid those practices being discriminatory.

The EOC has also issued a code of practice to endeavour to eliminate sex and marriage discrimination. Breach of the code is not unlawful but in proceedings under the SDA 1975 an industrial tribunal can take into account any failure to follow the provisions of the code.

Race discrimination

Discrimination on racial grounds in employment is made unlawful by the Race Relations Act 1976 (RRA 1976) which is very similar, and in some cases identical, to the Sex Discrimination Act 1975. The RRA 1976 also applies, in a similar way as the SDA 1975, to certain self-employed persons.

'Racial grounds' are colour, race, nationality or ethnic or national origins. Although in Britain, but not in Northern Ireland, there is no law against religious discrimination, the expression ethnic origins can include religious groupings if they are of a particular ethnic origin.

◆ Mandla v Dowell Lee (1983)

A Sikh boy was refused a place at a school because the boy wore a turban instead of the regulation school cap. Although Sikhs were a religious grouping, they were of common ethnic origin and therefore discrimination against Sikhs was racial discrimination.

In the same way as for sex discrimination, racial discrimination by an employer is prohibited at all stages of employment commencing with the recruitment stage and going through to dismissal.

The definition of 'discrimination' in racial discrimination follows the same pattern as for sex discrimination

- direct discrimination means treating on racial grounds one person less favourably than another person
- indirect discrimination is applying a requirement or condition which appears to be non-racial, but which creates a greater obstruction for members of one racial group than another to their disadvantage, and which requirement or condition cannot be justified.

Direct discrimination would be a refusal to employ or promote someone because of his or her colour.

Indirect discrimination is more difficult to recognise. There must be some condition or requirement not obviously discriminatory, for example a prohibition on having a beard. That condition must be applied equally to everyone and yet significantly fewer people in one racial group can, in practice, comply with the requirement, to their detriment.

If, however, the need for the condition or requirement can be justified in the circumstances, then there is no unlawful discrimination.

◆ Singh v Rowntree Mackintosh Ltd. (1979)

The employers, who manufactured confectionery, had a works rule forbidding beards. Mr Singh, a Sikh, applied for a job but his religion prevented him shaving off his beard. Accordingly, he did not get the job.

Although there was a condition forbidding beards, and this discriminated against Sikhs, the condition was justified on the grounds of the employer's need for the preparation of confectionary in hygienic conditions.

As with sex discrimination, an employer may legitimately discriminate on racial grounds when being of one racial grouping is necessary for the particular job. This is covered in section 5 RRA 1976 and is limited to situations where being of one racial group is a genuine occupational qualification for the job. This arises in four situations but it is possible that the only relevant situation is if the job is working in a place where food and drink is provided in a particular setting, which requires a person of a particular racial group, for example a waiter or waitress in a Chinese or Indian restaurant.

There are certain exceptions to the race discrimination laws, but the only one of any real relevance is the exception for positive discrimination which applies in similar circumstances to positive sex discrimination.

A person who considers that he or she has been unlawfully discriminated against may present a complaint to an industrial tribunal, and if the tribunal is satisfied that the complaint is proved, then compensation may be ordered to be paid by the discriminator to the person discriminated against.

The Commission for Racial Equality (CRE) is a body created under the race relations legislation with duties towards the elimination of racial discrimination. The CRE may carry out investigations and issue non-discrimination notices and it has also issued a code of practice. Breach of the code by itself has no legal consequences, but such a breach can be taken into account by an industrial tribunal when dealing with a complaint under the RRA 1976.

HEALTH AND SAFETY AT WORK

Health and safety at work is a subject which, like consumer protection, is tackled both on the criminal and the civil front. Indeed, health and safety at work can be viewed as being the equivalent of consumer protection in that it is employee protection. Because it is tackled both on the criminal and the civil front, there are a variety of duties owed concerning health and safety of employees.

There are the various common law duties which are civil duties owed by an employer to an employee. There are also statutory obligations. These arise under two principal Acts of Parliament

- Occupiers' Liability Act 1957
- Health and Safety at Work etc. Act 1974.

The first of these Acts has been looked at in some detail in Chapter 3.

The Health and Safety at Work etc. Act 1974 creates very general obligations and also gives cover to numerous Regulations. The intention being that all criminal health and safety legislation will eventually come under that Act. Both the Act and some of the regulations will be examined in this Chapter.

Common law duties

The employers' common law duties (for definition of 'common law', see Chapter 1) create civil responsibilities and are generally divided into five headings

- to provide a safe place of work including safe access to the work area
- to provide a safe system of work
- to provide adequate and safe equipment and materials
- to employ competent fellow employees
- to protect from risk of injury.

The first of these duties relates to the premises and the method of getting to the workplace. An employer should, for instance, ensure that the premises are properly maintained and safe for use at all times.

◆ BELL V DEPARTMENT OF HEALTH AND SOCIAL SECURITY (1989)

Mrs Bell was employed in the office of the DHSS. The floors of the passages in the offices were pseudo marble with a history of being slippery if wet. The DHSS did not provide tea or coffee for its employees but there was a fourth floor kitchen, either to make drinks, or to obtain hot water to make drinks, in the various offices. There was a history of spillages of water on the passage floors. On the afternoon in question Mrs Bell slipped on some spilt liquid on the passage floor and suffered injuries. The DHSS was aware of the danger of the floors being slippery while wet but it only distributed a memorandum asking staff to be more careful with mugs of hot water and suggesting saucers or a tray as a method to avoid spilling the liquid. The judge decided that more should have been done to avoid the problem, for example by providing more places for hot water thereby reducing the distance it had to be carried, or by putting down some non-slip surface over the pseudo marble. Accordingly, the employer had failed to comply with the common law duty of providing a safe place of work or safe means of access to it.

The other duties, such as systems of work, materials and equipment and competent fellow workers are all concerned with the method of working.

None of these duties is absolute, the duty on the employer is to take reasonable care, but the duty to supply safe equipment is amended by the Employers' Liability (Defective Equipment) Act 1969 which says that if an injury is caused by defective equipment which is due to a manufacturing fault the employer is liable to the employee. If therefore, an hotelier buys kitchen equipment and an accident happens at work due to that equipment being faulty, the employer is liable to the injured employee under the duty to provide safe equipment but that does not prevent the employer suing the supplier of the equipment.

These common law duties create civil rights and duties in the same way as the common duty of care under the Occupiers' Liability Act 1957. Indeed, in the case of *Bell v DHSS 1989*, Mrs Bell succeeded in showing not only a breach of the employer's common law duties to her as an employee, but also a breach of the employer's statutory duty of care under the Occupiers' Liability Act 1957. Before going on to look at criminal liability which might arise under the same facts under the Health and Safety at Work etc. Act 1974, it is important to consider the employer's compulsory duty to insure for civil responsibility.

Employers' liability insurance

Every employer must maintain a policy of insurance to cover his or her civil liability for injury to, or disease contracted by employees. This obligation arises under the Employers' Liability (Compulsory Insurance) Act 1969.

The insurance has to be with certain approved insurers and those insurers issue annual certificates of insurance which the employer must display at the workplace, for instance on the staff notice board.

An employee who has a civil claim against the employer can be sure that, should he or she succeed in a claim against the employer, then the insurer will be able to pay that claim.

Health and Safety at Work etc. Act 1974

The Health and Safety at Work etc. Act 1974 (H&SAWA 1974) creates criminal responsibility only. In other words if the employer falls foul of the H&SAWA 1974 the employer will be prosecuted and can be punished for the breach of the Act. The employee has no right to sue an employer for injuries caused by a breach of the 1974 Act but the facts of such a breach will almost certainly be a breach also of the employer's civil responsibilities.

The 1974 Act creates certain general duties of employers to employees.

Section 2 Health and Safety at Work etc. Act 1974

(1) It shall be the duty of every employer to ensure so far as is

reasonably practicable the health, safety and welfare at work of all his employees.

(2) . . . the matters to which that duty extends include in particular

  (a) *the provision and maintenance of plant and systems of work that are, so far as is reasonably practicable, safe and without risks to health;*

  (b) *arrangements for ensuring, so far as is reasonably practicable, safety and absence of risks to health in connection with the use, handling, storage and transport of articles and substances;*

  (c) *the provision of such information, instruction, training and supervision as is necessary to ensure, so far as is reasonably practicable, the health and safety at work of his employees;*

  (d) *so far as is reasonably practicable as regards any place of work under the employer's control, the maintenance of it in a condition that is safe and without risks to health and the provision and maintenance of means of access to and egress from it that are safe and without such risks;*

  (e) *the provision and maintenance of a working environment for his employees that is, so far as is reasonably practicable, safe, without risks to health and adequate as regards facilities and arrangements for their welfare at work.*

There are duties placed on employees.

Section 7 Health and Safety at Work etc. Act 1974

It shall be the duty of every employee while at work

  (a) *to take reasonable care for the health and safety of himself and of other persons who may be affected by his acts or omissions at work; and*

  (b) *as regards any duty or requirements imposed on his employer or any other person . . . to co-operate with him so far as is necessary to enable that duty or requirement to be performed or complied with.*

Reinforcing the employer's duties under the H&SAWA 1974 are further duties.

- Employers with at least five employees are under a duty to prepare and keep up to date a written health and safety policy statement and to bring such a statement to the attention of staff for example by displaying it on the staff notice board (section 2(3) H&SAWA 1974 and the Employers' Health and Safety Policy Statements (Exception) Regulations 1975).
- Employers must display a poster in a specified form about the general duties under the H&SAWA 1974 and certain other information. If the poster is not displayed then staff must be given a leaflet containing the same information (Health and Safety Information for Employees Regulations 1989).
- Employers must make facilities available, including time off for training, for safety representatives. Safety representatives are employees appointed for that purpose by a trade union recognised by the employer. Additionally, employers should consult with safety representatives on safety matters. (Safety Representatives and Safety Committee Regulations 1977).

The enforcement of the H&SAWA 1974 and all safety regulations is by local authorities and the Health and Safety Executive who may appoint inspectors. Inspectors have powers to issue improvement notices and prohibition notices. The former may be served if the inspector considers one of the statutory duties is being contravened and such a notice requires steps to be taken to remedy that contravention (section 21 H&SAWA 1974). Prohibition notices can be served if an inspector thinks that there is a risk of serious personal injury in which case the notice prohibits the activities causing that risk until specified safety measures have been taken.

A feature of the H&SAWA 1974 is the wide powers to make regulations for securing the health and safety of people at work. There is also power, where appropriate, for regulations to be supplemented by Approved Codes of Practice. The codes of practice are not legal requirements, but a breach of a code of practice may be used as evidence in criminal proceedings to show that the statutory obligations have been contravened.

In fact the H&SAWA has been supplemented by numerous Regulations many of which are supported by associated codes of practice.

One of the sets of regulations made under the H&SAWA 1974 has already been looked at in Chapter 3 namely the Workplace (Health, Safety and Welfare) Regulations 1992. Those regulations are reinforced by a code of practice and together form a complete set of rules for safety of workplaces.

The Management of Health and Safety at Work Regulations 1992

The Management of Health and Safety at Work Regulations 1992 take the H&SAWA 1974 a stage further by making more explicit what is required of employers under that Act.

The main requirements of these regulations for employers are

- to carry out a risk assessment to identify what needs to be done to comply with health and safety laws in relation both to employees and others who may be affected by the activities of that business
- to put into effect appropriate arrangements and management systems as highlighted by that assessment to ensure the health and safety of employees and others
- to keep a record of both the risk assessment and the safety arrangements unless there are less than five employees
- to appoint at least one competent person who may be either internal or from outside (such as a consultant) to assist with complying with all health and safety laws
- to have emergency procedures in place
- to cooperate and coordinate safety procedures where employers share the same workplace (e.g. employees of contract caterers in an office block)
- to instruct staff in various aspects of safety of their jobs and in their workplace.

Hazardous substances

The Control of Substances Hazardous to Health Regulations 1994 (COSHH) create further specific duties owed by employers to employees concerning substances hazardous to health. Such substances are defined in the regulations and include substances labelled as being toxic, harmful, corrosive or irritant. Other substances such as concentrated dust of any kind when present in the air and certain micro-organisms also come within the definition of substances hazardous to health.

The first duty under the COSHH is for employers to carry out an assessment of any working practices where employees might be exposed to any substances which could be hazardous to their health. The purpose of the assessment is to identify the risk to health and decide what steps should be taken to eliminate or minimise that risk.

Where there is a risk to health then the employer should try to eliminate the risk altogether for example by changing working practices or using instead a harmless substance. If the risk cannot be eliminated it should be controlled without resorting, in the first instance, to merely providing protective clothing; however, if the measures taken cannot provide adequate control without such protective clothing, then the employer must provide such clothing.

Breach of the regulations is a criminal offence and as with many Regulations there is also a supplementary code of practice.

Other safety regulations

There are several other main safety regulations

- The Noise at Work Regulations 1989 – these Regulations specify certain action levels of noise. Two of these action levels are concerned with exposure to noise during the working day, for example working with noisy machinery during the day, and the third action level deals with one-off loud sounds, all of which could cause damage to the ears and loss of hearing. The obligation under these Regulations is to ascertain whether noise exposure could reach an action level, and if it could, to take appropriate action which action could be reducing the noise levels by sound insulation, reducing the time spent by employees working in noisy areas and providing ear protection.
- The Electricity at Work Regulations 1989 are concerned with all aspects of electricity at work, both the safe use of electrical equipment, and the repair and maintenance work of electrical wiring and insulation.
- The Pressure Systems and Transportable Gas Containers Regulations 1989 require an examination schedule to be drawn up for all pressure systems such as steam boilers, cafe-sets etc., and for the systems to be inspected at periods specified in that schedule. Usually the inspection will be carried out by an insurance company engineer and it is likely that inspections will take place every 14 months.
- The Provision and Use of Work Equipment Regulations 1992 lay down criteria for both the selection and safe use of all types of work equipment.
- The Health and Safety (Display Screen Equipment) Regulations 1992 provide for an ergonomic approach to the use of computer screens at workstations.
- The Manual Handling Operations Regulations 1992 require the avoidance of manual handling tasks which could involve a risk of injury and an assessment of those tasks which cannot be avoided. The purpose of the assessment is to see what can be done to minimise the risk of injury.

- The Gas Safety (Installation and Use) Regulations 1994 apply a range of gas safety precautions in particular, that only registered gas fitters carry out work on gas fittings in the workplace.

Reporting and recording accidents and illness

An employer is obliged to report certain injuries and dangerous occurrences. The report must be made, in the case of most catering and hospitality establishments, to the local authority.

The Reporting of Injuries, Diseases and Dangerous Occurrences Regulations 1985 (RIDDOR) require the following to be notified in writing to the enforcing authority within seven days

- the death of any person as a result of an accident at work
- major injury to any person as a result of an accident at work – such injury includes most fractures, loss of sight in an eye, amputation and burns and electrical shocks requiring immediate treatment
- acute illness as a result of exposure to certain materials
- any other injury resulting in a stay in hospital for more than 24 hours
- injury due to an accident at work resulting in a person being away from work for more than three days.

In any case falling within the first three categories, the death, injury or illness must be notified by the quickest method (for example telephone) to the enforcement authority.

Certain dangerous occurrences also have to be notified immediately to the enforcement authority and these are listed in Part 1 of Schedule 1 to RIDDOR 1985, and include a fire or explosion caused by an electrical short-circuit or overload.

Employers who have at least ten employees must keep an accident book in which certain particulars of accidents must be kept and all employers are required to keep records of notifiable accidents, illnesses etc.

First aid

Every employer is required by the Health and Safety (First Aid) Regulations 1981 to provide adequate equipment and facilities for first aid for employees who are injured or become ill at work.

Employers should make sure that there are an adequate number of trained persons to give first aid to employees. Usually this obligation is met by making sure that an adequate number of staff hold a current first aid certificate.

The 1981 Regulations are supplemented by a code of practice designed to give practical guidance to employers as to how comply with the 1981 Regulations.

TERMINATION OF EMPLOYMENT

There are numerous ways employment may be terminated. Employment, as has already been seen, is a contractual relationship and may therefore be terminated by agreement and in the case of a fixed term contract of employment it expires at the end of the fixed term if not renewed. Contracts of employment may also specify that they terminate on the employee reaching a specified retirement age.

Apart from these situations, a contract can usually be terminated by one party or the other by notice. The giving of notice by an employer is dismissal, but if the employee gives notice to the employer, then it is resignation. Either way, the giving of a notice to terminate the employment will bring it to an end on the date specified in the notice.

Dismissal

Dismissal may be 'summary' or 'on notice', summary dismissal is only justified in certain circumstances which will be considered later. Notice to terminate employment does not have to be in writing, but it must be clear that it is notice to terminate the employment on a specified date.

The length of notice to be given by an employer to an employee to terminate the employment is whichever is the longer of the contractual notice period or the statutory minimum notice period. The contractual notice period should be specified in the written particulars given to the employee under section 1 EP(C)A 1978.

The statutory minimum period of notice to be given by an employer to an employee is set out in Table 9.1 but there is no statutory minimum period for someone employed for less than one month.

TABLE 9.1

Number of years of continuous employment	Minimum number of notice in weeks
less than 2	1
at least 2 but less than 3	2
at least 3 but less than 4	3
at least 4 but less than 5	4
at least 5 but less than 6	5
at least 6 but less than 7	6
at least 7 but less than 8	7
at least 8 but less than 9	8
at least 9 but less than 10	9
at least 10 but less than 11	10
at least 11 but less than 12	11
12 or more	12

Notice given by an employer must not be less than the statutory minimum. If an employer terminates a contract of employment by giving no notice, or shorter than the notice to which the employee is entitled, then, unless he or she was entitled to dismiss the employee summarily the employer will have wrongfully dismissed the employee. Wrongful dismissal is a breach of contract and the employer will be liable to compensate the employee. The compensation payable is the net amount of wages the employee would have received for working during the notice period. A complaint of wrongful dismissal can be made either to an industrial tribunal or to a county court.

If an employer pays such compensation, he or she can dismiss an employee without notice and this is known as making a payment in lieu of notice. Dismissing an employee without notice subject to making a payment in lieu of notice, constitutes a breach of contract but the only practical consequence will be that any restrictive covenant on the part of the employee in the contract of employment, will be unenforceable. Accordingly, if an employer wishes to dismiss an employee to leave straight away, he or she may do so, but the employer has to give the employee pay in lieu of notice.

In certain circumstances, however, an employer is entitled to dismiss an employee without either notice or pay in lieu of notice. This is known as summary dismissal. This is usually only possible where the employee is guilty of some gross misconduct. Examples of gross misconduct would be theft from the employer, refusal to carry out proper instructions or other serious misconduct, for example a waiter being drunk on duty.

Resignation

An employee may resign by giving notice to his or her employer. The minimum period of notice to be given (after one months employment) is one week's notice unless the contract of employment specifies a longer period.

As with dismissal there can also be a 'summary resignation' by the employee, that is resignation without notice, but this can only be done if the employer is guilty of some serious breach of contract. The expression 'summary resignation' is not used, instead it is commonly known as constructive dismissal and entitles the employee to compensation for wrongful dismissal.

Written reasons for dismissal

An employee who is dismissed after having been employed for at least two years is entitled to request from his or her employer, written reasons for the dismissal, and the employer is obliged to reply with the correct reason, or reasons, within 14 days of such a request.

An employee who is dismissed while she is pregnant or during her maternity leave must be given written reasons for her dismissal whether or not she requests such reasons and even though she may not have been employed for two years.

If the employer fails to reply, or gives inadequate or false reasons, then the employee may make a complaint to an industrial tribunal, and if the tribunal considers the complaint to be well founded then the employer will be obliged to pay the employee compensation equal to two weeks pay.

Restrictive covenants

Contracts of employment, especially of senior employees and those with special skills or knowledge of the employer's business, often contain what are termed 'restrictive covenants'. Such covenants are designed to restrain the employees concerned from competing with the employer when they leave employment. This is done by preventing them either setting up their own business, or going into the employment of a competitor, within a certain period of time after leaving employment, and in circumstances in which they can pose a threat to the previous employer's business.

Restrictive covenants were met in Chapter 3 under the guise of brewery ties and it will be recalled that the courts will treat restrictive covenants as being void unless they are reasonable in all the circumstances, both from the point of view of the parties and from the public interest point of view.

The question of reasonableness will usually be tested by looking to see if the covenant is only to protect some legitimate interest of the employer. Such interests tend to be twofold – identity of the employer's customers and the employer's trade secrets. To be valid, the restraint must be no more than is required to protect the employer's interest. So, if an employer's business draws its customers from within five miles of the business premises, a covenant to prevent the employee being involved in any way in a competing business within ten miles of those premises will fail because it will be wider than necessary.

If the employee is wrongfully dismissed, or the employee is constructively dismissed due to the employer's breach of the contract of employment, the employer will be unable to enforce the restrictive covenant, whether or not it would otherwise have been valid.

Retirement

If there is a compulsory retirement age namely an age at which employees must retire then, since the Sex Discrimination Act 1986 the age must be the same for men and women despite the fact that the State Pension age is 65 for men and 60 for women.

Retirement age should be distinguished from pension age but there is a European Court of Justice case (*Barber v Guardian Royal Exchange Group 1990*) involving a pension under an occupational pension scheme which the court decided is 'pay' within the meaning of Article 119 EC Treaty and hence men and women are entitled to equal pension ages under such a scheme. That judgement does not apply to state schemes which can still have different commencement ages for pensions for men and women.

Redundancy

Subject to certain conditions, employees who are made redundant are entitled to a redundancy payment from their employer. The conditions are that the employee

- must have been dismissed due to redundancy
- at the date of termination of employment must have been employed continuously by that employer for at least two years.

There are two qualifications to those conditions. The first qualification is that employment before the employee was 18 years old does not count towards continuous employment and hence a person cannot qualify for a redundancy payment before their twentieth birthday. Second, if the business is taken over as a going concern, the continuity of employment of any employees in the business is preserved so that if a person has been employed for one year before the business had a new proprietor, the employee has to work a further year in the business following the takeover to qualify for the right to a redundancy payment.

The first condition for entitlement to a redundancy payment is that the employee must have been dismissed due to redundancy. This involves consideration of what is dismissal and what is a redundancy. 'Dismissal' has a special meaning in the EP(C)A 1978 and means

- the employer terminates the contract
- the contract of employment was for a fixed period and that period expires without being renewed
- the employee terminates the contract where he or she is entitled to do so, due to the employer's serious breach of the contract (constructive dismissal).

Redundancy must be the reason for the dismissal and redundancy can arise in two situations

- the employer ceases to carry on the business in which the employee is employed or intends to close that business either completely or in the place where the employee is employed
- fewer employees are required where the redundant employee is employed, either because the business was overstaffed in the first place or because of a fall-off in business.

In some circumstances the right to a redundancy payment either does not arise or can be lost.

- If there is a normal retirement age in the business which is the same for male and female employees and which is less than 65 years of age then if the redundant employee has reached that age he or she will not be entitled to any redundancy pay. Whether or not there is a normal retirement age, any employee who is 65 or over will not qualify for a redundancy payment.
- If the redundant employee unreasonably refuses an offer of a suitable alternative job made by his or her employer, which offer is made before the end of his or her employment, and is of a job to start within four weeks of the end of the old job, then the employee will not be entitled to redundancy pay.
- If the contract of employment was for a fixed period of two years or more, the employee may agree in writing to the exclusion of the redundancy

payment rights, in which case, if the dismissal is as a result of the non-renewal of that contract at the end of the term, then the employee has no right to redundancy pay.

- If the employee fails to make a written claim for payment or to apply to an industrial tribunal within six months of being made redundant for the tribunal to decide if he or she is entitled to redundancy payment, then the employee will be out of time to claim redundancy pay, although there is some limited power to allow late claims.

The amount of the redundancy pay is based on the employee's length of service, age and pay but in the case of employees aged 64, the amount is reduced by one twelfth for each complete month since the employee's 64th birthday. The calculation is by a formula

- half a week's pay for each year of continuous service during ages 18 to 21 inclusive
- one weeks pay for each year of continuous service during ages 22 to 40 inclusive
- one and a half weeks pay for each year of continuous service during ages 41 to 64 inclusive.

A weeks pay is calculated in accordance with the EP(C)A 1978 and is based on average gross pay, subject to a maximum, which is usually reviewed every year.

Where an employer intends to make a number of employees redundant at the same time or period then an obligation may arise to notify the Department of Employment. This obligation arises if the employer intends to make either ten or more employees redundant within 30 days, or 100 or more employees redundant within a period of 90 days. Failure to notify the Department of Employment of redundancies when obliged to do so renders the employer liable to criminal prosecution. There is also a requirement to notify and consult with a recognised trade union of impending redundancies in similar situations.

References

An employee is not entitled to a reference and an employer is not obliged to give a reference for either a current on past employee. The only exception is where there is an enforceable agreement to provide a reference as is often the case where an unfair dismissal claim is settled by agreement.

It is, however, usual practice to give references. An employer who gives a reference can be liable in the tort of negligence to either a future employer (for a reference which is too good) or to the employee/ex-employee (for one too bad). Consequently it is important for references to be truthful and usually limited to factual matters.

A disclaimer of responsibility is usually added into a reference to exclude liability for a negligent reference. Such a disclaimer will not protect a deliberate untruth and in any event will have to pass the reasonableness test in the Unfair Contract Terms Act 1977 to be effective.

UNFAIR DISMISSAL

The right

The right not to be unfairly dismissed is entirely created by statute and is analogous to a statutory tort. It was originally created by the Industrial Relations Act 1971, but that Act has now been repealed and the right is now to be found in the EP(C)A 1978.

Section 54 Employment Protection (Consolidation) Act 1978

(1) In every employment to which this section applies every employee shall have the right not to be unfairly dismissed by his employer.
(2) This section applies to every employment except insofar as its application is excluded by or under any provision of this part or by sections 141 to 149.

As can be seen from section 54, only employees can complain of unfair dismissal. A self-employed person cannot claim unfair dismissal even if the worker only works for the one 'employer' as was seen at the outset of this Chapter in the case of *O'Kelly v Trust House Forte plc (1983)*.

An employee can only complain of unfair dismissal if he or she has been dismissed, and for the purposes of unfair dismissal (as with redundancy), dismissal has a special meaning

- the employee's employment is terminated by the employer with or without notice
- a fixed term contract of employment comes to an end without being renewed
- the employee terminates the contract due to a serious breach of the contract by the employer (constructive dismissal).

Also, where a female employee is entitled to return to work after maternity absence but the employer refuses to have her back then the employee is treated as having been dismissed on the day she was due to return to work.

An employee who resigns in a situation which is not a constructive dismissal cannot claim unfair dismissal compensation because he or she has not been dismissed. However, an employee who resigns when faced with a 'resign or be fired' option by an employer will be treated as having been dismissed.

Certain employees are excluded from the right to make a claim for unfair dismissal. The employees who are excluded are those who do not have the qualifying period of employment and certain other employees in certain situations considered below.

Qualifying period of employment

Subject to certain exceptions (considered below) an employee must have been employed continuously in the business for two years regardless of the number of hours worked each week before he or she qualifies for the right not to be unfairly dismissed. So if an employee is dismissed before two years of service he or she cannot make an unfair dismissal claim.

However, an employee does not even have to have two years service in four circumstances in order to bring an unfair dismissal claims

- if the dismissal is for being a member of a trade union or taking part in its activities (or proposing to do either) or the dismissal is for not being a member of a trade union
- if the dismissal is for pregnancy or some connected reason – taking maternity leave or other pregnancy of childbirth-connected grounds
- if the dismissal is for raising certain health and safety concerns etc., as specified in section 57A EP(C)A 1978
- if the dismissal is for asserting the employee's employment rights.

A change of employer does not break continuity if the employer takes over the business as a going concern. In certain limited circumstances, the continuity of employment can be broken. The rules are set out in Schedule 13 to the EP(C)A 1978.

The qualifying period of continuity of employment has to be calculated up to the effective date of termination. This date is generally the date the contract of employment terminates, but if the employee is dismissed without notice, or adequate notice, then the effective date of termination will be extended to when the statutory minimum period of notice would have expired.

Other excluded employees

Apart from those employees without the necessary qualifying period of employment, the other main categories of employees excluded from the right to complain of unfair dismissal are as follows.

- Employees lose the right to complain of unfair dismissal once they have reached the normal retirement age in their employment (provided that age is the same for both male and female employees) or the age of 65 whichever is the lower age.
- Employees who normally work outside Great Britain are excluded from the right to complain about unfair dismissal.
- Employees who are employed under a fixed term contract of one year or more can validly agree in writing to exclude their unfair dismissal rights. It should be noted here that other attempts to exclude the unfair dismissal rights are ineffective.
- Employees who are taking part in a strike or other industrial action at the time they are dismissed have no unfair dismissal rights. But if the strike (or other action) was official, in the sense of having union authorisation, or there was no union involved, then all the employees involved in the strike or industrial action must be dismissed and not reinstated or re-engaged within three months in order for those employees to lose the right to complain of unfair dismissal. In practice this means that an employer faced with a strike or other action needs to discover whether the strike has official backing, and if it has not, then he or she can selectively dismiss the employees without fear of unfair dismissal claims.
- Employees who fail to make their complaint to an industrial tribunal prior to three months after the effective date of termination, lose the right to unfair dismissal compensation, but there are limited powers to allow an extension of time.

Automatically unfair dismissals

Not every dismissal is unfair but certain dismissals are treated as being automatically unfair, in other words, if the dismissals are made in certain situations then the employee automatically becomes entitled to unfair dismissal compensation provided (in most cases) they have the qualifying period of employment and are not excluded.

These automatically unfair dismissals situations are

- Union related dismissals – dismissal for being a member of a union or proposing to become a trade union member, dismissal for taking part in the activities of a trade union, and dismissal for non-membership of, or refusal to join a trade union. These are all automatically unfair dismissals (section 152 Trade Union and Labour Relations (Consolidation) Act 1992. For these union related dismissals there is no need for the employee to have completed any qualifying period (two years) and additional compensation (a 'special award') is payable in such cases.

- Dismissal of a woman because she is pregnant, or for a reason connected with her pregnancy, is an automatically unfair dismissal and two years service is not necessary (section 60 EP(C)A 1978.

- If the reason for the dismissal of the employee was redundancy, but the circumstances constituting the redundancy apply equally to one or more other employees in similar positions, who have not been dismissed, and either the reason the employee was made redundant in preference to the others was union or pregnancy related as above, or he or she was selected for redundancy for one of the reasons in section 57A or section 60A (see below), then the dismissal will be an automatically unfair dismissal (section 59 EP(C)A 1978).

- A dismissal because of a transfer of a business as a going concern, or reasons connected with it, is automatically unfair. So, if employees are dismissed by the seller of a business at the request of the buyer because the buyer has his or her own staff that he or she wishes to use in that business, such dismissals will be automatically unfair. There is one exception which is that if the dismissal is for an economic, technical or organisational reason involving changes in the workforce, then the dismissal may not be automatically unfair (Transfer of Undertakings (Protection of Employment) Regulations 1981).

- Dismissal in connection with certain health and safety issues (section 57A EP(C)A 1978) or for asserting a statutory employment right (section 60A EP(C)A 1978).

- A dismissal for not disclosing a 'spent' conviction (see the Rehabilitation of Offenders Act 1974) is generally regarded as being an automatically unfair dismissal.

Non-automatically unfair dismissals

Apart from those cases the question whether a dismissal is fair or unfair (subject to the employee having the necessary qualifying period of continuous employment and not being excluded from the right) is governed by section 57 EP(C)A 1978.

Section 57 Employment Protection (Consolidation) Act 1978

(1) In determining whether the dismissal of an employee was fair or unfair, it shall be for the employer to show

- *(a) what was the reason (or, if there was more than one, the principal reason) for the dismissal; and*
- *(b) that it was a reason falling within subsection (2) or some other substantial reason of a kind such as to justify the dismissal of an employee holding the position which that employee held.*

(2) In subsection (1)(b) the reference to a reason falling within this subsection is a reference to a reason which

- *(a) related to the capability or qualifications of the employee for performing work of the kind which he was employed by the employer to do; or*
- *(b) related to the conduct of the employee; or*
- *(c) was that the employee was redundant; or*
- *(d) was that the employee could not continue to work in the position which he held without contravention (either on his part or on that of his employer) of a duty or restriction imposed by or under an enactment.*

(3) Where the employer has fulfilled the requirements of subsection (1), then the determination of the question whether the dismissal was fair or unfair, having regard to the reasons shown by the employer, shall depend on whether in the circumstances (including the size and administrative resources of the employer's undertaking) the employer acted reasonably or unreasonably in treating it as a sufficient reason for dismissing the employee; and that question shall be determined in accordance with equity and the substantial merits of the case.

(4) In this section, in relation to an employee,

- *(a) 'Capability' means capability assessed by reference to skill, aptitude, health or any physical or mental quality;*
- *(b) 'Qualifications' means any degree, diploma or other academic, technical or professional qualification relevant to the position which the employee held.*

A complaint of unfair dismissal is made to an industrial tribunal, and at the tribunal, it is for the employer to prove the reason for the dismissal and that it was one of the five potentially valid reasons for dismissal

- incapability or lack of qualifications
- misconduct
- redundancy
- contravention of some statutory restriction, for example dismissal of a driver who has been banned by a court from driving
- some other substantial reason.

After that, the tribunal has to decide whether, in the circumstances, the employer acted reasonably in treating that reason as a sufficient reason for dismissing the employee. In deciding this question the tribunal considers the size of the employer and whether the employer followed a fair disciplinary procedure such as that recommended in the ACAS Code of Practice Number 1.

The fifth potentially valid reason for dismissal namely 'some other substantial reason' has shown up a number of interesting sub-reasons which can justify dismissal in limited circumstances. Many of these reasons are involved with reorganisation of the business, or necessary changes for the continued health of the business, or to protect the interests of the business in some way or the other. For instance, employees who refuse to accept a change in their terms and conditions of employment, e.g. because the business has to reorganise or take other means to survive, may find that their dismissal is not unfair if they refuse to accept those changed terms and conditions.

Remedies for unfair dismissal

A complaint of unfair dismissal must be made to an industrial tribunal within three months of the effective date of termination and if the tribunal decides that the employee was unfairly dismissed then the remedies available are either an order for reinstatement or re-engagement, or an award of compensation payable by the employer.

If an Order is made for reinstatement or re-engagement of the employee, but the employer refuses to comply, then the tribunal will make an award of compensation plus additional compensation for the failure to comply with the Order.

Unfair dismissal compensation is generally awarded under two heads

- a basic award – this is calculated in almost identical fashion to the calculation of redundancy pay

- compensatory award – this is the amount the tribunal considers appropriate, subject to a maximum which is reviewed each year. The factors taken into account by the tribunal will include loss of earnings, and loss of pension rights, and whether or not the former employee has obtained a new job or is likely to obtain one.

◆ SELF EXAMINATION QUESTIONS ◆

1 Albert is starting up a restaurant business and appoints Bernard as the chef. The terms of the appointment include terms as to split shifts, days off, holidays and the rate of pay. What are Albert's legal obligations to ensure that Bernard has information about the terms of his appointment?

2 A few months after starting work, Bernard has a road accident which means he will be off work for at least two weeks. Albert obtains the services of a chef from an agency to cover for Bernard's absence but he refuses to pay Bernard anything because he is having to pay the agency more for the replacement chef. What is the legal position and what can Bernard do about it?

3 Twenty months after starting the restaurant business Albert sells it to Charles as a going concern. Charles wants to change the menu from French cuisine (which is Bernard's strength) to a menu featuring traditional English cooking. Bernard objects to the change and the relationship between the two deteriorates to such an extent that five months after taking over the restaurant Charles dismisses Bernard and recruits a new chef. Discuss the different legal aspects of that dismissal.

4 The new chef recruited by Charles is David. One day when working in the kitchen, David slips on some fat spilt on the floor by another of the kitchen staff. In the fall David breaks his arm and has to be taken to hospital. What are Charles' various obligations arising from this incident?

5 Unfortunately David is likely to be off work due to his injury for some considerable time. Charles needs a chef and cannot get one on a temporary basis. Discuss the situation should David be dismissed because his injury makes him unfit to carry on working for the time being.

6 Charles dismisses David and advertises for a new chef. There are a number of applicants including a qualified chef who is of Asian ethnic origin but who has lived all his life in Britain and attended catering college in England. Charles informs that applicant that he will not be appointed because Charles wants traditional English cuisine cooked by an English chef. Discuss the implications of this.

See Appendix for suggested answers.

Appendix

SUGGESTED ANSWERS TO SELF EXAMINATION QUESTIONS

Chapter 1

1 A directive is a European law which is binding on the member countries as
   to the objective to be achieved but leaves to the government of each
   member country the choice of the method to achieve that objective.
   In the UK the Government will choose how to implement those European
   objectives into national law and in the case of Council Directive
   93/13/EEC the method used is by secondary legislation namely a
   statutory instrument. That statutory instrument is national law and
   becomes effective in accordance with national law.

   European directives are addressed to the governments of member
   countries and do not as a rule confer rights or obligations on individuals.
   Those rights and obligations arise under the national laws made to
   implement the directives.

   However, where the time for the implementation of the directive has
   expired without it being implemented and where the provisions are
   sufficiently clear and precise an individual can rely on unconditional rights
   in the unimplemented directive but only as between the individual and the
   defaulting government.

   In the case of *Francovich v Italian Republic (1992)*, the European Court
   of Justice went further, deciding that a defaulting government is liable to
   pay compensation if loss is sustained by an individual because of failure to
   implement a directive in time.

   Accordingly, the six months delay in implementing the Unfair Contract
   Terms Directive could result in compensation claims against the UK
   Government by UK citizens either under the principle of vertical direct
   effect or under the Francovich case.

2 Klaus is liable to be prosecuted for a criminal offence under the Food
   Safety Act 1990. That prosecution will be by the environmental health
   officer. If he is found guilty he will be punished – that may involve payment
   of a fine which he will have to pay himself – he cannot rely on an insurance
   policy to pay the fine because it is not possible to insure against a crime.
   The amount of the fine will not in any way be calculated by reference to
   the loss suffered by the ill customers.

   Klaus is also liable to be sued in the civil courts individually by the
   customers who became ill by eating his food. However those customers
   cannot sue for the tort of breach of statutory duty because the Food Safety
   Act 1990 does not create any civil liability (it is a criminal law only).
   Instead the customers may sue Klaus under the tort of negligence. If the
   customers win their civil court action then the customers will be awarded
   damages (compensation) calculated to compensate them for their loss, pain
   etc. arising from their food poisoning. If Klaus has appropriate insurance
   then his insurance company will pay the civil compensation.

   ◆

Chapter 2

1 The two forms of business organisation available to Angela are to be a sole
   trader or to form a single member private limited company. The advantage
   of being a sole trader is the lack of formality in setting up and running the
   business. A company has to be formed which involves preparation of
   company documents, submitting them to the Registrar of Companies and
   payment of a fee. There are also additional record keeping and
   administrative duties.

   The main advantage of a small company is the limitation of liability. If
   the company becomes insolvent Angela will not have her personal assets
   taken to pay the company's creditors. As a sole trader Angela would be at
   risk personally if the business failed and she could be made bankrupt.

2 As Beatrice does not wish to make a loan one of the options available is to
   enter into partnership with Angela. The drawback to that suggestion is that
   it leaves Beatrice exposed to liability for the business debts. A limited
   partnership is another option, as under such a partnership Beatrice could
   have limited liability. Another option is for Beatrice and Angela to form a
   company together. The company documentation could set down the
   management responsibilities. Profits could be divided according to
   shareholding after payment of a salary to Angela.

3 Angela's successful business formula could be used as the basis for a franchising option. She has a successful business which can be replicated in other locations under individual franchise agreements. The franchisees would pay fees to Angela for the benefit of her formula and know-how. Another option is to take on partners to help share the responsibilities of the extended business. It is important to choose partners carefully.

A further possibility is to form a company and run an expanded operation with a board of directors to share the decision making and the operation of the business.

◆

Chapter 3

1 Edward and Felicity's most direct route for authority to purchase another brewer's beer is to approach the brewery who granted the lease to see if the brewery will agree an amendment to the lease. But in any event Edward and Felicity may be able to take advantage of the Supply of Beer (Tied Estates) Order 1989 to be able to buy in a 'guest' beer.

2 Opening up seven letting bedrooms has a number of consequences. The premises will require a fire certificate which may not have been the case before. There may be a need to apply for planning permission because this may involve a material change of use. Another matter to be considered is the question of insurance for any potential liability to guests under the Occupiers Liability Act 1957. There may also be a change to the basis of charge for business rates.

3 The signs which Edward and Felicity want to put up will require express planning permission unless covered by a deemed consent in the Town and Country Planning (Control of Advertisements) Regulations 1992. But deemed consent will not be relevant if the public house is within an Area of Special Control. Edward and Felicity also need to consider if putting up the signs would be in breach of any of the clauses in the lease – the consent of the brewery may be necessary to the new signs and they may not be too keen to agree to the display of the sign from another brewery.

4 Edward and Felicity may be able to negotiate for the grant of a new lease when their existing lease runs out. In any event Edward and Felicity may be able to rely on Part 2 of the Landlord and Tenant Act 1954. Unless before the lease was granted a court order was obtained to exclude the provisions of the 1954 Act Edward and Felicity will be entitled to a new lease when

their existing lease expires. The brewery may be able to object to the grant of a new lease if one of the seven grounds of objection can be established. However, Edward and Felicity must bear in mind that a new lease will be at a new rent.

◆

Chapter 4

1 Unwind Caterers is a business name. As a consequence the business stationery, invoices etc. must show Arnold's and Bertram's names to show that they are the partners who are the proprietors of the business.

Additionally there must be an address at which service of any documents can be made – this will usually be the office address so that any important matters come quickly to the attention of either Arnold or Bertram. The VAT registration number also needs to be shown on invoices, bills or other documents which will be issued in respect of taxable supplies.

2 There is no requirement to register a logo but it is desirable to do so if money is to be spent in promoting that logo as the visible corporate sign of the business. Registration would be as a trade mark under the Trade Marks Act 1994 and the advantage is that once registered it will protect the business against use of the same or very similar logo by a competing business.

3 Despite the description as a booking fee, the proposed charge is in fact an advance deposit because by deducting the fee from the final bill the payment is part payment as of the accommodation charge. Consequently, the business must treat the payment as VAT inclusive at the time of receipt but can reclaim that VAT if the 'guest' does not take up the accommodation.

4 The guests' televisions give rise to a need for a Hotel Comprehensive Licence for each hotel – it is important to note that the licence is for the hotel not for the whole of the business. Because the hotel is licensed no public entertainment licence is necessary but the playing of recorded music will be a breach of music copyright unless licences are obtained from the Performing Right Society and Phonographic Performance Limited.

◆

Chapter 5

1 Megabig Hotels may not be able to rely on or enforce the conditions on

the back of the registration form for various reasons. First, it is quite possible that contracts for accommodation at the hotels are concluded before guests are asked to sign the registration form. Bookings made by telephone or post will create a contract before the guests arrive. In any event, guests are unlikely to appreciate that the registration form contains contract conditions and it will not be possible to enforce those conditions if they are not brought to the attention of guests.

Second, if the conditions do form part of the contract the Unfair Contract Terms Act 1977 may nullify or restrict the effect of those conditions. Finally, as the conditions are standard printed conditions they are likely to fall foul of the Unfair Terms in Consumer Contracts Regulations 1994 and be ineffective if they cause a significant imbalance in the rights and obligations under contracts for accommodation.

2 If the Ocean Hotel is a hotel as defined in section 1 of the Hotel Proprietors Act 1956 then the proprietor of the hotel is in breach of the common law duty to offer accommodation to travellers. The offer of a room at the Station Hotel does not satisfy that duty. Breach of such a duty is both a criminal offence and a civil wrong.

The Ocean Hotel may also be in breach of section 29 of the Sex Discrimination Act 1975. Such a breach is not a criminal offence but can be the subject of a civil action by Sally. Refusal of accommodation on the ground that she is female is direct unlawful sex discrimination. The Equal Opportunities Commission may be willing to advise or assist Sally in connection with such a claim or investigate the accomodation policy of the hotel.

3 Mountbatten Hotel may have civil liability to Derek

- for the loss of his wallet – that liability is strict if the Mountbatten Hotel is a hotel as defined in section 1 of the Hotel Proprietors Act 1956. If it is not then liability will depend on whether the hotel took reasonable care for the security of Derek's belongings
- for his bruises either under the Occupier's Liability Act 1957 or the common law tort of negligence
- for the assault by the fellow guest under the principle in the case of Chordas *v* Bryant 1988.

The Mountbatten Hotel could face a prosecution under section 3 of the Health and Safety at Work etc. Act 1974 in respect of the wet marble floor because it is likely to expose guests to risks to their health and safety.

Chapter 6

1 (a) The distinction between criminal and civil responsibility (as explained in Chapter 1) lies in the fact that in the former the objective is to punish an offence against society while the latter aims to remedy a wrong against an individual.

Crimes are prosecuted by a prosecutor on behalf of society in the criminal courts. Civil wrongs can be the subject of civil court proceedings instigated by the wronged individual.

In the case of consumer protection the law recognises that certain wrongs against individuals which would normally be a matter for civil remedy are matters where the criminal law should become involved to protect individuals generally

(b) The restaurateur is liable to be prosecuted by the local authority under any one of a number of criminal laws

- section 1 Trade Descriptions Act 1968 – false description of goods (including food) supplied
- section 14 Food Safety Act 1990 – selling food not of the nature, substance or quality demanded
- section 15 Food Safety Act 1990 – falsely labelling or presenting food.

Each of these offences is a strict liability offence subject to a 'due diligence' defence.

2 The Package Travel, Package Holidays and Package Tours Regulations 1992 do not apply to Jill and Trevor's weekend break because there is not a combination of accommodation and tourist services – the booking is for the hotel including use of all the hotel facilities and so none of the criminal consequences of those regulations apply.

Criminal liability may arise under section 14 of the Trade Descriptions Act 1968, namely the criminal offence of making in the course of a business, a false statement as to any services, accommodation or facilities. False in this context means to a material degree and so the criminal court would have to consider whether the brochure description of the hotel facilities was false using that test.

It is also an ingredient of the offence that the person making the false statement did so knowingly or recklessly. On the assumption that the brochure was prepared by the hotelier there is likely to be little doubt, but if the brochure was put together, say, by the local tourist board there could be a defence to a criminal charge under section 14 of the 1968 Act.

3 Justin and Tracey will have to display the following consumer protection notices

- in the reception area of their hotel – a list of accommodation prices (Tourism (Sleeping Accommodation Price Display) Order 1977)
- at the entrance to the restaurant – a list of food and drink prices (Price Marking (Food and Drink on Premises) Order 1979)
- on both notices and in a notice at the hotel entrance a statement as to the surcharge for credit cards (Price Indications (Method of Payment) Regulations 1991)
- on the wine list and near the restaurant bar (if any) – the measures for all types of drinks (Weights and Measures (Intoxicating Liquor) Order 1988) and the alcoholic strengths of drinks (Food Labelling (Amendment) Regulations 1989).

Failure to display these notices is a criminal offence.

◆

Chapter 7

1 (a) The likelihood is that Rita may be prosecuted for either (or both) of the following offences

- selling food for human consumption which fails to comply with the food safety requirements (section 8 Food Safety Act 1990)
- failure to keep food at the correct temperature as required by the Food Safety (Temperature Control) Regulations 1995.

Rita is the manager and as such can be prosecuted personally (section 20 FSA 1990).

(b) Rita can defend the prosecution on the basis that she has taken all reasonable precautions and exercised all due diligence to avoid food being kept at the incorrect temperature and becoming unsafe to eat. The defence is in section 21 of the Food Safety Act 1990 and applies to both offences with which Rita is likely to be charged. The court will have to decide whether her system is sufficient to satisfy the statutory defence – if so she will be entitled to be acquitted.

(c) If Rita is convicted she may well be fined. She could be made the subject of a court order under section 11 FSA 1990 to ban her from further involvement in the management of a food business. Such an order will only be made if the court considers that such a ban would be proper in all the circumstances.

2 All the foods in question are highly perishable and have a 'use by' date. It is an offence to sell food after its use by date and Rita can be prosecuted for doing so.

   The date marking requirements are in the Food Labelling Regulations and so a conviction for selling food past its use by date is not an offence in respect of which the court has power to make a prohibition order under section 11 FSA 1990 to ban Rita from management of a food business.

3 An improvement notice can be served under section 10 FSA 1990 if it is considered that the proprietor is failing to comply with the hygiene regulations.

   Nerys can appeal against the improvement notice to a magistrates court (section 37 FSA 1990). However, if the toilet does lead directly off the kitchen then there is no point in making an appeal against that part of the improvement notice because the Food Safety (General Food Hygiene) Regulations 1995 make that illegal.

   So far as the food bin is concerned the rule is that food waste should be in closeable containers unless the use of open containers is appropriate. Nerys could argue on appeal that open waste bins are appropriate.

   The rule about flyscreens is not absolute because flyscreens are only required for outside openable windows 'where necessary'. This means that flyscreens are not a legal requirement where the circumstances are such that they are not necessary for the purposes of food hygiene and safety. Nerys may be able to say at the appeal that in the circumstances flyscreens are not legally required.

   The magistrates' court can cancel, modify or confirm the improvement notice and to the extent the notice is confirmed Nerys must comply as failure to do so is a criminal offence.

◆

Chapter 8

1 John and Marie's residential licence only allows residents at the hotel to buy alcoholic drinks. The dining room could be made into a public restaurant but then non-residents would not be able to have alcoholic drinks with their meals. To overcome this but retain the advantages which go with a residential licence, John and Marie could apply for a combined licence and then the restaurant would have the equivalent of a restaurant licence.

   To turn the bar into a family room John and Marie should be considering applying for a children's certificate. This would allow families with children under 14 to use the bar together.

2 The problems now are basically two-fold. First, the new premises do not have a licence and there is no guarantee a licence can be obtained. Second, the existing premises should not have been altered without the prior approval of the licensing justices (section 20 LA 1964). The licensing justices might not be prepared to licence the next door premises and have no power to approve the alterations and so the premises must be restored to their original condition.

Those problems could have been avoided by obtaining a provisional licence for the new premises and prior consent to the alterations.

Cecil can offer to surrender the existing licence and apply for a new licence of the enlarged premises but he is very much at the mercy of the licensing justices.

3 A full on-licence allows the supply of alcoholic liquor on the licensed premises during the permitted hours for drinking on or off the premises.

Since the Licensing Act 1988, the general weekday permitted hours have been 11am to 11pm. Accordingly, unless a restriction order is in force, Margaret's on-licence will cover the period of Mr and Mrs Jones' daughter's wedding reception without the need for any special arrangements.

The twinning association's disco is to be held off the premises. Those premises are not covered by Margaret's licence. To run the bar at the village hall Margaret will need to apply for an occasional licence.

The bar requested by the rotary club will close 90 minutes after the end of the general permitted hours. To cover that period Margaret will need to apply for a special order of exemption. As the event is annual it should satisfy the test of being a 'special' event.

Chapter 9

1 Section 1 of the Employment Protection (Consolidation) Act 1978 requires employers to give employees within two months of starting the job written particulars of their employment. Such written particulars are not the contract of employment itself but is evidence of the main terms and conditions of that contract. The particulars must include rate of pay, hours of work, holiday entitlement and holiday and sickness pay.

It is not an offence to fail to give this written statement but if an employee complains to an industrial tribunal that he or she has not received the particulars the tribunal may write some of the statement itself.

2 Bernard is entitled to be paid by Albert statutory sick pay for his sickness absence after the first three days he is off ill. The amount of sick pay is fixed by law. However, this assumes that Bernard's contract of employment (as evidenced by the section 1 written particulars) does not specify a more generous sick pay scheme operated by Albert – if it does then Bernard is entitled to sick pay under that scheme. The situation is the same even if Bernard was entirely to blame for the road accident.

Sick pay (statutory or otherwise) comes within the definition of 'wages' in the Wages Act 1986 and so Bernard can issue an industrial tribunal application under that Act to recover from Albert the sick pay to which he is entitled.

3 The sale of the restaurant to Charles will be a transfer of an undertaking within the Transfer of Undertakings (Protection of Employment) Regulations 1981. Consequently, Bernard's continuity of employment will be preserved. When Bernard is dismissed by Charles, although Charles will only have been Bernard's employer for five months Bernard will have over two years service to his credit and therefore will qualify for the rights to redundancy pay and not to be unfairly dismissed.

The dismissal of Bernard is not for redundancy because a new chef is recruited. Bernard is not, therefore, entitled to any redundancy pay.

Bernard can complain he has been unfairly dismissed. It may be possible to claim that his dismissal is for a reason connected with the transfer namely the changeover to English cuisine in which case Bernard may be able to claim that it is an automatically unfair dismissal. More likely it will not be automatically unfair and the question of fairness of the dismissal will be for the tribunal to decide after having heard the evidence and decided the category of reason for dismissal.

4 The immediate matters for Charles are to notify the local environmental health officer by telephone and record the incident in the accident book. The Reporting of Injuries, Diseases and Dangerous Occurrences Regulations 1985 are relevant here and the telephone notification is required because of the fractured arm. A written notification (on an official form) must be sent within a week to the local authority.

The environmental health officer will almost certainly visit the restaurant and will want to see Charles' safety policy (under the Health and Safety at Work etc. Act 1974) and his risk assessment (under the Management of Health and Safety at Work Regulations 1992). The officer will also want to see what safety arrangements Charles has laid down for dealing with fat spillages (a common cause of kitchen accidents). A prosecution could follow from the accident if Charles has not done everything reasonably practicable to prevent this type of accident.

The other aspect of the incident is a possible civil claim by David for compensation for his injuries. Such a claim may be based on the tort of negligence or under the Occupiers Liability Act 1957 or even for breach of statutory duty relying on the obligations in the Workplace (Health, Safety and Welfare) Regulations 1992. Such a civil claim will be handled on behalf of Charles by the insurance company with whom he has insured under the Employer's Liability (Compulsory Insurance) Act 1969.

5 We are not told how long David has been in employment. If less than two years he will not be able to present a claim for unfair dismissal. If he has been employed by Charles at least two years then he has the right not to be unfairly dismissed. It is not unfair to dismiss someone injured at work. The question of unfairness depends on the two factors set out in section 57 of the Employment Protection (Consolidation) Act 1978. As David is incapable of doing his job due to his injury there is a potentially fair ground for dismissal. The industrial tribunal will then decide the issue of fairness on the question of the reasonableness of Charles' decision to dismiss for that reason and the tribunal will consider what steps Charles took to find out how long it would be before David would be fit to do his job and the difficulties facing Charles in running the business in the meanwhile.

6 The job applicant has been subjected to direct race discrimination under section 1 of the Race Relations Act 1976 because he has been treated less favourably than others – if he had been English he would have been considered for the job. That discrimination is unlawful under section 4 of the Race Relations Act 1976 because Charles has discriminated against the applicant in the arrangements he has made for determining who should be offered employment.

The remedy for unlawful race discrimination in employment is an application to an industrial tribunal and so Charles may receive from the tribunal office a copy of a complaint made by the job applicant under the 1976 Act. It is not possible to justify direct discrimination (compare with indirect discrimination) but in any event Charles appears to have failed to consider the possibility, especially in the light of the job applicant's training, that he might be just as suitable and able as a native English person to prepare traditional English cuisine.

Table of Cases

Important cases are reported in law reports. The letters after the case name indicate where the report can be found. For example, Meah *v* Roberts [1978] 1 All ER 97 shows that a report of that case can be found in the first volume in 1978 of the All England Law Reports commencing at page 97. There are many different law reports and a list of abbreviations can be found in all law libraries and most public libraries.

Table of Legislation

Statutory Instruments are identified by their statutory instrument number. European legislation can be found printed in the Official Journal (OJ) of the European Union L series.

GENERAL INDEX

For cases and legislation see separate indices.